Clinician's Pocket Reference

THE SCUT MONKEY'S HANDBOOK

Appleton Clinical Manuals

Ayres, et al.: Medical Resident's Manual, 4th edition
Ellis and Beckmann: A Clinical Manual of Gynecology
Ellis and Beckmann: A Clinical Manual of Obstetrics
Gomella, et al.: Clinician's Pocket Reference,
4th edition

Forthcoming titles

A Clinical Manual of Cardiology
A Clinical Manual of Nephrology
A Clinical Manual of Nuclear Medicine
Surgical Resident's Manual, 2nd edition

FOURTH EDITION

Clinician's Pocket Reference

THE SCUT MONKEY'S HANDBOOK

**Developed at the University of Kentucky
College of Medicine, Lexington, Kentucky**

Editor
Leonard G. Gomella, M.D.

Surgical Resident, Department of Surgery, Division of
Urology, University of Kentucky Medical Center,
Lexington, Kentucky

Associate Editor
G. Richard Braen, M.D.

Associate Professor, Emergency and Internal Medicine;
Director, Department of Emergency Medicine,
University of Kentucky Medical Center,
Lexington, Kentucky

Assistant Editor
Michael J. Olding, M.D.

Surgical Resident, Department of Surgery, New York
Hospital, New York, New York

With 128 Illustrations

A Capistrano Publication
APPLETON-CENTURY-CROFTS / Norwalk, Connecticut

Edition Four
Copyright© 1983 by Capistrano Press, Ltd.
12882 Valley View, Suite 15, Garden Grove, California 92645

Previously published as
So You Want to Be a Scut Monkey
Medical Student's and House Officer's
Clinical Handbook
Previous editions copyrighted 1979, 1980, 1981 by
Leonard G. Gomella and Michael J. Olding

85 86 87 88 89/10 9 8 7 6 5

Library of Congress Cataloging in Publication Data
Main entry under title:
Clinician's pocket reference.
    Based on a house manual used at the University of
Kentucky College of Medicine.
    Bibliography: p.
    Includes index.
    1. Medicine, Clinical—Handbooks, manuals, etc.
I. Gomella, L. G. (Leonard G.)   II. Olding, M. J.
III. Braen, G. Richard.   IV. University of Kentucky.
College of Medicine.   [DNLM: 1. Clinical competence—
Education—Handbooks.   2. Diagnosis, Laboratory—
Handbooks.   W   18   C643]

RC55.C555   1983   616   82-24430
ISBN 0-8385-1163-5

Publisher, B. Wallace Hood, Jr.
Acquisitions Editor, Carmen Germaine Warner
Production Editor, Barbara L. Halliburton
Art, John W. Brown
Internal Design, Alice Harmon

Printed in the United States of America

*"Blessed are the ignorant,
     for they need not unlearn."*

G. Richard Braen, M.D.
Associate Professor
University of Kentucky
College of Medicine

*"We don't drive the trucks,
     we only load them."*

Nick Pavona, M.D.
University of Kentucky
Class of 1980

Contributors

Patrick J. Bryant, Pharm.D.
Fellow in Clinical Pharmacology, College of
Pharmacy, University of Kentucky,
Lexington, Kentucky

The Department of Clinical Dietetics
University of Kentucky Medical Center,
Lexington, Kentucky

Sue Fosson, M.A.
Division of Educational Development,
University of Kentucky Medical Center,
Lexington, Kentucky

Patricia L. Gomella, M.D.
Pediatric Resident,
University of Kentucky Medical Center,
Lexington, Kentucky

Dennis G. Karounos, M.D.
Medical Resident,
University of Kentucky Medical Center,
Lexington, Kentucky

John A. Morris, Jr., M.D.
Chief Resident, Department of Surgery,
University of Kentucky Medical Center,
Lexington, Kentucky

Bud Nave, A.A.S., R.R.T., C.R.T.T.
Educational Coordinator, Respiratory Therapy
Division, University of Kentucky Medical Center,
Lexington, Kentucky

Nick A. Pavona, M.D.
Resident Physician, Department of Occupational
Medicine, University of Kentucky Medical Center,
Lexington, Kentucky

Contents

Preface

The *Clinician's Pocket Reference* is based on three previous editions of a University of Kentucky house manual entitled *So You Want to Be a Scut Monkey, Medical Student's and House Officer's Clinical Handbook*. The "Scut Monkey" Program at the University of Kentucky College of Medicine began in the summer of 1978. It was devloped by members of the Class of 1980 to help ease the often frustrating transition from the preclinical to the clinical years of medical school. Working with the College of Medicine's Division of Educational Development, members conducted interviews with third and fourth year students, house officers, and faculty to develop a list of essential information and skills that third year students should be familiar with at the start of their clinical years. The "Scut Monkey" Program was developed around this core of material. A random sampling of 44 other medical schools around the country indicated that a similar need existed elsewhere.

The "Scut Monkey" Program consists of reference manuals (similar to this edition) and a series of workshops conducted at the start of the third year. Held originally as a pilot program for the University of Kentucky College of Medicine Class of 1981, the orientation is now an official part of the third year curriculum. It is the responsibility of each new fourth year class to conduct the orientation for the new third year students. We feel that much of the success of the program is due to the fact that it is a program developed and taught by students for other students. This method has allowed us to maintain perspective on those areas that are critical not only for learning while on the wards but also for delivering effective patient care. This program could not have been conducted without the full support of the Office of the Dean. Detailed information on the "Scut Monkey" Orientation Program is available on request.

The program was presented at the 1980 National Convention of the American Medical Students Association, and since that time over four dozen medical schools have requested not only information on the workshops but also copies of the manuals. These requests and feedback from members of the Class of 1980 who found that the book was useful to interns and residents as well as to students have led to the extensive revision and publication of this manual. The original text of the fourth edition was prepared using a computer-assisted editing program.

We would like to express special appreciation to D.K. Clawson, M.D., Dean of the University of Kentucky College of Medicine, for his extensive support of the "Scut Monkey" Program and his encouragement to make this manual available outside the University of Kentucky Medical Center.

Many persons have made the first three editions of this book possible. The majority (more than 40) were members of the Classes of 1980 and 1981 who made their contributions while still medical students. Although we cannot list each one by name, we wish to note our appreciation and gratitude for their efforts. Continuing contributions to the program by Len Heller, Ed.D, and his staff at the Division of Educational Development have been outstanding, and the cooperation of Roy Jarecky, Ed.D., Terrence Leigh, Ed.D., and the entire Office of Academic Affairs is gratefully acknowledged. We are also thankful for the assistance of Darreldean Winkler, a clinical nutritionist at the College of Medicine. Many faculty members at the College of Medicine have been kind enough to review the majority of chapters in this book. We wish to thank our friends at the Ohio State University College of Medicine for allowing us to modify their selection entitled "So You Want To Be A Toad" that is used in the first chapter. We would also like to acknowledge Sheila Sullivan and Jane Keeble for their efforts in preparing this manuscript for publication and Capistrano Press, Ltd. for their enthusiastic support of our manual.

The "Scut Monkey" Project is meant to be a continuing endeavor. Comments and feedback are always welcome. We trust the benefits of this manual will adequately reflect the effort and enthusiasm with which it was compiled.

Leonard G. Gomella, M.D.

1

"So You Want to Be a Scut Monkey?"

An introduction to clinical medicine

THE HIERARCHY

Most services may be expected to have at least one each of the following physicians on the team.

The Intern

In some programs, known euphemistically as the first year resident. This is the person charged with the day-to-day responsibilities of patient care. This duty, combined with a total lack of seniority, usually serves to keep the intern in the hospital more than the other members of the team and may limit teaching of medical students. Any question concerning details in the evaluation of the patient, e.g., whether Mrs. Farkle gets a CBC (complete blood count) this morning or this evening is usually referred first to the intern.

Adapted with permission from Epstein A, Frye T (eds): "So You Want to Be a Toad"; Ohio State University, College of Medicine.

The Resident

The member of the house staff who has completed at least one year of postgraduate medical education. The resident is usually on call less often than the intern, is in charge of the overall conduct of the service, and is the person you might ask a question such as, "What are the kinds of things that might give Mrs. Farkle a WBC (white blood cell count) of 142,000?" You might also ask your resident for an appropriate reference on the subject or perhaps to arrange a brief conference on the topic for everyone on the service.

The Attending Physician

Also called simply "The Attending," and on nonsurgical services, "the attending." This is a physician who has completed postgraduate education and is now a member of the faculty. The attending is morally and legally responsible for the care of all patients whose charts are marked with the attending's name. All major therapeutic decisions made on the care of these patients are ultimately passed by the attending. In addition, this is the person responsible for teaching and evaluating house staff and medical students. This is the member of the team you might ask, "Why are we treating Mrs. Farkle with busulfan?"—if the attending does not ask you first.

The Fellow

Fellows are physicians who have completed their postgraduate education and elected to do extra study in one special field, e.g., nephrology, high-risk obstetrics, or retinal surgery. They may or may not be active members of the team and are not obligated to teach medical students but usually will be happy to do so if asked any questions. This is the person you might ask to help you read Mrs. Farkle's bone marrow smear.

TEAMWORK

The medical student, in addition to being a member of the medical team, must interact with members of the professional team of nurses, dietitians, pharmacists, and all others who provide direct care for the patient. Good working relations with this group of professionals can make your work go smoother; bad relations with them can make your rotation miserable.

Nurses are generally good-tempered, but overburdened. They respond very favorably to polite treatment. Leaving a mess in a patient's room after the performance of a floor procedure, standing by idly while a 98 lb LPN (licensed practical nurse) struggles to move a 350 lb patient onto the chair scale, or obviously listening to three ringing telephones while room call lights flash are acts guaranteed not to please. Do not let anyone talk you into being an acting nurse's aide or ward secretary, but try to help when you can.

You will occasionally meet a staff member who is having a bad day, and you will be able to do little about it. Returning hostility is unwarranted at these times, and it is best to avoid confrontations except when necessary for the care of the patient.

When faced with ordering a diet for your first sick patient, you will no doubt be confronted with the inadequacy of your education in nutrition. Fortunately for your patient, there are dietitians available. Never hesitate to call one.

In matters concerning drug-drug interactions, side effects, individualization of dosages, alteration of drug dosages in disease, and equivalence of different brands of the same drug, it never hurts to call the pharmacist. Most medical centers have a pharmacy resident who follows every patient on a floor or service and who will gladly answer any questions you have on medications. The pharmacist or pharmacy resident can very often provide pertinent articles on a requested subject.

YOUR HEALTH AND A WORD ON "AGGRESSIVENESS"

In your months of curing disease both day and night, it becomes easy to ignore your own right to keep yourself healthy. Numerous bad examples are available among the medical and surgical interns who sleep three hours a night and get most of their meals from vending machines. Do not let anyone talk you into believing that you are not entitled to decent meals and sleep. If you offer yourself as a sacrifice, it will be a rare rotation on which you will not become one.

You may have the misfortune some day of reading an evaluation that says a student was not "aggressive enough." This is an enigmatic notion to everyone. Does it mean that the student refused to attempt to start an intravenous (IV) line after eight previous failures? Does it mean that the student was not consistently the first one to shout out the answer over the mumblings of fellow students on rounds? Whatever constitutes "aggressiveness" must be a dubious virtue at best.

A more appropriate virtue might be ASSERTIVENESS IN OBTAINING YOUR EDUCATION. Ask GOOD questions, have the house staff show you floor procedures and review your chartwork, read about your patient's illness, participate actively in your patient's care, and take an interest in other patients on the service. This approach avoids the need for victimizing your patients and comrades that the definition of "aggression" requires.

ROUNDS

Rounds are meetings of all members of the service for discussing the care of the patient. These occur daily and are of three different kinds:

Morning Rounds

Also known as "work rounds," these take place from 6:30 to 8:00 A.M. on most services and are attended by residents, interns, and students. This is the time for discussing what happened to the patient during the night, the progress of the patient's evaluation or therapy or both, the laboratory and radiological tests to be ordered for that patient, and, last but not least, talking with the patient. Know about your patient's most recent laboratory reports and progress—this is a chance for you to look good.

Ideally, differences of opinion and any glaring omissions in patient care are politely discussed and resolved here. Writing new orders, filling out consultations, and making any necessary telephone calls are best done right after morning rounds.

Attending Rounds

These vary greatly depending on the service and on the nature of the attending. The same people who gathered for morning rounds will be here, with the addition of the attending. At this meeting the patients are often seen again (especially on the surgical services); significant new laboratory, radiographic, and physical findings are described (most often by the student caring for the patient); and new patients are formally presented to the attending (again, most often by the medical student).

The most important thing for the student on attending rounds is to know the patient. Be prepared to concisely tell the attending what has happened to the patient. Also be ready to give a brief presentation on the patient's illness, especially if it is unusual. The attending will probably not be interested in those details that do not affect therapeutic decisions, e.g., the fact that Mrs. Farkle tripped and fell the previous evening but did herself no harm. Additionally, the attending will probably not wish to hear a litany of normal laboratory values, only the pertinent ones, e.g., Mrs. Farkle's platelets are still $350,000/mm^3$ in spite of her bone marrow disease. You do not have to tell everything you know on rounds, but you must be prepared to do so.

Open disputes among house staff and students are bad form on attending rounds. For this reason there is an unwritten rule of the road that any differences of opinion that have not been previously discussed shall not be initially discussed in the presence of the attending.

Check-out or Evening Rounds

Usually only on Surgery and Pediatrics. Expect to convene sometime between 3 and 7 P.M. on most days. All new data are presented by the person who collected them (usually the student). Orders are again written, laboratory work desired for early the next day is requested, and those unfortunates on call compile a "scut list" of work to be done that night and a list of patients who need close supervision.

Bedside Rounds

Basically the same as any other rounds except that tact is at a premium. The first consideration at the bedside must be for the patients. If no one else on the team says good morning and asks how they are feeling, do it yourself; this is not a presumptuous act on your part. Keep this encounter brief and then explain that you will be talking about the patient for a while. If handled in this fashion, the patient will often feel flattered by the attention and will listen to you with interest.

Certain things in a hallway presentation are omitted in the patient's room. The patient's race and sex are usually apparent to all and do not warrant inclusion in your first sentence. The patient must NEVER be called by the name of the disease; e.g., Mrs. Farkle is not "a 45-year-old CML (chronic myelogenous leukemia)" but "a 45-year-old WITH CML." The patient's general appearance need not be reiterated. Descriptions of evidence of disease must not be prefaced by words such as "outstanding" or "beautiful." Mrs. Farkle's massive spleen is not beautiful to her, and it should not be to the physician or student either.

At the bedside, keep both feet on the floor. A foot up on a bed or chair conveys impatience and disinterest to the patient and other members of the team.

Although you will probably never be called upon to examine a patient during bedside rounds, it is still worthwhile knowing how to do so considerately. Bedside examinations are often done by the attending at the time of the initial presentation or by one member of a surgical service on postoperative rounds. First, warn the patient that you are about to examine the patient's wound or affected part. Ask the patient to uncover whatever needs to be exposed rather than boldly removing the patient's clothes yourself. If the patient is unable to do so alone, you may do it, but remember to explain what you are doing. Remove only as much clothing as is necessary, and then promptly cover the patient again. In a ward room, remember to pull the curtain.

Bedside rounds in the intensive care unit (ICU) call for as much consideration as they do in any other room. That still, naked soul on the bed might not be as "gorked out" as the resident (or anyone else) might believe and may be hearing every word you say. Again, exercise discretion in discussing the patient's illness, plan, prognosis, and personal character as it relates to the disease.

READING

Time for reading is at a premium on many services, and for that reason it is important to use it effectively. Unless you can remember everything you learned in the first 15 months of medical school, you will probably want to review the basic facts about the disease that brought your patient into the hospital. These facts are most often found in the same core texts that got you through the preclinical years. Unless specifically directed to do so, avoid the temptation to sit down with the *Index Medicus* and try to find all the latest articles on a disease you have not read about for the last seven months; you do not have the time.

The appropriate time to head for the *Index Medicus* is when a therapeutic dilemma arises and only the most recent literature will adequately advise the team. You may wish to obtain some direction from the attending, the fellow, or the resident before plunging into the library on your only Friday night off call this month.

THE WRITTEN HISTORY AND PHYSICAL

Much has been written on how to obtain a useful medical history and perform a competent physical examination, and there is not much to add to it. Three things worth emphasizing are your own physical findings, your impression, and your own differential diagnosis.

Trust and record your own physical findings, even if other examiners have written things different from those you found. You just may be right, and if not, you have learned something from it. Avoid the temptation to copy another examiner's findings as your own when you are unable to do the examination yourself. It would be an unusually cruel resident who would make you give Mrs. Farkle her fourth rectal examination of the day, so simply write "rectal per resident." DO NOT do this routinely just to avoid doing a complete physical examination. Check with the resident first.

Although not always emphasized in physical diagnosis, your clinical impression is probably the most important part of your write-up. Reasoned interpretation of the medical history and physical examination is what separates physicians from the computers touted by the tabloids as their successors. Judgment is learned only by boldly stating your case, even if you are wrong more often than not.

The differential diagnosis, i.e., your impression, should include only those entities that you consider when evaluating your patient. Even under duress, try to avoid including every possible cause of your patient's ailments. List only those things that you are seriously considering, and include in your plan those things that you intend to do to exclude each one. Save the exhaustive list for the time your attending asks for all the causes of a symptom, syndrome, or abnormal laboratory value.

THE PRESENTATION

The object of the presentation is to BRIEFLY and CONCISELY (usually in a few minutes) describe your patient's reason for being in the hospital to all those members of the team who do not know the patient and the story. Unlike the write-up, which contains all the data you obtained, the presentation may include only the pertinent positive and negative evidence of a disease and its course in the patient. It is hard to get a feel for what is pertinent until you have seen and done a few presentations yourself.

Practice is important. Try never to read from your write-up, as this often produces dull and lengthy presentations. Most attendings will allow you to carry note cards, but this method can also lead to trouble unless content is carefully edited.

Presentations are given in the same order as a write-up: identification, chief complaint, history of the present illness, past medical history, family history, social history, review of systems, physical examination, laboratory and x-ray data, clinical impression, and plan. Only pertinent positives and negatives from the review of systems should be given. These and truly pertinent items from other parts of the interview often can be added to the history of the present illness.

Finally, length and content of the presentation vary greatly according to the wishes of the attending and resident, but you will learn quickly what they do and do not want.

RESPONSIBILITY

Your responsibilities as a student should be clearly defined on the first day of a rotation by either the attending or the resident. Ideally, this enumeration of your duties should also include a list of what you might expect concerning teaching, floor skills, presentations, and all the other things for which you are paying several thousand dollars a year.

On some services you may feel like a glorified unit secretary (clinical rotations are called "clerkships" for good reason!), and you will not be far wrong. This is NOT what you are going into hock for. The scut should be divided among the house staff.

You will frequently be expected to call for a certain piece of laboratory data or to go review an x-ray film with the radiologist. You may then mutter under your breath, "Why waste my time? The report will be on the chart in a day or two!" You will feel less annoyed in this situation if you consider that every piece of data ordered is vital to the care of your patient.

The student's responsibility may be summarized in three words: KNOW YOUR PATIENT. The whole service relies to a great extent on a well-informed presentation by the student. The better informed you are, the more time there is for education, and the better your evaluation will be. A major part of becoming a physician is learning responsibility.

ORDERS

Orders are the physician's instructions to the nursing staff on the care of the patient. These may include the frequency of vital signs, medications, respiratory care, laboratory and x-ray studies, and nearly anything that you can imagine.

There are many formats for writing concise admission, transfer, and postoperative orders. Some rotations may have a precisely fixed set of routine orders, but others will leave you and the intern to your own devices. It is important in each case to avoid omitting instructions critical to the care of the patient. Although you will be confronted with a variety of lists and mnemonics, ultimately it is helpful to devise your own system and commit it to memory. Why memorize? Because when you are an intern and it is 3:30 A.M., you may overlook something if you try to think it out.

One system for writing admission or transfer orders uses the mnemonic A.D.C. Van Dissel. (See Chapter 3 for details.)

The word *stat* is the abbreviation for the Latin word *statim*, which means "immediately." When added to any order, it puts the requested study in front of all the routine work waiting to be done by the laboratory. Ideally, this order is reserved for the truly urgent situation, but in practice it is often inappropriately used. Most of the blame for this situation rests with physicians who either fail to plan ahead or who order stat results when routine studies would do.

Student orders may require cosignature by a physician, although at some institutions students are allowed to order routine laboratory studies. Do not ask a nurse or pharmacist to act on an unsigned student order; it is illegal for them to do so.

The intern is usually responsible for most orders. The amount of interest shown by the resident and attending varies greatly, but ideally you will review the orders on routinely admitted patients with the intern. Have the intern show you how to write some orders on a few patients, then take the initiative and write the orders yourself and review them with the intern.

THE DAY

The events of the day and the effective use of time are two of the most distressing enigmas encountered in making the transition from preclinical to clinical education. For example, there are no typical days on surgical services, as the operating-room schedule prohibits making rounds at a regularly scheduled time every day.

The following are suggestions that will help on any service:

Schedule special studies early in the day. The free time after work rounds is usually ideal for this. Also, call consultants early in the morning. Often they can see your patient that same day or at least early the next day.

Try to take care of all your business in the radiology department in one trip unless a given problem requires viewing a film promptly. DO NOT make as many separate trips as you have patients.

Make a point of knowing when certain services become unavailable, such as electrocardiograms (ECGs), contrast-study scheduling, and blood drawing. Be sure to get these procedures done while it is still possible to do so.

Make a daily work or "scut" list and write down laboratory results as soon as you obtain them. Few people can keep all the daily data in their heads without making errors.

Try to arrange your travels around the hospital efficiently. If you have patients to see on four different floors, try to take care of all their needs in one trip, e.g., do postoperative examinations, remove sutures, write progress notes, and call for consultations.

Strive to work thoroughly but quickly. If you do not try to get work done early, you never will (this is not to say that you will succeed even if you do try!). There is no sin in leaving at 5:00 P.M. or earlier if your obligations are COMPLETED at that time.

A PARTING SHOT

From this preview, the clinical years may seem like a badly written episode of "Mission Impossible." Trying to tell you adequately about them on paper is not unlike trying to make someone into a swimmer on dry land. It is hoped, however, that this chapter will give you some insight into what it takes to become a "scut monkey."

2
History and Physical

Basic History and Physical
Heart Murmurs

BASIC HISTORY AND PHYSICAL

History

Identification: Name, age, race, sex, home, referring physician, and the informant (patient, relative, chart, etc.)

Chief Complaint: State, in patient's own words, the current problem.

History of the Present Illness (HPI): State the course of the present illness, how and when it began, diagnostic tests done, pertinent positive and negative review of systems, related illnesses, risk factors.

Past Medical History (PMH): Illnesses, hospitalizations, surgery, current and past medical problems, current medications, allergies, blood transfusions, trauma, exposure to environmental agents, tobacco and alcohol use; for pediatric patients: prenatal and birth history, feedings, food intolerance, immunization history

Review of Systems (ROS)

GENERAL: Weight loss, weight gain, weakness, fever, chills, fatigue, sweats

SKIN: Rashes, pruritus, lesions

HEAD: Trauma, headache, tenderness

EYES: Vision, changes in the visual field, glasses, last prescription change, photophobia, blurring, diplopia, spots, inflammation, discharge

EARS: Hearing changes, tinnitus, pain, discharge, vertigo

NOSE: Sinus problems, nosebleeds, obstruction, polyps

THROAT: Teeth, tongue, gums, dentures, lesions, hoarseness

RESPIRATORY: Chest pain, wheezing, dyspnea, cough, amount and color of sputum, hemoptysis

CARDIOVASCULAR: Blood pressure, chest pain, dyspnea, rheumatic fever, murmurs, orthopnea, number of pillows used at night, cyanosis, edema, claudication

GASTROINTESTINAL: Appetite, dysphagia, nausea, vomiting, hematemesis, indigestion, pain, diarrhea, constipation, melena, bloating, anal discomfort, hemorrhoids, stool shape and color, jaundice

GENITOURINARY: Frequency, urgency, dysuria, hematuria, nocturia, incontinence, venereal disease, discharge, sterility, impotence

GYNECOLOGICAL: Gravida/para/abortions, last period, frequency, duration, flow, dysmenorrhea, spotting, menopause, contraception, last pelvic and Pap smear

ENDOCRINE: Polyuria, polydypsia, polyphagia, temperature intolerance, thyroid difficulties, glycosuria, hormone therapy

SKELETOMUSCULAR: Arthritis, trauma, swelling

HEMATOLOGY: Anemia, bleeding tendency, easy bruising, lymphadenopathy

NEUROPSYCHIATRIC: Syncope, seizures, weakness, coordination, sensations, memory, mood, sleep pattern, emotional disturbances, drug and alcohol problems

Family History: Medical problems in any blood relatives (especially cancer, tuberculosis [TB], allergy, asthma, heart disease, kidney, ulcers, diabetes, hemophilia)

Social History: Marital status, present and past employment, support, exposure to environmental agents, religion, hobbies, beliefs, living conditions, water supply; for pediatric patients: sleep and play habits

Physical Examination

General: Level of consciousness, mood, development, race and sex; state if patient is in any distress or if assuming an unusual position.

Vitals: Temperature, pulse, respirations, blood pressure (right arm, left arm, sitting, standing), height, weight

Skin: Rashes, eruptions, scars, tatoos, moles, hair pattern

Nodes: Location, size, tenderness, motility, consistency (cervical, supraclavicular, epitroclear, axillary, femoral)

HEENT:

HEAD: Size and shape, tenderness, trauma, bruits

EYES: Pupil size, shape, reactivity, extraocular muscle movements, vision (20/20, etc.), fields, fundi (disc color, size, margins, cupping, spontaneous venous pulsations, hemorrhages, exudates, arteriovenous [A-V] ratio, nicking), conjunctiva and sclera, arcus senilis, lids, enophthalmos, exophthalmos

EARS: Tenderness, discharge, external canal, tympanic membrane (intact, dull or shiny, bulging, motility, fluid or blood, injected)

NOSE: Tenderness, obstruction, lesions, exudate, inflammation

THROAT: Lips, teeth, gums, tongue, pharynx (lesions, erythema, exudate, tonsillar size, presence of crypts)

Neck: Motility, tenderness, jugular venous distention (JVD), nodes, masses, thyroid, location of larynx, bruits, hepatojugular reflux (HJR)

Chest: Symmetry, deformity, lesions, percussion, breath sounds, rales, rhonchi, rubs, fremitus, egophony, pectoriloquy

Heart: Rate, rhythm, gallop, murmurs, rubs, point of maximal impulse (PMI), thrill (See table for heart murmurs)

Breast: Symmetry, masses, nipple discharge, retraction, skin dimpling, tenderness

Abdomen: Shape (scaphoid, flat, distended, obese), scars, bowel sounds, tenderness rebound, guarding, masses, liver (span in midclavicular line) splenomegaly, bruits, costovertebral angle tenderness, percussion (tympanic, shifting dullness)

Male Genitals: Penis, circumcision, scrotal swelling, testicular size and tenderness, hernia, masses

Pelvic: See Chapter 4

Rectal: Hemorrhoids, fissures, skin tags, sphincter tone, masses, tenderness, fluctuance, stool in vault, occult blood, prostate size, shape, masses, tenderness

Extremities: Range of motion, clubbing, cyanosis, edema, joint swelling, tenderness, hair pattern, temperature, pulses (radial, brachial, femoral, popliteal, posterior tibial, dorsalis pedis) calf tenderness, Homan's sign, cords

Neurological

ORIENTATION
MEMORY
INTELLIGENCE
ABSTRACT THINKING

CRANIAL NERVES:
I	Smell
II	Vision, fields and fundi
III, IV, VI	Pupillary response, ptosis, volitional eye movements, pursuit eye movements
V	Corneal reflex, facial sensation, open jaw against resistance
VII	Close eyes tight, show teeth, smile or whistle
VIII	Watch tick, finger rub, Weber-Rinne (Air conduction lasts longer than bone conduction in a normal person.)
IX, X	Palate moves in midline, speech
XI	Shoulder shrug, push head against resistance
XII	Stick out tongue

MOTOR: Strength, finger squeeze, heel and toe walking

CEREBELLUM: Heel to shin, finger to nose

SENSORY: Pain, vibration, position, stereognosis

Useful dermatome levels:
C4	Top of shoulder
C6	Thumb
C7	2 & 3 digits
C8	4 & 5 digits
T4	Nipple line
T6	Xyphoid
T8	Costal margin
T10	Umbilicus
L1	Groin
L5	Top of foot
S1	Little toe

REFLEXES: Biceps C5-C6, triceps C7-C8, brachioradialis C5-C6, quadriceps L3-L4, ankle S1-S2, Babinski, Hoffman, snout, other pathological reflexes

Laboratory Data: CBC, SMA-6, chest x-ray (CXR), ECG, etc.

Assessment (Impression):   Differential diagnosis

Plan: Additional labs, medical treatment, consults, etc.

Signature

Title

HEART MURMURS

The following table describes the various types of heart murmurs. Fig. 2-1 on p 20 gives a graphic representation.

Heart Murmurs

TYPE (pitch)	DESCRIPTION
(A) Aortic Stenosis (medium)	Heard best in aortic area, rarely at apex Transmitted to carotids (neck) A_2 decreased, ejection click often heard at apex Paradoxical splitting of S_2 Left ventricular hypertrophy (LVH) with lift at apex
(B) Aortic Insufficiency (high)	Heard best at aortic area and lower left sternum Wide pulse pressure, LVH with apical lift
(C) Pulmonic Stenosis (medium)	Pulmonic area, transmitted to back and neck A_2 decreased, P_2 delayed, click often heard Right ventricular hypertrophy (RVH) with parasternal lift
(D) Pulmonic Insufficiency (low)	Heard best at pulmonic area RVH usually present
(E) Mitral Stenosis (low rumbling)	Heard best at apex in left lateral decubitus position Opening snap (OS), often increased S_1 and P_1 Presystolic accentuation, right ventricular (RV) lift, pulmonary hypertrophy
(F) Mitral Insufficiency (loud, high)	Heard best at apex, transmitted to axilla S_1 may be masked by murmur
(G) Atrial Septal Defect (medium)	Systolic ejection murmur at upper left sternal border Midsystolic murmur at lower left sternal border S_2 wide with fixed splitting, RVH with lift
(H) Ventricular Septal Defect (high, harsh)	Heard best at lower left sternal border S_1 often masked by murmur Holosystolic with peak intensity at midsystole
(I) Patent Ductus (medium)	Machinery, continuous type Heard best at left first and second interspace

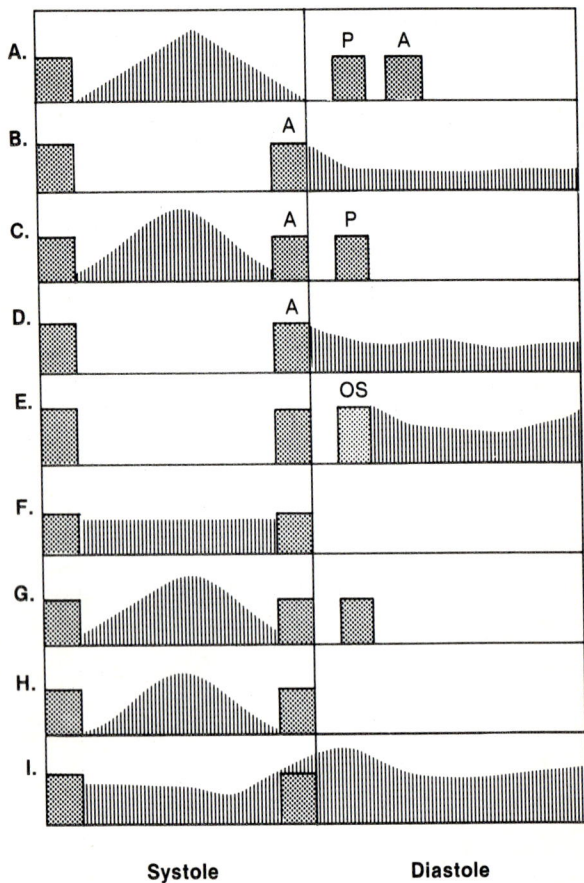

Systole   **Diastole**

Fig. 2-1 Graphic representation of common heart murmurs.

3
Chartwork

HOW TO WRITE ORDERS

The following is a useful format for writing concise admission, transfer, and postoperative orders. It involves the mnemonic A.D.C. VAN DISSEL.

This stands for Admit, Diagnosis, Condition, Vitals, Activity, Nursing procedures, Diet, Ins and outs, Specific drugs, Symptomatic drugs, Extras, and Labs.

A.D.C. VAN DISSEL

Admit: Location, team, floor, attending, house officer, etc.

Diagnosis: And procedure if post op orders, allergies if any

Condition: Stable, critical, etc.

Vitals: Frequency of temperature, pulse, blood pressure (BP), central venous pressure (CVP), pulmonary capillary wedge pressure (PCWP), weight

Activity: Bed rest, ad lib, ambulate four times a day (qid), bathroom privileges, etc.

Nursing Procedures

BED POSITION: Elevate head of bed (HOB) 30 degrees

PREPS: Enemas, scrubs, showers

RESPIRATORY CARE: Percussion and postural drainage (P&PD); turn, cough, and deep breathe (TC&DB); nasotracheal (NT) suctioning

DRESSING CHANGES, WOUND CARE

NOTIFY HOUSE OFFICER IF: Temperature >102 F, BP <90, etc.

Diet: Nothing by mouth (NPO), clear liquid, regular, etc.

Ins and Outs: Refers to all "tubes" a patient may have

RECORD DAILY INTAKE AND OUTPUT (I&O)

IV FLUIDS: Specify type and rate

DRAINS • Nasogastric (NG) to low wall suction
• Foley to gravity drain
• Hemovac to accordion suction

ENDOTRACHEAL TUBES, ARTERIAL LINES, SWAN-GANZ LINES

Specific Drugs: Diuretics, antibiotics, hormones, etc.

Symptomatic Drugs: Pain medications, laxatives, "sleepers"

Extras: ECGs, x-rays, and other studies

Labs: CBC, SMA-6, state times desired

PROBLEM-ORIENTED PROGRESS NOTE

1. List each medical, surgical, psychiatric problem separately: pneumonia, pancreatitis, congestive heart failure (CHF), etc.

2. Give each problem a call number: 1, 2, 3 . . . .

3. Retain the number of each problem throughout the hospitalization.

4. When a problem is resolved, mark it as such and delete it from the daily progress note.

5. Evaluate each problem by number in the following SOAP format:

SOAP

Subjective
- How the patient feels, any complaints
- What you notice about the patient: mental state, etc.

Objective
- Vital signs
- Physical exam
- Lab data, etc.

Assessment
- Evaluation of the data and any conclusions that can be drawn

Plan
- Any new labs or medications
- Changes or additions to nurses' orders
- Discharge or transfer plans

DISCHARGE SUMMARY/NOTE

Date of Admission:

Date of Discharge:

Admitting Diagnosis:

Discharge Diagnosis:

Attending and Service Caring for Patient:

Referring Physician: And address if available

Procedures: Include surgery, invasive procedures like lumbar punctures (LPs), etc.

Brief History, Pertinent Physical and Lab Data: On admission

Hospital Course:

Condition at Discharge:

Discharge Medications:

Disposition: Where the patient was sent

Discharge Instructions and Follow-up: Clinic return date, etc.

Problem List:

PREOPERATIVE NOTE

Pre Op Diagnosis:

Procedure:

Labs: Results of CBC, electrolytes, prothrombin time (PT), partial thromboplastin time (PTT), urinalysis, etc.

CXR: Results

ECG: Results

Blood: For example, type and cross (T&C) 2 units whole blood or not needed

Orders: Written

Permit: Signed and on chart

OPERATIVE NOTE

Immediately following surgery.

Pre Op Diagnosis:

Post Op Diagnosis:

Procedure:

Surgeons:

Findings:

Anesthesia: Local, spinal, general endotracheal

Fluids: Amount and type during case, e.g., normal saline (NS), blood, albumin

EBL: Estimated blood loss

Drains: State location and type of drain, e.g., Penrose in left upper quadrant (LUQ), T-tube in midline

Specimens: State any sent to pathology lab

Complications:

Condition:

NIGHT OF SURGERY NOTE

Procedure:

Level of Consciousness:

Vital Signs:

I&O:

Hematocrit and Labs:

Physical Exam: Chest, heart, abdomen, extremities; examine the dressing for bleeding

Assessment:

Plan:

DELIVERY NOTE

_____-year-old (married or single) (state race) gravida (G) _____ now para (P) _____, abortion (Ab) _____ clinic (vs. nonclinic) patient with estimated date of confinement (EDC) _____ and a prenatal course (describe any problems). Any comments concerning labor (e.g., pitocin induced, premature rupture of membranes). Taken to the delivery suite and prepped and draped in the usual sterile fashion. Under controlled conditions delivered a _____ lb _____ oz (_____ gm) viable male or female infant under _____ (general, spinal, pudendal) anesthesia. Delivery was via SVD (spontaneous vaginal delivery) with midline episiotomy (or forceps or cesarean section). Apgars were _____ at one minute and _____ at five minutes. State delivery date and time. Cord blood sent to lab and placenta expressed intact with trailing membranes. Uterus explored. Lacerations of the _____ degree repaired by standard method with good hemostasis and restoration of normal anatomy.

EBL
MBT (maternal blood type)

RT (rubella titers)
Condition of mother
Hematocrit (HCT) (predelivery and postdelivery)
VDRL test (or plasmacrit)

OUTPATIENT PRESCRIPTION WRITING

Drug Name, Type

Disp: Amount of drug

Sig: Patient instructions

EXAMPLE
- Dalmane, 30-mg capsules
- DISP: #30 (thirty)
- SIG: One, by mouth at bedtime, for sleep as needed

SHORTHAND FOR LABORATORY VALUES

Fig. 3-1 shows a common way to record lab values in a patient's chart.

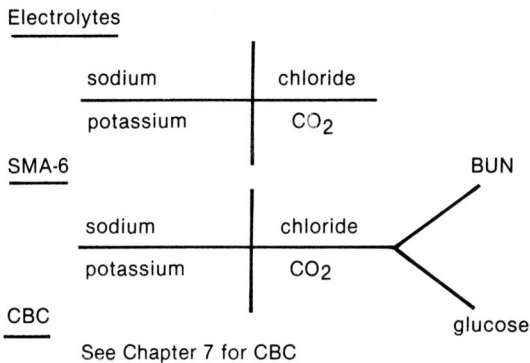

Fig. 3-1 Shorthand for laboratory values.

4

Procedures

Included in this chapter are common therapeutic and diagnostic procedures. Where appropriate, guides for differential diagnosis are included.

ARTERIAL BLOOD SAMPLING

Indications

- Blood gas determinations
- When arterial blood is needed for chemistry determinations (e.g., ammonia levels)
- Monitoring arterial pressure directly

Procedure

1. If the sample is being drawn for the determination of blood gases, use a heparinized syringe. For a chemistry determination, no heparin is required. Otherwise, the procedure is identical.

2. Obtain a blood gas kit (contains a preheparinized syringe) or a small syringe (3 to 5 ml) with a small gauge needle (22 to 25 gauge). "Heparinize" the syringe by drawing up about 1 ml of a 1:1000 solution of heparin, pulling the plunger all the way back, and discarding the heparin. The small amount of heparin that coats the needle and syringe is sufficient for anticoagulation.

3. Arteries in the order of preference are radial, brachial, and femoral. If using the radial artery, perform the Allen test to verify the patency of the ulnar artery. You do not want to damage the radial artery if there is no flow in the ulnar artery. To perform the test, have the patient make a tight fist. Occlude both the radial and ulnar arteries at the wrist and have the patient open his hand. While maintaining pressure on the radial artery, release the ulnar artery. If the ulnar artery is patent, the hand should flush red.

4. If using the femoral artery, use the mnemonic NAVEL to aid in locating the important structures in the groin. From lateral to medial they are Nerve, Artery, Vein, Empty space, Lymphatic. Palpate the artery carefully. You may wish to inject 1% lidocaine subcutaneously for anesthesia that does not distort the anatomy, but this often turns a "one-stick procedure" into a "two-stick procedure." Palpate the artery proximally and distally with two fingers or trap the artery between two fingers placed on either side of the vessel. Hyperextension of the joint will often bring the radial and brachial arteries closer to the surface.

5. Prep the area with either a povodine-iodine solution or alcohol swab.

6. Hold the syringe like a pencil with the needle bevel up and enter the skin at a 60 to 90 degree angle. Often you can feel the arterial pulsations as you approach the artery. Maintain a slight negative pressure on the syringe.

7. Obtain blood on the downstroke or upon slow withdrawal (after both sides of the artery have been punctured). Aspirate very slowly. A good arterial sample, because of the pressure in the vessel, should require only minimal back pressure. If a glass syringe or special blood-gas syringe is used, the barrel will usually fill spontaneously.

8. If the vessel cannot be located, redirect the needle without coming out of the skin.

9. Withdraw the needle quickly and apply FIRM pressure at the site for at least five minutes even if the sample was not obtained. Arterial bleeding due to inadequate pressure can cause a large hematoma.

10. If the sample is for a blood gas, expel any air from the syringe, mix the contents thoroughly by twirling the syringe between your fingers (if ANY blood clots in the syringe, the blood gas cannot be run on the machine!), and make the syringe airtight with a cap or cork. Place the syringe in an ice bath if more than a few minutes will elapse before the sample is processed and mark the lab slip with the inspired oxygen concentration and the time.

BLOOD CULTURES

Indications

- The routine work-up of a fever
- When a subclinical bacteremia is suspected

Chills and fever usually ensue from one-half to two hours after sudden entry of bacteria into the circulation. In actual practice, it is very difficult to predict when the number of bacteria in the blood stream is at a maximum. If a bacteremia is suspected, several sets of cultures are usually needed to improve the chances of culturing the organism. Ideally, more than one set of cultures should be done at a time to help determine if a positive culture is a contaminant or a true pathogen. (*Staphylococcus epidermitis* is the most common contaminant of blood cultures. On rare occasions, however, it may be the causative organism.) A "set" of blood cultures is actually two different cultures: one aerobic and one anaerobic.

Procedure

1. Apply a tourniquet to an extremity and choose a site for the venipuncture. Paint the site three times with an iodine-based disinfectant; start at the center and spiral out to the periphery. Wipe off the area over the vein with alcohol.

2. Clean the tops of the culture tubes or bottles with iodine solution.

3. Use an 18 to 22 gauge needle (or smaller if needed) and a 10 to 20 ml syringe. Enter the skin over the prepped vein. BE CAREFUL NOT TO TOUCH THE NEEDLE. Enter the vein and draw off about 10 ml of blood. Remove the tourniquet and compress the venipuncture site.

4. Carefully place a NEW, STERILE 18 to 22 gauge needle on the syringe. Place a few milliliters of blood in each of the culture tubes or bottles and submit the samples to the lab promptly. Results are usually available in 12 to 48 hours.

CHEST TUBE (CLOSED THORACOSTOMY)

Indications

- Pneumothorax
- Hemothorax
- Tension pneumothorax
- Empyema

Procedure

Materials

- Chest tube (24 to 36 for adults)
- Water-seal drainage system (Pleurevac)
- Towel, gloves, prep solution
- Scalpel, kelly clamp, scissors
- Silk suture
- Anesthetic
- Syringes

Technique

1. Check a chest x-ray film, if possible. Site of insertion varies with the indication. In general, for a simple pneumothorax, choose a high anterior site, such as the second intercostal space, midclavicular line, or subaxillary position. Since fluid tends to settle in the lowest part of the chest, place a low lateral chest tube in the fifth to eighth intercostal space in the midaxillary or posterior axillary line for a hemothorax. For a traumatic pneumothorax, use a low, lateral tube since this condition is usually associated with bleeding.

2. If the procedure is elective, sedation may be helpful. Prep the area with antiseptic and drape it with towels. Use 1% lidocaine (with or without epinephrine) to anesthetize the skin and periosteum of the rib; start at the center of the rib and gently work over the top. (Remember, the neurovascular bundle runs under the rib).

3. Make a 2 to 3 cm transverse incision over the center of the rib. Use a hemostat to bluntly dissect over the top of the rib.

4. Puncture the parietal pleura with the hemostat. Insert a gloved finger into the pleural cavity to gently clear any clots or adhesions and to make certain the lung is not accidentally punctured by the tube.

5. Carefully insert the tube into the desired position. Attach the end of the tube to a water-seal or Pleurevac suction

system. A "thoracic catheter" chest tube has multiple holes and is best for draining fluid. The "trocar" chest tube has only two holes and is usually best for a simple pneumothorax.

6. Suture the tube in place. Place a heavy silk (0 or 2-0) suture through the incision next to the tube. Tie the incision together, then tie the ends around the chest tube. Alternatively, a purse string suture can be placed. Make sure all of the suction holes are beneath the skin before the tube is secured.

7. Wrap the tube with vaseline gauze and cover with plain gauze. Make the dressing as airtight as possible with tape.

8. Start suction (usually −20 cm) and take a chest x-ray film immediately to check the placement of the tube.

9. To remove a chest tube, make sure the pneumothorax or hemothorax is cleared. Check for an air leak by having the patient cough; observe the water-seal system for bubbling.

10. Take the tube off suction and cut the retention suture. Have the patient perform the Valsalva maneuver while you apply pressure with vaseline gauze and 4 x 4 gauze squares. Pull the tube rapidly and make an airtight seal with tape. Check a chest x-ray film for pneumothorax.

Complications

- Infection
- Bleeding
- Lung damage
- Subcutaneous emphysema

DEEP LINES (CENTRAL VENOUS CATHETERS)

A "deep line" is a catheter introduced into the superior vena cava, inferior vena cava, or one of their main branches.

Indications

- Administration of fluids and medications, especially during resuscitation (Remember that most peripheral veins collapse during a cardiac arrest or shock.)
- Administration of hyperalimentation solutions (These are so hypertonic that they damage peripheral veins.)
- Measurement of CVP
- Insertion of a Swan-Ganz catheter or transvenous pacemaker.

Procedures

There are several different techniques for inserting a deep line, including the subclavian, internal jugular, external jugular, antecubital, and femoral. Only the first two are commonly used.

The Subclavian Technique

1. Use sterile technique (povodine-iodine prep, gloves, and a sterile field) whenever possible.

2. Place the patient head down in the Trendelenberg position (this helps to engorge the veins and prevent air embolism) with his head turned to the opposite side. The right side is preferred for deep line placement since the dome of the pleura is lower and there is more of a direct path to the right atrium. It may be helpful to place a towel roll behind the patient's shoulder.

3. Use a 25 gauge needle to make a small skin wheal with 1% lidocaine 1 cm below the midclavicle. At this point a larger needle such as a 22 gauge can be used to anesthetize the deeper tissues.

4. Attach a large-bore, deep-line needle (a 14 gauge needle with a 16 gauge catheter at least 8 to 12 inches long) to a 10 to 20 ml syringe and introduce it into the site of the skin wheal.

5. Place a finger in the suprasternal notch and direct the needle towards this finger. Keep the needle parallel to the lateral border of the clavicle and parallel to the skin.

6. Apply constant back pressure as the needle is advanced deep to the clavicle but above the first rib (Fig. 4-1).

7. Free return of blood indicates entry into the subclavian vein. Bright red blood that forcibly enters the syringe indicates that the subclavian artery has been entered. If this occurs, remove the needle and apply firm pressure for 10 minutes.

8. If an Intracath is being used, remove the syringe, place a finger over the needle hub, and advance the catheter an appropriate distance through the needle. Then withdraw the needle slightly and snap the protective cap over the end of the needle.

9. If an Intrafusor is being used, advance the catheter while maintaining back pressure on the syringe and lock it into position. Then withdraw the needle slightly and snap the protective cap over the tip of the needle.

10. Attach the catheter to the appropriate IV solution and place the IV bottle below the level of the deep-line site to insure a good backflow of blood into the tubing. If there is no backflow, the catheter is probably kinked or not in the proper position.

11. Securely suture the assembly in place with 3-0 silk. Apply an occlusive dressing with povidone-iodine ointment.

12. Obtain a chest x-ray film to verify placement of the catheter tip and to rule out pneumothorax. The catheter tip should lie in the superior vena cava in the vicinity of the right atrium, at about the fifth thoracic vertebra.

Internal Jugular Technique

1. Use sterile technique as for the subclavian.

2. Place the patient in the Trendelenberg position. (See the subclavian technique.)

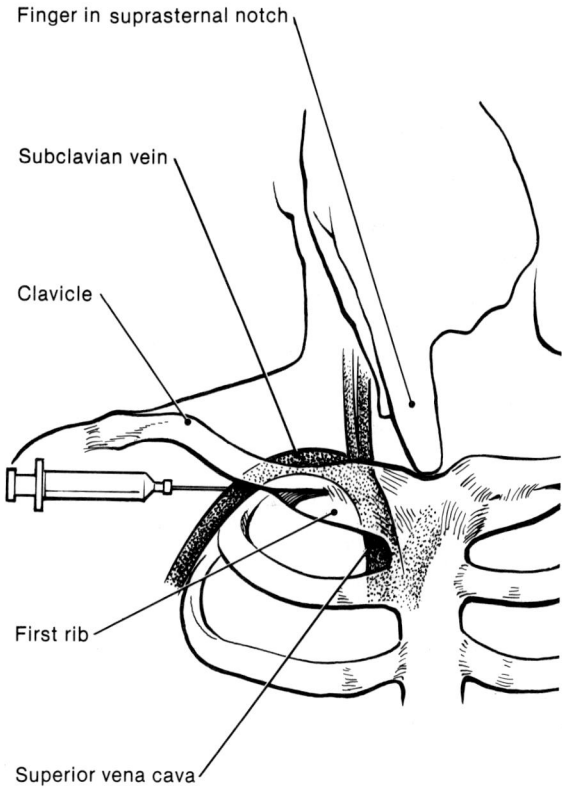

Fig. 4-1 Technique for catheterization of the subclavian vein.

3. Locate the triangle formed by the clavicle and the two heads of the sternocleidomastoid muscle. Use a 25 gauge needle and 1% lidocaine to raise a small skin wheal in the center of this triangle. Change to a 22 gauge needle to anesthetize the deeper layers, and then use gentle aspiration, with the same needle, to initially locate the internal jugular vein (Fig. 4-2).

4. Attach a large-bore, deep-line needle (14 gauge needle with a 16 gauge catheter at least 12 inches long) to a 10 to 20 ml syringe. Direct the needle through the skin wheal caudally, parallel to the sagittal plane and at a 30 degree angle to the frontal plane. If the vein is not entered, withdraw the needle slightly and redirect it 5 to 10 degrees more laterally. Apply constant backpressure.

5. If bright red blood forcibly fills the syringe, you have punctured the carotid artery. Remove the needle and apply firm pressure for 10 minutes.

6. Follow steps 8 to 12 as described for the subclavian technique.

Deep Line Removal

1. Turn off the IV flow.

2. Cut the retention sutures and gently withdraw the catheter.

3. Apply pressure for at least two to three minutes and apply a sterile dressing.

Complications

- Pneumothorax: Listen to the chest and check a chest x-ray film taken after the insertion of the deep line.
- Arterial puncture with hematoma: Withdraw the needle and apply firm pressure. BE VERY CAUTIOUS IN ATTEMPTING AN INTERNAL JUGULAR PUNCTURE ON THE OPPOSITE SIDE AFTER ENTERING THE ARTERY.

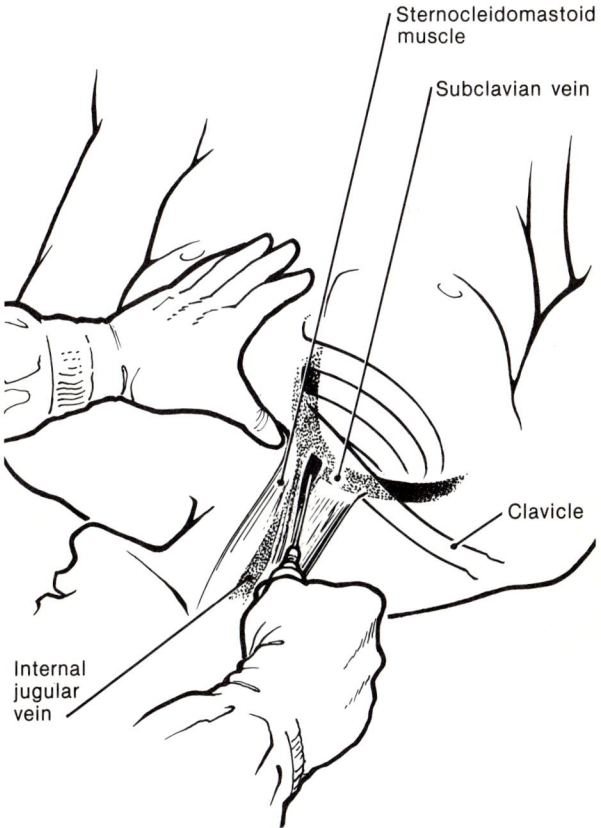

Fig. 4-2 Technique for catheterization of the internal jugular vein.

LIFE-THREATENING TRACHEAL AND CAROTID COM-PRESSION CAN OCCUR IF THERE ARE BILATERAL CAROTID HEMATOMAS.
- Catheter tip embolus: NEVER withdraw the catheter back through the needle. It can shear off the tip.
- Air embolus: Make sure that the open end of a deep line is ALWAYS covered with a finger. Studies have shown that as little as 50 to 100 ml of air in a vein can be fatal. If you suspect that air embolization has occurred, place the patient head down and turned on his left side to keep the air in the right atrium. Obtain a STAT portable chest film to see if air is present in the heart.

DOPPLER PRESSURES

Indication

- Evaluation of peripheral vascular disease

Procedure

Materials

- Doppler flow monitor
- Conductive jel (lubricant jelly can also be used)
- Blood pressure cuff

Technique

1. Determine the blood pressure in each arm.

2. Measure the pressures in the popliteal arteries by placing a blood pressure cuff on the thigh. The pressures in the dorsalis pedis arteries (on the top of the foot) and the posterior tibial arteries (behind the medial malleolus) are determined with a blood pressure cuff on the calf.

3. Apply conductive jelly and place the Doppler probe over the artery. Inflate the blood pressure cuff until the pulsatile flow is no longer heard. Deflate the cuff until the flow returns. This is the systolic or Doppler pressure. It should be noted that the Doppler cannot routinely determine the

diastolic pressure and that a palpable pulse need not be present to use the Doppler.

4. The ankle-brachial (A/B) index is often computed from Doppler pressure. It is equal to the pressure in the ankle (usually the posterior tibial) divided by the systolic pressure in the arm. An A/B index <0.4 is usually associated with significant peripheral vascular disease.

ELECTROCARDIOGRAMS

Basic ECG reading can be found in Chapter 19.

Procedure

1. Start with the patient in a comfortable, recumbent position. Explain the procedure to dispel any myths about "electrocution." Instruct the patient to lie as still as possible to cut down on artifacts in the tracing.

2. Plug in the ECG machine and turn it on. Allow the stylus tip to warm up. Most ECG paper is heat sensitive.

3. Attach the electrodes.

Patient Cables

The standard ECG machine has five lead wires, one for each limb and one for the chest leads. By design, these are color coded in the following fashion:

RA: White—right arm
LA: Black—left arm
RL: Green—right leg
LL: Red—left leg
C: Brown—chest

Limb Electrodes

The limb electrodes are flat, rectangular plates held in place by rubber or velcro straps that encircle the limb. Electrode paste can be used beneath the plates (be sure to rub it vigorously on the skin) to improve electrical contact. It is often much easier and neater to use alcohol pads beneath the plates for this purpose. Place each electrode on the limb indicated, wrist or ankle, usually on the ventral surface. In case of amputation or a cast, the lead may be placed on the shoulder or groin with almost no effect on the tracing.

Chest (Precordial) Electrodes

The chest electrode is brown and designated by the letter C. It is attached to a suction cup that is attached in sequence to each of the positions (see the following) on the precordium. Be sure to apply a small amount of electrode paste to each of the positions prior to running the ECG. This makes locating the proper positions much quicker and easier (Fig. 4-3).

PRECORDIAL LEADS

V1 = fourth intercostal space, to the RIGHT of the sternal border
V2 = fourth intercostal space, to the LEFT of the sternal border
V3 = midway between leads V2 and V4
V4 = midclavicular line, above the fifth interspace
V5 = anterior axillary line at the same level as V4
V6 = midaxillary line at the same level as leads V4 and V5

4. Once the machine is warmed up and the electrodes are positioned or ready for positioning, make sure that the paper speed is set at 25 mm/sec.

5. It is helpful to center the stylus so that the ECG baseline falls on the central, thick horizontal line of the recording paper.

6. With the paper running, push the standardization button several times. Make sure the sensitivity switch is set so that the 1 millivolt standardization pulse will have an amplitude of 10 small boxes or two large boxes of height. (Usually the standardization is set at 1, although sometimes it may be necessary to change the standardization to get a good tracing.)

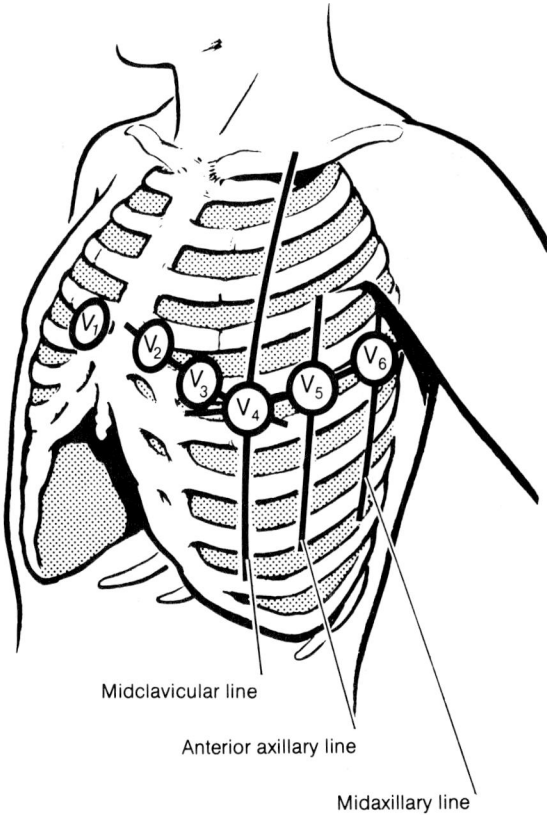

Fig. 4-3 Location of precordial chest leads.

7. Record the leads in the order dictated on the lead selector switch. The order is I, II, III, AVR, AVL, AVF, V1, V2, V3, V4, V5, and V6. Note that there is only one position "V" on the selector switch for the chest leads. YOU will select each of the different precordial leads by changing the position of the suction cup electrode.

8. Mark each lead correctly on the strip. This can be done by using the lead marker device with one of the various codes, e.g., use "dots" to identify each of the standard limb leads (I, II, III), "dashes" for each of the augmented limb leads (AVR, AVL, AVF), and "dots" preceded by "dashes" for each of the precordial leads. Or simply use up to six "dots" for the limb leads (I to AVF) and the same "dots" preceded by "dashes" for each of the precordial leads. Or simply use a ball-point pen to mark each lead as it is running on the machine.

9. Each recording of a lead should be about six seconds long; this can be measured by allowing two of the three-second vertical markers at the top of the strip to pass. It is also useful to run a 30-second lead II rhythm strip at the end of V6.

10. Label the tracing with the patient's name, date, time, any other useful information, and your name. It should take four to eight minutes to get a routine "twelve lead ECG."

Helpful Hints

1. The second rib is the sternal angle, and the second intercostal space is directly inferior to the sternal angle. Feel down two more intercostal spaces and you have the fourth intercostal space to position V1 and V2.

2. When you start seeing a solid blue line at the top or bottom of the strip, you are about to run out of paper. ALWAYS leave enough paper for the next user.

3. Learn the color scheme for the leads; it could be very useful in an emergency.

- Red and green go to the legs: "Christmas on the bottom" or "When driving your car you use your left leg to brake (red light) and your right leg to go (green light)."
- Black and white go to the arms: "Remember white is right and black is left."
- Brown is for the chest.

FEVER WORK-UP

The true definition of a "fever" can vary from service to service. General guidelines to follow are

- Temperature > or = 101.6 F orally on a medicine or surgery service
- Temperature > or = 101 F rectally or 100 F orally in pediatric patients less than 4 months old

When evaluating a patient for a "fever," consider if it is an oral, rectal, or axillary temperature (rectal temperatures are about 1 degree higher than oral; axillary temperatures are about 1 degree lower than oral); has the patient drunk any hot or cold liquids around the time of the determination; and is the patient on any antipyretics like aspirin or acetaminophen.

General Fever Work-up

1. Quickly review the chart and medication record if the patient is not familiar to you.

2. Examine the patient to locate any obvious sources of fever.

EARS: Especially in children

NOSE AND THROAT: Again especially in children

LUNGS: Note the presence of rales, rhonchi, decreased breath sounds, or dullness to percussion.

ABDOMEN: Presence or absence of bowel sounds, guarding, rigidity, tenderness, bladder fullness, or CVA (costovertebral angle) tenderness

GENITOURINARY: Is there a Foley catheter in place, what does the urine look like grossly and microscopically?

RECTAL EXAM: Tenderness or fluctuance to suggest an abscess

PELVIC EXAM: Especially in the postpartum patient

WOUNDS: Check all wounds for evidence of inflammation, pus, or fluctuance.

EXTREMITIES: Check around all IV sites for signs of inflammation; check for signs of thrombophlebitis.

MISCELLANEOUS: Consider the possibility of a drug fever (check the eosinophil count on the CBC) or nasogastric-tube fever. Do all this before you begin to investigate the less common or less obvious causes of a fever.

Laboratory Studies

CBC With Differential

Urinalysis

Cultures as Indicated: Urine, blood, sputum, wound, (spinal fluid ESPECIALLY in children less than 4 to 6 months old)

Chest X-ray

Abdominal X-rays: If the physical exam indicates a possible abdominal etiology

More Aggressive Procedures: If indicated; for example, lumbar puncture, thoracentesis, paracentesis

Miscellaneous Fever Facts

Causes of Fever in the Post Op Patient: Think of the "Five Ws."

WIND: Atelectasis secondary to intubation and anesthesia, the most common cause of a fever immediately post op. To treat, have the patient up and ambulating, getting incentive spirometry, P&PD, and NT suctioning.

WATER: Urinary tract infection; may be secondary to a Foley catheter

WOUND: Infection

WALKING: Phlebitis

WONDER DRUGS: Drug fever (especially with some cephalosporins)

If you are on an obstetrics service, you may want to extend this to the "Seven Ws" to include

WOW: Breast (mastitis)

WOMB: Endometritis

These are common only in postpartum patients.

Elevated White Cell Counts: Commonly elevated secondary to catecholamine discharge after a stress such as surgery or childbirth

Temperatures of 103 F to 105 F: In adults think of lung, kidney, or septicemia.

Lethargy, Combativeness, Inappropriate Behavior: Do a lumbar puncture to rule out meningitis. DO NOT wait for opisthotonus.

Elderly Patients: Can be "low sick" without many of the typical manifestations; may be hypothermic or deny any tenderness. You must be very aggressive with the elderly.

Infants: Can become very ill very quickly; you must be aggressive with them also.

GASTROINTESTINAL TUBES

Indications

- Gastric or upper intestinal decompression
- Pyloric or intestinal obstruction, ileus
- Lavage of the stomach in a gastrointestinal (GI) bleed or drug overdose
- Prevention of emesis with concomitant aspiration in an obtunded patient or for the relief of nausea and vomiting
- "Resting the bowel": Especially after GI tract surgery or with pancreatitis
- Feeding a patient who is unable to swallow

Types of Gastrointestinal Tubes

Nasogastric Tubes

LEVIN: A 48-inch-long straight rubber or plastic tube with a single lumen, a perforated tip, and four to five side holes for the aspiration of gastric contents. Sometimes it is necessary to cut off the tip to allow for the aspiration of larger pills or tablets. The size varies from 10 to 18 French (1 French unit = ⅓ mm).

SALEM-SUMP: A 48-inch-long double lumen tube, with the smaller tube acting as an air intake vent. This is the best tube for irrigation and lavage since it will not collapse upon itself. If a Salem-sump tube stops working even after it is repositioned, often a "shot" of air from a catheter-tipped syringe in the air vent will clear the tube. Both the Salem-sump and Levin tubes have radiopaque markings.

Intestinal Tubes

CANTOR TUBE: A 9-foot-long single lumen tube with a rubber balloon at the tip. The balloon is partially filled with mercury which allows it to gravitate into the small bowel with the aid of peristalsis. Used for decompression when the bowel is obstructed distally.

MILLER-ABBOTT TUBE: A 9-foot-long double lumen tube with a rubber balloon at the tip. One lumen is used for aspiration; the other connects to the balloon. After the tube is in the stomach, inflate it with 5 to 10 ml of air, inject 2 to 3 ml of mercury, and then deflate the balloon. Functioning and indications are essentially the same as for the Cantor tube. DO NOT tape these intestinal tubes to the patient's nose or the tube will not descend. The progress of the tube can be followed on an x-ray film.

Miscellaneous

SENGSTAKEN-BLAKEMORE TUBE: A triple lumen tube used exclusively for the control of bleeding esophageal varices by tamponade. One lumen is for aspiration, one is for the gastric balloon, and the third is for the esophageal balloon.

FEEDING TUBES: Virtually any NG tube can be used as a feeding tube, but a pediatric NG tube is often used because its small size is less irritating to the patient. Other types are Keogh feeding tubes and a variety of weighted feeding tubes made of soft plastic. These weighted tubes tend to travel down into the duodenum. This position helps prevent regurgitation during tube feeding.

Procedure for Insertion of Nasogastric Tubes

1. Inform the patient of the nature of the procedure and encourage cooperation if the patient is able.

2. Lubricate the distal 3 to 4 inches of the tube with a water-soluble jelly (K-Y Jelly or viscous 2% lidocaine) and insert

the tube gently along the floor of the nasal passageway. Maintain gentle pressure that will allow the tube to pass into the nasopharynx.

3. When the patient can feel the tube in the back of his throat, ask him to swallow small amounts of water through a straw as you advance the tube 2 to 3 inches at a time.

4. To be sure that the tube is in the stomach, aspirate gastric contents or blow air into the tube and listen over the stomach with your stethoscope for a "pop" or "gurgle."

5. NG tubes are usually attached either to low wall suction or to intermittent suction (this type allows the tube to fall away from the gastric wall between suctions).

6. Feeding and pediatric feeding tubes in adults are more difficult to insert because they are more flexible. A stiff guide wire can be used or the smaller NG tube can be attached to a larger, stiffer tube by wedging both into a gelatin capsule. Pass the tube in the usual fashion and allow it to remain in the stomach for 10 to 15 minutes. After this time, the capsule dissolves, and the larger tube can be removed.

7. Tape the tube securely in place but do not allow it to apply pressure to the ala of the nose. Patients have been disfigured because of ischemic necrosis of the nose caused by a poorly positioned NG tube.

Complications

- Inadvertent passage into the trachea may provoke coughing or spasm in the patient.
- If the patient is unable to cooperate, the tube often becomes coiled in the oral cavity.
- The tube is irritating and may cause a small amount of bleeding in the mucosa of the nose, pharynx, or stomach. The drying and irritation can be lessened by throat lozenges.

HEELSTICK

Although called a "heelstick," any highly vascularized capillary bed can be used (finger, ear lobe, or great toe).

Indication

- Frequently used to collect blood samples from infants

Procedure

Materials

- Alcohol swabs
- Lancet
- Capillary or caraway collection tubes
- Clay

Technique

1. Choose a highly vascularized capillary bed. Warm the heel for 5 to 10 minutes by wrapping it in a warm washcloth.

2. Wipe the area with an alcohol swab. Use Fig. 4-4 to choose the site on the foot.

3. Use a 4 mm lancet and make a quick, deep puncture so that there is a free flow of blood. Wipe off the first drop of blood. Gently squeeze the heel and touch a collection tube to the drop of blood. The tube should fill by capillary action. Seal the end of the tube in clay.

4. Most labs can usually do laboratory determinations on small samples from the pediatric age group. A caraway tube can hold 0.3 ml of blood. One to three caraway tubes can be used for most routine tests. For a capillary blood gas, the blood is usually transferred to a 1 ml heparinized syringe and placed on ice.

5. Wrap the foot with 4 x 4 gauze squares or apply a Band-Aid.

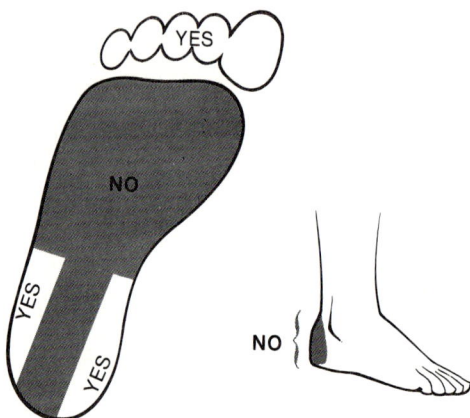

Fig. 4-4 Suggested sites for heelsticks. Use of these sites helps prevent osteomyelitis.

IV TECHNIQUES

Indication

- To establish an intravenous access for the administration of fluids, blood, or medications

Procedure

Materials

- IV fluid
- Connecting tubing
- Tourniquet
- Alcohol swab
- Intravenous cannulas (a catheter over a needle, like Angiocath, Jelco)
- Antiseptic ointment, dressing, and tape (It helps to rip the tape into strips and to flush the air out of the tubing before you begin.)

Technique

1. The upper, nondominant extremity is the site of choice
   for an IV. Choose a distal vein so that if the vein is lost,
   you can reposition the IV more proximally. Avoid veins
   that cross a joint space. Also avoid the leg since there is a
   high incidence of thrombophlebitis with IVs placed there.
   If no extremity vein can be found, try the external jugular.
   If all these fail, the only alternatives are a deep line or a
   cutdown.

2. Apply a tourniquet above the proposed IV site. Use the
   techniques described in the section on venipuncture to
   help expose the vein. Carefully clean the site with an
   alcohol or povidone-iodine swab.

3. Stabilize the vein distally with the thumb of your free
   hand. Using the catheter-over-needle assembly (Intracath
   or Angiocath), either enter the vein directly or enter the
   skin alongside the vein first and then stick the vein along
   the side at about a 20 degree angle. Once the vein is
   punctured, blood should appear in the "flash chamber."
   Advance a few more millimeters to be sure that BOTH
   the needle AND the tip of the catheter have entered the
   vein. Carefully withdraw the needle as you advance the
   catheter into the vein (Fig. 4-5). NEVER WITHDRAW THE
   CATHETER BACK OVER THE NEEDLE SINCE THIS PRO-
   CEDURE CAN SHEAR OFF THE PLASTIC TIP AND
   CAUSE A CATHETER EMBOLUS. Apply pressure with
   your thumb over the vein just proximal to the site to prevent significant blood loss while you connect the IV line
   to the catheter.

4. Observe the site with the IV fluid running for signs of
   induration or swelling that indicate improper placement
   or damage to the vein. See Chapter 11 for choosing IV
   fluids and how to determine infusion rates.

5. Tape the IV securely in place, apply a drop of povidone-
   iodine or antibiotic ointment and a sterile dressing.
   Ideally, the dressing should be changed every 24 to 48
   hours to help reduce infections. Armboards are also useful to help maintain an IV site.

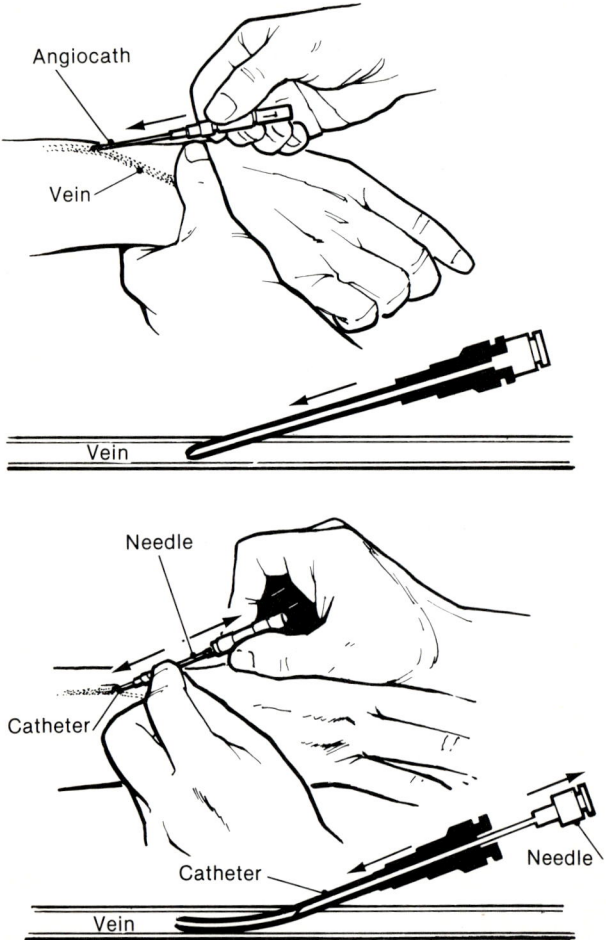

Fig. 4-5 To insert a catheter over a needle (Jelco or Angiocath), stabilize the skin and vein with gentle traction. Enter the vein and advance the catheter while removing the needle.

6. If the veins are deep and difficult to locate, a small 3 to 5 ml syringe can be mounted on the catheter assembly. Proper position inside the vein is determined by aspiration of blood. If blood specimens are needed on a patient who also needs an IV, this technique can be used to start the IV and to collect samples at the same time.

7. If venous access is limited, a "butterfly" or "scalp vein" needle can sometimes be used. This is a small metal needle with plastic "wings" on the side. It is very useful in infants, who often have poor peripheral veins but prominent scalp veins, and in adults who have small, fragile veins.

LUMBAR PUNCTURE

Indications

- Diagnostic purposes: Analysis of cerebrospinal fluid (CSF) for blood, as in subarachnoid hemorrhage, or pus, as in meningitis
- Measurement of CSF pressure or its changes with various maneuvers (Valsalva, etc.)
- Injection of various agents: Contrast media for myelography, antitumor drugs, analgesics, antibiotics

Contraindications

- Increased intracranial pressure, papilledema, mass lesion
- Infection near the puncture site
- Septicemia
- Planned myelography or pneumoencephalography
- Coagulation disorders

Anatomical Considerations

The objective of a lumbar puncture is to obtain a sample of cerebrospinal fluid from the subarachnoid space. Specifically, during a lumbar puncture the fluid is obtained from the lumbar cistern, the volume of CSF located between the termination of the spinal cord (the conus medularis) and the termination of the dura mater at the coccygeal ligament. The cistern is surrounded by the subarachnoid membrane and the overlying dura. Located within the cistern are the filum terminale and the nerve roots of the cauda equina. When an LP is done, the main body of the spinal cord is avoided and the nerve roots of the cauda are simply pushed out of the way by the needle.

The termination of the spinal cord in the adult is usually between L1 and L2, and in pediatric patients between L2 and L3. The safe site for a lumbar puncture is the interspace between L4 and L5. An imaginary line drawn between the iliac crests (the supracristal plane) intersects the spine at either the L4 spinous process or the L4-L5 interspace exactly.

A spinal needle introduced between the spinous processes of L4 and L5 penetrates the layers in the following order: skin, supraspinous ligament, interspinous ligament, ligamenta flava, epidural space (contains loose areolar tissue, fat, and blood vessels), dura, "potential space," subarachnoid membrane, subarachnoid space (lumbar cistern) (Fig. 4-6).

Procedure

Materials

- A sterile, disposable LP kit
- Sterile gloves
- Povidone-iodine paint
- Other spinal needles if a specific size is desired

Technique

1. Discuss the relative safety and lack of comfort to the patient to dispel any myths. Some prefer to call the procedure a "subarachnoid analysis" rather than a spinal tap. As long as the procedure and the risks are outlined, most patients will agree to the procedure. Have the patient sign a consent form if he is able.

2. Place the patient in the lateral decubitus position close to the edge of the bed or table. The patient (held by an

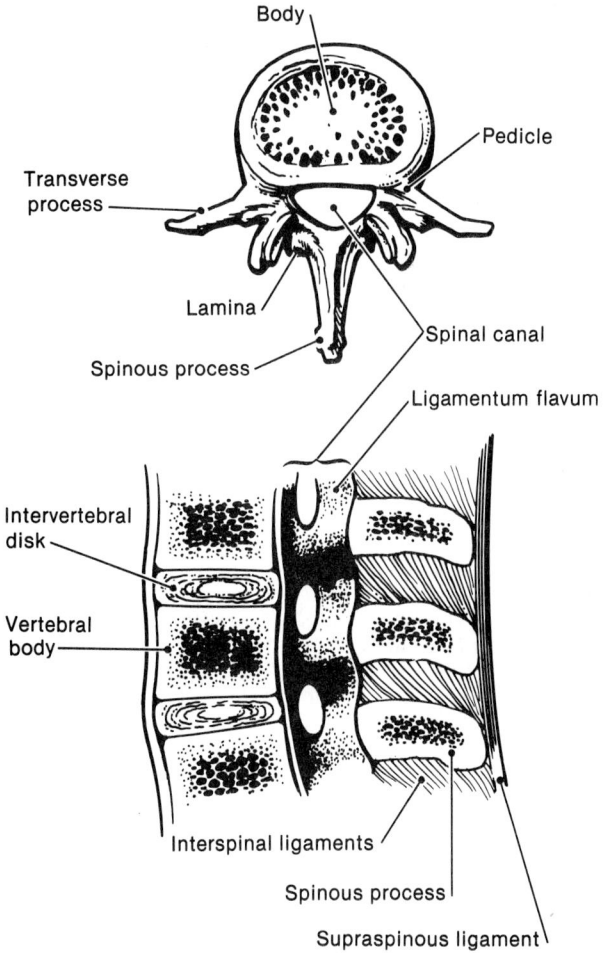

Fig. 4-6 Basic anatomy for a lumbar puncture.

assistant, if possible) should be positioned with his knees pulled up towards his stomach and his head flexed onto his chest. This enhances flexion of the vertebral spine and widens the interspaces between the spinous processes. Place a pillow beneath the patient's side to prevent sagging and insure alignment of the spinal column. In an obese patient, the sitting position may be preferred to minimize the distortion of anatomy caused by the fat (Fig. 4-7).

3. Palpate the supracristal plane and carefully determine the location of the L4-L5 interspace.

4. Open the kit, put on sterile gloves, and prep the area with povidone-iodine solution in a circular fashion and covering several interspaces. Next, drape the patient.

5. With a 25 gauge needle and 1% lidocaine, raise a skin wheal over the L4-L5 interspace. Anesthetize the deeper structures with a 22 gauge needle.

6. Examine the 21 gauge spinal needle with stylet and then insert it into the skin wheal into the spinous ligament. Hold the needle between your index and middle fingers, with your thumb holding the stylet in place. Direct the needle cephalad at a 30 to 45 degree angle, in the midline and parallel to the bed (Fig. 4-7).

7. Advance through the major structures and "pop" into the subarachnoid space through the dura. An experienced operator can feel these layers, but an inexperienced one may need to periodically remove the obturator to look for return of fluid. Direct the bevel of the needle parallel to the long axis of the body so that the dural fibers are separated rather than sheared. This method helps cut down on "spinal headaches."

8. If no fluid returns, it is sometimes helpful to rotate the needle slightly. If still no fluid appears, and you think that you are within the subarachnoid space, 1 ml of air can be injected since it is not uncommon for a piece of tissue to clog the needle. NEVER inject saline or distilled water. If

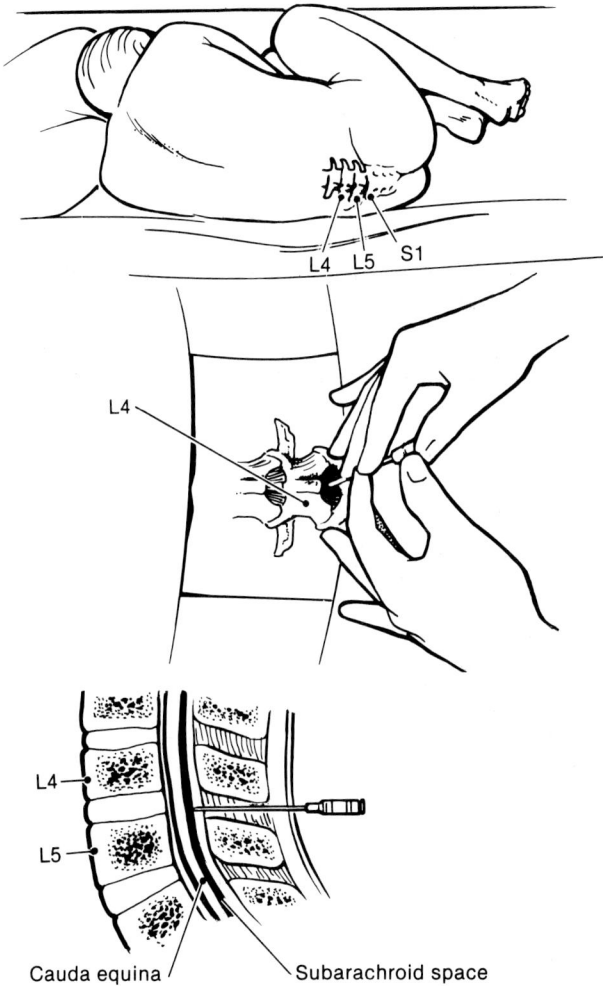

Fig. 4-7 Place the patient in the lateral decubitus position and locate the L4–L5 interspace. Control the spinal needle with two hands and pass it into the subarachnoid space.

no air returns and if spinal fluid cannot be aspirated, the bevel of the needle probably lies in the epidural space; advance it with the obturator in place.

9. When fluid returns, attach a manometer and stopcock and measure the pressure. Normal opening pressure is 70 to 180 mm water. Increased pressure may be due to a tense patient, CHF, ascites, subarachnoid hemorrhage, infection, or a space-occupying lesion. Decreased pressure may be due to needle position or obstructed flow (you may need to leave the needle in for a myelogram since if it is moved, the subarachnoid space may be lost).

10. Collect 0.5 to 2.0 ml samples in serial, labeled containers. Send them to the lab in this order:

    • 1st tube for bacteriology: Gram stain, routine culture and sensitivity (C&S), acid-fast bacilli (AFB), and fungal cultures and stains
    • 2nd tube for glucose and protein
    • 3rd tube for cell count: CBC with differential
    • 4th tube for special studies: VDRL test, etc.

    NOTE: Some people prefer to send the first and last tubes for CBC since this procedure permits a better differentiation between a subarachnoid hemorrhage and a traumatic tap. In a traumatic tap, the number of red blood cells (RBCs) in the first tube should be much higher than in the last tube. In a subarachnoid hemorrhage, the cell counts should be equal, and xanthochromia of the fluid should be present, indicating the presence of old blood.

11. Withdraw the needle and place a dry, sterile dressing over the site.

12. Instruct the patient to remain recumbent for 6 to 12 hours and encourage an increased fluid intake to help prevent "spinal headaches."

Complications

- Spinal headache: The most common complication, this appears within the first 24 hours after the puncture. It goes away when the patient is lying down and is aggravated when he sits up. It is usually characterized by a severe throbbing pain in the occipital region and can last for weeks. It is thought to be caused by intracranial traction caused by the acute volume depletion of CSF and by persistent leakage from the puncture site. To help prevent spinal headaches, keep the patient recumbent for 6 to 12 hours, encourage the intake of fluids, use the smallest needle possible, and keep the bevel of the needle parallel to the long axis of the body to help prevent a persistent CSF leak.

- Trauma to nerve roots or to the conus medullaris: Much less frequent (some anatomical variation does exist, but it is very rare for the cord to end below L3). If the patient suddenly complains of paresthesia (numbness or shooting pains in the legs), the procedure should be stopped.

- Herniation of either the cerebellum or the medulla: Occurs rarely, during or after a spinal tap, usually in a patient with increased intracranial pressure. This complication can often be reversed medically if it is recognized early.

- Meningitis

The following table gives the differential diagnosis of CSF.

MEASUREMENT OF ORTHOSTATIC BLOOD PRESSURE

Changes in blood pressure and pulse when a patient moves from the supine to the upright position are very sensitive guides for detecting early volume depletion. Even before a person becomes overtly tachycardic or hypotensive because

Differential Diagnosis of Cerebrospinal Fluid

Condition	Color	Opening Pressure (mm H$_2$O)	Protein (mg/100 ml)	Glucose (mg/100 ml)	Cells (#/mm^3)
ADULT (NORMAL)	clear	70–180	15–45	45–80	0–5 lymphs
NEWBORN (NORMAL)	clear	70–180	20–120	2/3 serum glucose	40–60 lymphs
VIRAL INFECTION	clear or opalescent	norm or slightly increased	norm or slightly increased	normal	10–500 lymphs (polys early)
BACTERIAL INFECTION	opalescent, yellow, may clot	incr	50–1500	<, usually < 20	25–10,000 polys
GRANULOMATOUS (TB, FUNGAL)	clear or opalescent	often >	>, but usually <500	<, usually 20–40	10–500 lymphs
SUBARACHNOID HEMORRHAGE	bloody or xanthochromic after 2–8 hr	usually >	>	normal	WBC/RBC* ratio same as blood

*WBC = white blood cell; RBC = red blood cell

of volume loss, the demonstration of orthostatic hypotension aids in the diagnosis.

Procedure

1. Have the patient assume a supine position. Determine the blood pressure and pulse.

2. Then have the patient stand up. If he is unable to stand, have him sit at the bedside with his legs dangling.

3. After about one minute, determine the blood pressure and pulse again.

4. A drop in systolic blood pressure greater than 10 mm Hg or an increase in pulse rate greater than 10 suggests volume depletion.

Other Causes

- Peripheral vascular disease
- Surgical sympathectomy
- Diabetes
- Medications such as prazosin hydrochloride or reserpine

PERITONEAL LAVAGE

Indication

- Diagnostic peritoneal lavage (DPL): A technique for evaluating intra-abdominal trauma

Contraindications

- None are absolute.
- Relative ones include multiple abdominal procedures, pregnancy, and any coagulopathy.

Procedure

1. A Foley catheter and NG tube MUST be in place. Prep the abdomen from above the umbilicus to the pubis.

2. The site of choice is in the midline 1 to 2 cm below the umbilicus. Avoid the site of old surgical scars (danger of adherent bowel). If a subumbilical scar or pelvic fracture is present, a supraumbilical approach is acceptable.

3. Infiltrate the skin with 1% lidocaine with epinephrine. Incise the skin in the midline vertically and expose the fascia.

4. Either pick up the fascia and incise it or puncture it with the trocar and peritoneal catheter. Caution is needed to avoid puncturing any organs. After entering the peritoneal cavity, remove the trocar and direct the catheter inferiorly into the pelvis.

5. Gross blood indicates a positive tap. If no blood is encountered, instill 10 ml/kg (about 1 liter in adults) of lactated Ringer's solution or normal saline into the abdominal cavity.

6. Gently agitate the abdomen to distribute the fluid and after five minutes, drain off as much fluid as possible into a bag on the floor. Send the fluid for analysis (amylase, bile, bacteria, food fibers, hematocrit, cell count).

7. Remove the catheter and suture the skin.

8. A negative DPL does not rule out retroperitoneal trauma. A false-positive DPL can be caused by a pelvic fracture.

Findings That Suggest Intra-abdominal Trauma

- Hematocrit >2% (a hematocrit <1% is usually negative, and a hematocrit of 1% to 2% is equivocal)
- Inability to read newsprint through the drainage tubing
- Grossly bloody tap
- RBC count >100,000 cells/mm^3
- WBC >500 cells/mm^3
- Amylase >100 Somogi units
- Presence of bile, bacteria, or food fibers

Complications

- Infection
- Bleeding
- Perforated viscus

PERITONEAL (ABDOMINAL) PARACENTESIS

Peritoneal paracentesis is surgical puncture of the peritoneal cavity for the aspiration of fluid.

Indications

- To determine if ascitic fluid is a transudate or an exudate
- To determine if intra-abdominal bleeding is present or if a viscus has ruptured
- Therapeutic removal of fluid when distention is pronounced or there is respiratory distress associated with it

Contraindications

- Abnormal coagulation factors
- Uncertainty if distention is due to peritoneal fluid or to a cystic structure (ultrasound can help here)

Procedure

Materials

- Gloves
- Povidone-iodine prep
- Sterile towels
- Angiocaths or Jelcos (18 to 20 gauge with a 1½ inch needle)
- 20 to 60 ml syringe
- 1% lidocaine
- 5 ml syringe with a 25 gauge needle for anesthesia
- Appropriate sterile containers for the specimens
- Kits are also available

Technique

1. The presence of ascitic fluid is indicated by abdominal distention, the presence of shifting dullness, and the presence of a palpable fluid wave.

2. Have the patient sign an informed consent paper, if he is able. Have him empty his bladder

3. The entry site is usually the midline 3 to 4 cm below the umbilicus. Avoid old surgical scars since the bowel may be clinging to the abdominal wall. Alternatively, the entry site can be in the left or right lower quadrant or in the patient's flank, depending on the percussion of the fluid wave.

4. Raise a skin wheal with the 1% lidocaine over the proposed entry site. Using gloves, prep and drape the patient appropriately.

5. With the catheter mounted on the syringe, go through the anesthetized area carefully while gently aspirating. You will meet some resistance as you enter the peritoneum. When you get free return of fluid, leave the catheter in place, remove the needle, and begin to aspirate. Sometimes it is necessary to reposition the catheter because of abutting bowel.

6. Aspirate the amount needed for tests (20 to 30 ml). If for a therapeutic tap, do not remove more than 500 ml in 10 minutes. A liter is the maximum that should be removed at one time; this volume permits the fluids and electrolytes to equilibrate.

7. Quickly remove the needle, apply a sterile 4 x 4 gauze square, and apply pressure with tape.

8. Depending on the clinical picture of the patient, send samples for total protein, specific gravity, lactate dehydrogenase (LDH), amylase, cytology, culture, stains, CBC, or food fibers.

Causes of Ascitic Fluid

TRANSUDATIVE ASCITES: Cirrhosis, nephrosis, and congestive heart failure.

EXUDATIVE ASCITES: Tumors, TB, and other causes of peritonitis including a perforated viscus.

Other causes can be found in Chapter 5 under Ascites. The following table gives the differential diagnosis.

Differential Diagnosis of Ascitic Fluid

Lab Value	Transudate	Exudate
SPECIFIC GRAVITY	<1.016	>1.016
PROTEIN (ASCITIC FLUID)	<3 gm/100 ml	>3 gm/100 ml
PROTEIN (ASCITIC TO SERUM RATIO)	<0.5	>0.5
LDH (ASCITIC TO SERUM RATIO)	<0.6	>0.6
ASCITIC FLUID LDH	<200 IU	>200 IU
FIBRINOGEN (CLOT)	NO	YES

CBC: • Up to 1000 WBC/mm^3 (usually <100 WBC/mm^3) suggests a noninflammatory transudate
• >1000 WBC/mm^3 with an inflammatory exudate
• >100 RBC/mm^3 in tumor, trauma, or TB

FOOD FIBERS: • Found in most cases of a perforated viscus

CYTOLOGY: • Bizarre cells with large nuclei may represent reactive mesothelial cells and NOT a malignancy
• Malignant cells suggest a tumor

Complications

- Peritonitis
- Perforated viscus
- Hemorrhage

- Precipitation of hepatic coma if patient has severe liver disease
- Oliguria
- Hypotension

PELVIC EXAMINATION

The pelvic exam should be carried out in a comfortable fashion for both the patient and physician. An assistant should be present for the procedure, and a female assistant MUST be present if the examiner is a male. The patient should be draped appropriately and place her feet in the stirrups on the examining table. A low stool, a good light source, and all needed supplies should be prepared before the exam begins.

Materials

- Gloves
- A speculum and lubricant
- Slides, fixative, and a cervical spatula prepared for a Pap smear
- Materials for other diagnostic tests: Culture media to test for gonorrhea, sterile cotton swabs, plain glass slides, KOH and normal saline solutions, as needed

Inform the patient of each move in advance. It is often useful to engage in conversation as a distraction.

General Inspection

1. Observe the skin of the perineum for swelling, ulcers, or color changes.

2. Separate the labia to observe the clitoris and vestibule.

3. Observe the urethral meatus for developmental abnormalities, discharge, neoplasm, and abcess of Bartholin's gland.

4. Inspect the vaginal orifice for discharge, gaping of the edges, or protrusion of the walls.

5. Note the condition of the hymen.

Speculum Examination

1. Use a speculum moistened with warm water NOT with lubricant (lubricant will interfere with Pap tests and slide studies). Check the temperature on the patient's leg to see if the speculum is comfortable.

2. Because the anterior wall of the vagina is close to the urethra and bladder, do not exert pressure in this area. Pressure should be placed on the posterior surface of the vagina. With the speculum directed at a 45 degree angle to the floor, spread the labia and insert the speculum fully. Turn the speculum parallel to the floor and open fully. The cervix should pop into view with some manipulation.

3. Inspect the cervix for color, lacerations, growths, nabothian cysts.

4. Inspect the cervical os for size, shape, color, discharge.

5. Inspect the vagina for secretions and obtain specimens for a Pap smear, other smear, or culture (see Tests for Vaginal Infections and Pap Smear).

6. Inspect the vaginal wall; rotate the speculum as you draw it out to see the entire canal (Fig. 4-8).

Bimanual Examination

1. For this part, stand up. Although there is some difference of opinion, many persons believe that a right-handed individual should use a gloved left hand in the vagina and the right hand for abdominal palpation. It is best to use whichever hand is comfortable.

2. Place lubricant on the first and second gloved fingers, and then, keeping pressure on the posterior fornix, introduce them into the vagina.

3. Palpate the tissue at five and seven o'clock between the first and second fingers and the thumb to rule out any abnormality of Bartholin's gland or duct. Likewise, palpate the urethra and paraurethral (Skene's) glands.

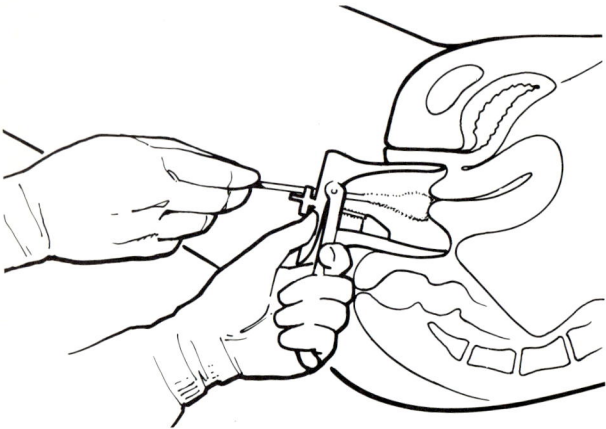

Fig. 4-8 The speculum is used both to examine the vagina and to obtain cervical scrapings for Pap smears. The spatula is rotated 360 degrees in the cervical os to obtain the sample.

4. Place the examining fingers on the posterior wall of the vagina to further open the introitus. Ask the patient to bear down. Is there evidence of prolapse, rectocele, or cystocele?

5. Palpate the cervix. Note the size, shape, consistency, motility and test for tenderness (the so-called "chandelier sign" or marked cervical tenderness is positive in pelvic inflammatory disease).

6. With your fingers in the vagina posterior to the cervix and your hand on the abdomen placed just above the symphysis, the corpus of the uterus can be forced between the two examining hands. Note size, shape, consistency, position, and mobility.

7. Move the fingers in the vagina to one or the other fornix and place the hand on the abdomen in a more lateral

position to bring the adnexal areas under examination. Palpate the ovaries, if possible, for any masses, consistency, and motility. Unless the Fallopian tubes are diseased, they usually are not palpable.

Rectovaginal Examination

1. Insert your index finger into the vagina and place the well-lubricated middle finger in the rectum.

2. Palpate the posterior surface of the uterus and the broad ligament for nodulation, tenderness, or other masses. Examine the uterosacral and rectovaginal septum.

3. It may also be helpful to do a test for occult blood while the stool specimen is available.

Pap Smear

There is some controversy with respect to the cost-benefit ratio, but it is generally agreed that a routine Pap smear should be done at least every one to two years.

1. With the unlubricated speculum in place, obtain vaginal pool material from the posterior vaginal fornix. Place a drop on a frosted slide that has the patient's name written on it in pencil. Smear the slide and fix it either in a bottle of 75% ethyl alcohol or with commercially available spray fixative.

2. Next, use a wooden cervical spatula to obtain a scraping from the squamocolumnar junction. Rotate the spatula 360 degrees around the external os, high up in the endocervical canal. (Some pathology labs also request that a specimen be obtained from the endocervical canal; use a cotton swab and smear it on a slide.) Smear and fix the slide (alcohol or spray).

3. Complete the appropriate lab slips.

Tests for Vaginal Infections

GC (Gonococcal) Culture

Use a sterile cotton swab to obtain a specimen from the endocervical canal and plate it out on Thayer-Martin media.

Saline Prep

If a patient has a thin, watery, greenish discharge, an infection with *Trichomonas vaginalis* may be present. Mix a drop of discharge with a drop of normal saline on a glass slide and cover the drop with a coverslip. It is important to observe the slide while it is still warm to see the flagellated, motile trichomonads. Alternatively, these can be seen by using a handing drop of saline and a concave slide.

Potassium Hydroxide Prep

If a thick, white, curdy discharge is present, the patient may have a *Candida albicans* (monilial) yeast infection. Prepare a slide with one drop of discharge and one drop of aqueous 10% KOH solution. The KOH dissolves the epithelial cells and debris and facilitates viewing of the hyphae and mycelia of the fungus that causes the infection. Smell the slide immediately after the KOH is applied. A distinctly fishy odor indicates a positive "whiff" test for infection with *Hemophilus*.

Gram Stain

Material can easily be stained in the usual fashion. Gram-negative intracellular diplococci (so-called GNIDs) are pathognomonic of *Neisseria gonorrhoeae*. The most commonly found bacteria in gram stains are large gram-positive rods (lactobacilli) which are normal vaginal flora.

PULSUS PARADOXUS

Definition

Pulsus paradoxus is an exaggeration of the normal inspiratory drop in arterial pressure. Inspiration decreases intrathoracic pressure. The result is increased right atrial and right ventricular filling with an increase in right ventricular output. Since the pulmonary vascular bed also distends, these changes lead to a delay in left ventricular filling and subsequently a decreased left ventricular output. This drop in systolic blood pressure is usually <10 mm Hg.

In the case of cardiac compression (e.g., acute asthma or pericardial tamponade), the right side of the heart fills more with inspiration and decreases the left ventricular volume to an even greater degree as a result of compression of the pericardial sac. This exaggerated decrease in left ventricular output drops the systolic pressure >10 mm Hg.

Differential Diagnosis

- Pericardial effusion
- Cardiac tamponade
- Adhesive pericarditis
- Chronic obstructive airways disease (COAD)
- Bronchial asthma
- Restrictive cardiomyopathies
- Hemorrhagic shock

Procedure

Qualitatively: Palpation of the radial pulse that "disappears" on normal inspiration

Quantitatively

1. Have the patient take a breath, let it out, and hold it. Determine the systolic blood pressure.

2. Ask the patient to breathe again. Once the patient is breathing normally, drop the pressure in the cuff SLOWLY until you hear his pulse during inspiration.

3. The difference in systolic pressure should be <10. If not, a so-called "paradox" exists.

SIGMOIDOSCOPY

Definitions

Sigmoidoscopy: Visual examination, with a lighted tube, of the last 25 cm of the GI tract

Proctoscopy: Roughly synonymous to sigmoidoscopy, but technically means examination of the last 12 cm

Procedure

Preparation

Enemas and cathartics are not routinely given before sigmoidoscopy, although some people prefer to give a mild prep such as a Fleet Enema just before the exam. An intravenous pyelogram (IVP) or a barium enema (BE) should not be scheduled just after sigmoidoscopy since the introduction of air into the colon may interfere with the x-ray study. Have the patient sign a consent form.

Materials

- Gloves
- Lubricant
- Hemoccult paper and developer
- Sigmoidoscope and light source
- Insufflation bag
- Tissues
- Long (rectal) swabs and a suction catheter
- Proctological examination table: Nice but not essential

Positioning the Patient

Sigmoidoscopy can be performed with the patient in bed lying on his side in the knee-chest position, but the best results are obtained with the patient in the "jackknife" position on the procto table (Fig. 4-9). Do not position the patient until all materials are at hand and you are ready to start.

Technique

1. Converse with the patient to create distraction and to relieve apprehension. Announce each maneuver in advance.

2. Observe the anal region for skin tags, hemorrhoids, fissures, etc. Do a careful rectal exam and Hemoccult test with a gloved finger and plenty of lubricant.

Sacrum

Rectum

Sigmoid colon

Umbilicus

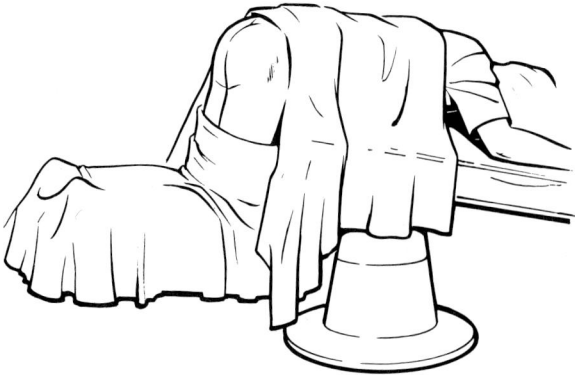

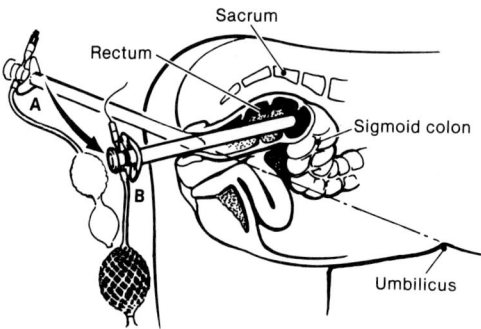

Fig. 4-9 Positioning the patient on a proctoscopic table facilitates the examination. The sigmoidoscope is advanced under direct vision as shown.

3. Lubricate the sigmoidoscope well and insert it with the obturator in place. Aim towards the patient's umbilicus initially. Advance 2 to 3 cm past the internal sphincter and remove the obturator.

4. Always advance under direct vision and make sure that the lumen is visible (Fig. 4-9). Insufflation (introducing air) may be used to help visualize the lumen, but remember this may be painful. It is necessary to follow the curve of the sigmoid towards the sacrum by directing the scope more posteriorly towards the back. A change from a smooth mucosa to concentric rings signifies entry into the sigmoid colon. The scope should reach 15 cm with ease. Use suction and the rectal swabs as needed to clear the way.

5. At this point, the sigmoid curves to the patient's left. Warn the patient that he may feel a cramping sensation. If you ever have difficulty negotiating a curve, do not force the scope.

6. After advancing as far as possible, slowly remove the scope; use a small rotary motion to view all surfaces. Observation here is critical. Remember to release the air from the colon before withdrawing the scope.

7. Inform the patient that he may experience mild cramping after the procedure.

Complications

- Bleeding (rare)
- Perforation (rare)

SKIN TESTING

Skin tests for delayed type hypersensitivity (type IV, tuberculin) are the most commonly administered and interpreted. Allergy tests (immediate wheal and flare) are rarely performed by the student or house officer.

Delayed hypersensitivity is caused by the activation of sensitized lymphocytes after contact with an antigen. The inflammatory reaction results from direct cytotoxicity and the release of lymphokines.

Indications

- Screening for current or past infectious agent (TB, mumps, fungus, etc.)
- Screening for immune competency (so-called "anergy screen") in debilitated patients

Procedure

Materials

- Appropriate antigen (usually 0.1 ml)
- A small, short needle (25, 26, or 27 gauge)
- 1 ml syringe
- Alcohol swab

Technique

1. The most commonly used site is the flexor surface of the forearm, approximately 4 inches below the elbow crease.

2. Prep the area with alcohol. With the bevel up, introduce the needle into the upper layers of the skin, but NOT into the subcutis. Inject 0.1 ml of antigen. The goal is to inject the antigen intradermally.

3. If done properly, you will raise a discrete white bleb, approximately 10 mm in diameter. The bleb should disappear soon, and no dressing is needed.

4. Mark the test site with a pen, and if multiple tests are being administered, identify each one. Also, document the site in the patient's chart.

Specific Skin Tests

Tuberculosis (PPD or Mantoux)

The solution of purified protein derivative (PPD) comes in three strengths: 1 TU, 5 TU, and 250 TU (tuberculin units). 1 TU is used if the patient is expected to be hypersensitive (history of a positive skin test); 5 TU is the standard initial screening test. A patient who has a negative response to a 5 TU test dose may react to the 250 TU solution. A patient who does not respond to the 250 TU is considered nonreactive to PPD. A patient may not react if he has not been exposed to the antigen or if he is anergic and unable to respond to any antigen challenge.

To interpret the PPD skin test, examine the injection site at 24, 48, and 72 hours. Measure the area of induration (the firm raised area), not the erythematous area.

- 0–5 mm induration — a negative response
- 5–10 mm induration — an equivocal test; repeat (possible atypical mycobacterium)
- >10 mm induration — a positive response

An equivocal PPD test may represent an infection with an atypical species of mycobacteria.

It is important to check the PPD test at intervals. If the patient develops a severe reaction to the skin test, apply 1% hydrocortisone cream to prevent skin sloughing.

The tine test for TB is useful only as a mass screening procedure. The PPD test is a much more sensitive and specific test and should be used on all hospitalized patients. A positive tine test is the presence of vesicles.

Anergy Screen

An anergy screen is based on the assumption that a patient has been exposed in the past to certain common antigens and a healthy patient is able to mount a reaction to them. To perform the screen, one can use an assortment of antigens such as mumps (positive test is an area of erythema >1.5 cm), *Candida*, dermatophyton, and SKSD (streptokinase-streptodornase). These are generally applied and read just like the PPD test.

Anergy screens are used to evaluate a patient's immunological status or his ability to withstand the stresses of surgery. They are also used in specific situations: if you suspect that a patient is PPD-positive, and he does not react to the test, do an anergy screen along with the PPD test to see if he can mount ANY response at all.

THORACENTESIS

Thoracentesis is the surgical puncture of the chest wall for aspiration of fluid from the pleural cavity.

Indications

- To differentiate whether a pleural effusion is a transudate or an exudate (infectious, traumatic, etc.)
- To remove pleural fluid in the event of large volumes causing respiratory distress

Contraindications

- Pneumothorax, hemothorax, or any major respiratory impairment on the contralateral side
- Coagulopathy (relative contraindication)

Procedure

With a Kit

A kit usually contains all that is needed, including an automatic valve that allows you to "pump" the fluid collected into a bag. A built-in safety hub prevents you from going in too far.

Without a Kit

A kit is usually not required when all that is desired is a small amount of pleural fluid for diagnosis. Use a 20 to 60 ml syringe and a 20 to 22 gauge, 1½ inch needle with a three-way stopcock. Since the needle does not have a safety hub, it is a good idea to clamp the needle with a hemostat to prevent it from going in too far. If not using a kit, you need to collect supplies like lidocaine, sterile containers, and sterile drapes.

Technique

1. The area of a pleural effusion will be dull to percussion, with decreased whisper and breath sounds. On a chest x-ray film you will see blunting of the costophrenic angles. These findings usually indicate that at least 300 ml of fluid are present. If you suspect that less than 300

ml are present, order a lateral decubitus chest film. Even effusions of only 100 to 200 ml should layer out on a decubitus film.

2. Have the patient sign an informed consent and have him practice the Valsalva maneuver or humming while sitting up comfortably.

3. The usual site for thoracentesis is the posterolateral aspect of the back, over the diaphragm but under the fluid level. Confirm the site by counting ribs on the chest x-ray film and percussing out the fluid level. Use the superior aspect of the rib below the fluid level as the site, thus avoiding the nerve, artery, and vein that run below the rib.

4. Use sterile technique with gloves, drapes, and povidone-iodine prep. The patient should be sitting up comfortably, leaning forward slightly.

5. Make a skin wheal over the proposed site with a 25 gauge needle and 1% lidocaine. Change to a 22 gauge, 1½ inch needle and infiltrate up and over the rib; try to anesthetize the deeper structures and the pleura. During this time you should be aspirating back for pleural fluid. Once fluid returns, note the depth of the needle. This gives you an approximate depth. Remove the needle.

6. Penetrate through the anesthetized area with the thoracentesis needle. MAKE SURE THAT YOU "MARCH" OVER THE TOP OF THE RIB to avoid the neurovascular bundle that runs below the rib (Fig. 4-10). Aspirate the amount needed. NEVER REMOVE MORE THAN 1000 ML PER TAP!

7. Have the patient hum or do the Valsalva maneuver as you withdraw the needle. This maneuver increases intrathoracic pressure and decreases the chance of a pneumothorax. Bandage with a Band-Aid strip or a 4 x 4 gauze square.

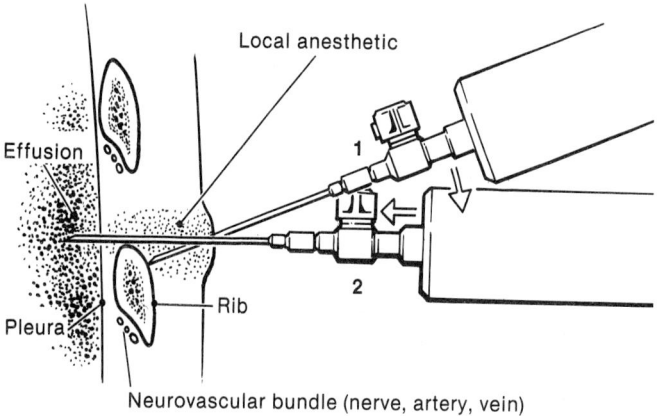

Fig. 4-10 The needle for thoracentesis is passed over the top of the rib to avoid the neurovascular bundle.

8. Obtain a chest x-ray film to evaluate the fluid level and to rule out a pneumothorax. An expiratory film is best because it helps reveal a small pneumothorax.

9. Distribute specimens in containers, label slips, and send them to the lab. Always order pH, specific gravity, protein, LDH, cell count and differential, glucose, gram stain and cultures, acid-fast cultures and smears, and fungal cultures and smears. Optional lab studies are cytology if you suspect a malignancy and amylase if you suspect an effusion secondary to pancreatitis (usually on the left).

Complications

- Pneumothorax
- Hemothorax
- Infection
- Pulmonary laceration
- Hypotension

Differential Diagnosis of Pleural Fluid

Common Causes of a Pleural Effusion: For a more complete differential, see Chapter 5 under Pleural Effusion.

TRANSUDATE: Nephrosis (renal failure), CHF, cirrhosis

EXUDATE: Infection (pneumonia, TB), malignancy, empyema, peritoneal dialysis, pancreatitis

The following table gives the differential diagnosis.

Differential Diagnosis of Pleural Fluid

Lab Value	Transudate	Exudate
SPECIFIC GRAVITY	<1.016	>1.016
PROTEIN (PLEURAL FLUID)	<3 gm/100 ml	>3 gm/100 ml
PROTEIN RATIO (PLEURAL FLUID TO SERUM RATIO)	<0.5	>0.5
LDH RATIO (PLEURAL FLUID TO SERUM RATIO)	<0.6	>0.6
PLEURAL FLUID LDH	<200 IU	>200 IU
FIBRINOGEN (CLOT)	NO	YES
CELL COUNT AND DIFFERENTIAL	very low WBC	WBC>2500/mm^3 suspect an inflammatory exudate (early polys, later monos)

(The causes of a grossly bloody tap are trauma, pulmonary infarction, tumor, and iatrogenic causes)

pH: The pH of pleural fluid is usually >7.3. If between 7.2–7.3, suspect TB or malignancy or both. If <7.2, suspect an empyema.

GLUCOSE: • Normal pleural fluid glucose is ⅔ serum glucose
• Pleural fluid glucose is MUCH, MUCH lower than serum glucose in effusions due to rheumatoid arthritis (0–16 mg/100 ml)

URINARY TRACT PROCEDURES

Bladder Catherization

Indications

- To prevent or relieve urinary retention in a postoperative or postpartum patient who is unable to void spontaneously
- To prevent or relieve urinary retention in a patient with lower urinary tract obstruction or paralysis
- To collect an uncontaminated urine specimen for diagnostic purposes
- To monitor urinary output in critically ill patients
- To perform tests of bladder function such as cystography or cystometrography

Catheters

FOLEY: Use a 16 to 18 French for adults (the higher the number, the larger the diameter). Irrigation catheters ("three-way") should be larger (20 to 22 French).

COUDÉ (COO-DAY):   An elbow-tipped catheter used especially in males with prostatic hypertrophy

Technique

1. Each insertion of a catheter implants bacteria into the bladder, so strict aseptic technique is mandatory.

2. Have the patient in a well-lighted area in a supine position, females with knees flexed wide and heels together to get adequate exposure of the meatus.

3. Check the balloon for leaks before insertion and place sterile lubricant jelly on the tip of the catheter.

4. Catheter kits should have povidone-iodine or some other type of prep solution. In females, use one ungloved hand to wipe from pubis to anus; hold the labia apart with the other, gloved hand. With uncircumsised males, retract the foreskin to prep the glans; use a gloved hand to hold the penis still.

5. The hand used to prep the penis or labia should not touch the catheter to insert it; a disposable forceps in the kit can be used to insert it. Or, the forceps can be used to prep, then the gloved hand can insert the catheter.

6. In the male, STRETCH the penis upwards perpendicular to the body to eliminate any internal folds in the urethra that might lead to a false passage. GENTLE pressure should be used to advance the catheter. The bulbous urethra is the most likely part to tear. Any resistance that is encountered may represent a stricture and requires urological consultation. In males with benign prostatic hypertrophy (BPH), a Coudé tip catheter may facilitate passage. Some tricks to use to get a catheter to pass in a male are to make sure that the penis is well stretched and to instill 30 to 50 ml of sterile jelly into the urethra with a catheter-tipped syringe. NEVER use a catheter guide wire to force the catheter. ANY MALE WHO IS UNCIRCUM- CISED SHOULD HAVE THE FORESKIN REPOSITIONED TO PREVENT MASSIVE EDEMA OF THE GLANS AFTER THE CATHETER IS INSERTED.

7. In both males and females, insert the catheter to the hilt of the drainage end. Compress the penis towards the pubis. These maneuvers insure that the balloon will be inflated in the bladder and not in the urethra. The balloon is inflated with 5 to 10 ml of sterile water or, occasionally, air. After inflation pull the catheter back so that the bal- loon will come to rest on the bladder neck. There should be good urine return when the catheter is in place. If no urine returns, attempt to irrigate with sterile saline. A CATHETER THAT WILL NOT IRRIGATE IS IN THE URETHRA, NOT THE BLADDER.

8. Catheters in females can be taped to the leg. In males, the catheter should be taped to the adbominal wall to decrease stress on the internal urethra. The catheter is usually attached to a gravity drainage bag or some device for measuring the amount of urine.

Clean-Catch Urine Specimen

A clean-catch urine is useful for routine urinalysis, is usually good for culturing urine from males, but is only fair for culturing urine from females because of the potential for contamination.

Technique

MALES

1. Expose the glans.

2. Clean it with an antiseptic solution and dry it with a sterile pad.

3. Collect a midstream urine in a sterile container after the initial flow has escaped.

FEMALES

1. Separate the labia widely to expose the urethral meatus; keep the labia spread throughout the procedure.

2. Cleanse the urethral meatus with antiseptic solution and rinse it with sterile water.

3. Catch the midstream portion of the urine in a sterile container.

In and Out Catheterized Urine for C&S

If urine is needed for analysis or for culture and sensitivity, especially in a female patient, a so-called "in and out cath" can be done. The incidence of inducing infection with this procedure is about 3%.

Technique

MALES

1. Drape the external genitals and soak the rayon balls in the catheter kit in either povidone-iodine or the equivalent.

2. Grasp the penis with one hand (unsterile). Clean the glans with the soaked rayon balls circumferentially from the meatus outward at least three times.

3. Insert the catheter until urine flows. DO NOT FORCE. Catch the urine in a sterile plastic tray and dispense it to specimen containers.

FEMALES

1. Drape the external genitals and soak the rayon balls in an antiseptic.

2. Spread the labia with two fingers (unsterile). Use one rayon ball to swab medially anterior to posterior. Next, use two rayon balls, one for each side, to swab the labia. Repeat this three times; use new rayon balls each time.

3. Insert the Foley catheter until urine begins to flow and catch the sample in a sterile tray. Dispense the urine to sterile specimen jars. Remove and discard the catheter.

Percutaneous Suprapubic Bladder Aspiration

This procedure is almost exclusively limited to the very young pediatric patient.

Indications

- When urine cannot be obtained by a less invasive method
- In the presence of urethral abnormalities
- In the presence of a urinary tract infection (UTI) that does not respond to apparently appropriate therapy

Technique

1. Immobilize the child. Do not attempt this procedure if the child has voided within the last hour.

2. Palpate the bladder above the pubic symphysis (the bladder sticks high above the pubis in a young child when it is full). Some suggest occluding the urethra by holding the penis in a male and by inserting a finger in the rectum to exert pressure in the female. Percuss out the limits of the bladder.

3. Obtain a 20 ml syringe with a 23 gauge, 1½ inch needle. Prep with betadine and alcohol 1.5 cm above the pubis.

4. Insert the needle perpendicular to the table in the mid-line; maintain negative pressure on the downstroke and on withdrawal.

5. If no urine is obtained, redirect the needle, without coming out completely, in a 30 to 40 degree angle caudad.

VENIPUNCTURE

Venipuncture (phlebotomy) is the puncture of a vein to obtain a sample of venous blood for analysis. (Blood cultures, IV techniques, and arterial punctures are discussed in other sections of this chapter.)

Procedure

Materials

- A tourniquet (a 1 ½-inch Penrose drain is acceptable)
- Alcohol prep sponge
- Proper specimen tubes (red top, purple top, etc.)
- Appropriate sized syringe for volume of blood needed (5 ml, 10 ml, etc.)
- An 18 to 22 gauge needle (Larger needles are uncomfortable and smaller ones can cause hemolysis or clotting. Remember, the larger the gauge number, the smaller the needle.)

Although the color and type of specimen tubes can vary from medical center to medical center, the following table lists the types of tubes used at the University of Kentucky and is provided as a general guide.

Technique

1. Collect the necessary materials before you begin.

2. The most commonly used sites for routine venipuncture are the veins of the antecubital fossa. Other sites that can

Specimen Tubes for Venipuncture

Tube Color	Additives	General Use
RED	None	Clot tube to collect serum for chemistry, crossmatching, serology
RED AND BLACK	Silicone gel for rapid clot	As above, but not for osmolality or blood bank work
BLUE	Sodium citrate (binds calcium)	Coagulation studies (best kept on ice)
PURPLE	Disodium EDTA (binds calcium)	Hematology, lipid profiles
GREEN	Sodium heparin	Ammonia, cortisol, ionized calcium (best kept on ice)
GREY	Sodium fluoride	Lactic acid
YELLOW	Transport media	Blood cultures

be used include the dorsum of the hand, the forearm, the saphenous vein near the medial malleolus, or the external jugular vein. If all the routine peripheral sites are unacceptable, the femoral vein can be used. REMEMBER, NEVER DRAW A BLOOD SAMPLE PROXIMAL TO AN IV SITE. IT MAY NOT BE A VALID COLLECTION BECAUSE OF THE HIGH CONCENTRATION OF IV FLUID IN THE VEINS THERE.

3. Apply the tourniquet at least 2 to 3 inches above the venipuncture site. Have the patient make a fist to help engorge the vein. If veins are difficult to locate, some helpful techniques include slapping the vein to cause reflex dilation, hanging the extremity in a dependent position, wrapping the extremity in a warm soak, or substituting a blood pressure cuff for the standard tourniquet.

4. Swab the site with the alcohol prep pad.

5. Use the syringe and needle with the bevel up and puncture the skin alongside the vein. After you are through the

skin, use the thumb of your free hand to stabilize the vein and prevent it from rolling.

6. Enter the vein on the side at about a 30 degree angle while applying gentle back pressure on the syringe. Withdraw the sample slowly to prevent the vein from collapsing. An alternative acceptable technique is to enter both the skin and vein in one stick, however this maneuver requires practice since the vein is often stuck through and through.

7. The Vacutainer system is a very useful method of blood collection, especially if several different sample tubes need to be filled. Mount a 20 or 22 gauge needle on the Vacutainer cup. Enter the vein as directed previously. Advance the collection tube onto the needle inside the Vacutainer. The vacuum inside the tube automatically collects the sample. If you hold the Vacutainer steady, serial tubes can be collected in this fashion.

8. After the blood is collected (by whatever method), remove the tourniquet, withdraw the needle, and apply firm pressure with the alcohol swab for two to three minutes. Elevation of the extremity is helpful.

9. If a needle and syringe were used, distribute the samples to the blood tubes. The best technique is to insert the needle into the tube and allow the vacuum to draw in the appropriate volume of blood for a given tube. Distribute the blood to the coagulation and CBC tubes first since clotting of the blood in the syringe can invalidate the results. Mix the tubes thoroughly.

10. If no peripheral veins can be located, puncture of the femoral vein can be attempted. Locate the femoral artery. The mnemonic for lateral to medial structures in the groin is NAVEL: Nerve, Artery, Vein, Empty space, Lymphatic. The femoral vein should be just medial to the femoral artery. After prepping the skin, insert the needle perpendicular to the skin and gently aspirate. The vein should be about 1 to 1½ inches below the skin. Apply firm pressure after collection of the sample since hematomas are frequent complications of femoral venipunctures.

VENOUS CUTDOWN

Indication

- Venous access when percutaneous puncture is not practical. Often used in pediatric patients.

Procedure

Materials

- Pre-packaged "cutdown" tray
- Lidocaine
- Sterile gloves
- Antiseptic prep paint
- Catheter of choice

Technique (Fig. 4-11)

1. The most common site for a cutdown is the greater saphenous vein. It is best located approximately one fingerbreadth anterior and superior to the medial malleolus. Other sites on the foot, hand, or arm can be used.

2. Apply a tourniquet proximal to the site. Children may need to be restrained. Prep the skin with antiseptic solution, drape the patient, and put on sterile gloves.

3. Infiltrate the skin over the vein with 1% lidocaine. Incise the skin transversely.

4. Spread the incision in the direction of the vein with a hemostat until the excess tissue is cleaned off. Lift the vein off the posterior tissues.

5. Pass two chromic or silk ties (3-0 or 4-0) behind the vein. Tie off the distal vein. The upper tie is used for traction.

6. Make a transverse nick in the vein. You may need a catheter introducer ("banana") to hold open the lumen of the vein.

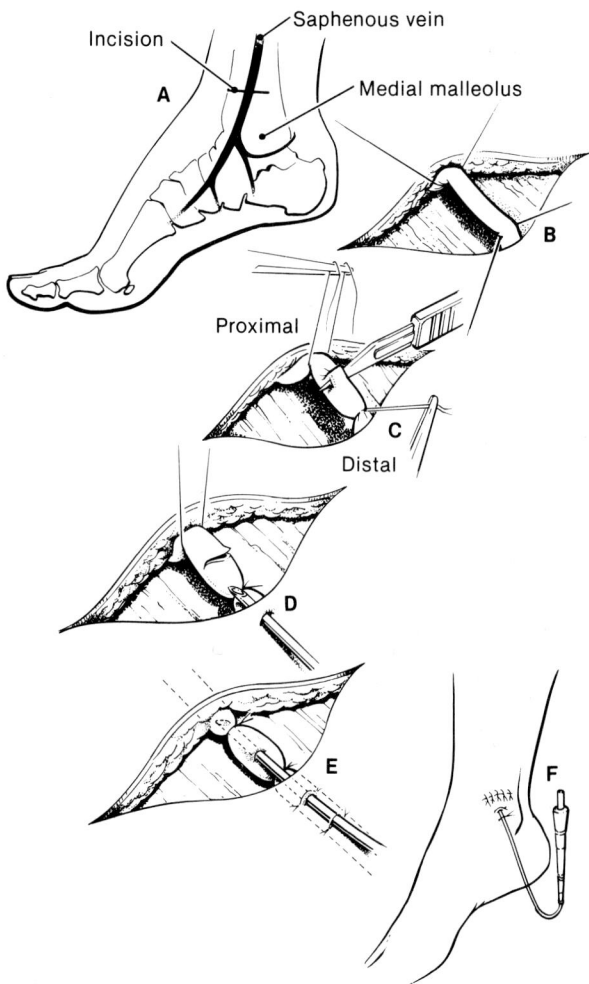

Fig. 4-11 Venous cutdown on the saphenous vein. Here the catheter is inserted through a separate stab wound.

7. Insert the plastic catheter or IV cannula into the vein, and tie the proximal suture to secure it in place. The catheter may also be inserted through a separate stab wound and then passed into the vein.

8. Attach the fluid, release the tourniquet, and close the skin with silk or nylon. Apply a sterile dressing.

5

Differential Diagnosis: Symptoms and Conditions

The following is a list of some common complaints and some of the more common conditions associated with them.

Abdominal Distention
Abdominal Pain
Anuria
Ascites
Anorexia
Arthritis
Constipation
Cough
Chills
Chest Pain
Coma
Diarrhea
Dysphagia
Dyspnea
Dysuria
Edema
Failure to Thrive
Flatulence
Fever of Unknown Origin

Frequency
Headache
Heartburn (Pyrosis)
Hematemesis
Hematuria
Hemoptysis
Hepatomegaly
Jaundice
Lymphadenopathy
   (Splenomegaly)
Melena
Nausea and Vomiting
Oliguria
Pleural Effusion
Seizures
Syncope
Vertigo
Weight Loss
Wheezing

ABDOMINAL DISTENTION

Ascites, intestinal obstruction, peritonitis, cysts (ovarian or renal), tumors, hepatosplenomegaly, aortic aneurysm, uterine enlargement (pregnancy), bladder distention, inflammatory mass

ABDOMINAL PAIN

Diffuse: Abdominal angina, early appendicitis, colitis, keto-acidosis, gastroenteritis, mesenteric thrombosis, mesenteric lymphadenitis, peritonitis, porphyria, sickle cell crisis, uremia, colic

Right Upper Quadrant: Dissecting aneurysm, gall bladder disease (cholecystitis, cholangitis, choledocholithiasis), hepatitis, hepatomegaly, pancreatitis, peptic ulcer disease, pericarditis, myocardial infarction, pleurisy, pneumonia, pulmonary embolus, pyelonephritis, renal colic

Left Upper Quadrant: Dissecting aneurysm, esophagitis, hiatal hernia, gastritis, pancreatitis, peptic ulcer disease, myocardial infarction, pericarditis, pleurisy, pneumonia, pulmonary embolus, pyelonephritis, renal colic, splenic rupture or infarction

Lower Quadrant: Aortic aneurysm, colitis, diverticulitis, intestinal obstruction, hernias, perforated viscus, pregnancy, ectopic pregnancy, endometriosis, mittleschmerz (ovulation), ovarian cyst or tumor (especially with torsion), pelvic inflammatory disease, renal colic, UTI, rectus hematoma, bladder distention

Right Lower Quadrant Specific: Appendicitis, cholecystitis (perforated), peptic ulcer (perforated), Crohn's disease, gastroenteritis, mesenteric lymphadenitis

ANURIA

See oliguria.

ASCITES

CHF, constrictive pericarditis, venous occlusion, cirrhosis, peritonitis (ruptured viscus, TB, pancreatitis, bile leak), tumors, trauma, Meigs' syndrome (ovarian fibroma), myxedema, anasarca (hypoalbuminemia)

(See Chapter 4 under Peritoneal Paracentesis for more details.)

ANOREXIA

Hepatitis, gastric carcinoma, anorexia nervosa, generalized debilitating diseases, digitalis toxicity, uremia, depression, CHF, pulmonary failure, radiation exposure, chemotherapy

ARTHRITIS

Osteoarthritis, bursitis, tendonitis, connective tissue disease (rheumatoid arthritis, systemic lupus erythematosis [SLE], rheumatic fever), gout, pseudogout, rheumatoid variants (ankylosing spondylitis, psoriatic arthritis, Reiter's syndrome), infection (bacterial, viral), trauma, sarcoidosis

CONSTIPATION

Dehydration, lack of exercise, medications (especially sedatives and narcotics), laxative abuse, anal fissures, ulcers, hemorrhoids, megacolon, spastic colon, chronic suppression of the urge to defecate, fecal impaction (often with paradoxical diarrhea), neoplasm, intestinal obstruction, vascular occlusion to the bowel, neurological disorders, depression

COUGH

Acute: Tracheobronchitis, pneumonia, pulmonary edema, foreign body, toxic inhalation, allergy, pharyngitis (viral or bacterial)

Chronic: Bronchitis (smoker), emphysema, cancer, TB, sarcoidosis, fungal infection, bronchiectasis, mediastinal lymphadenopathy

CHILLS

Infection (bacterial with a bacteremic abscess, viral, TB, fungal), neoplasm (Hodgkin's disease), connective tissue diseases, drug reactions, hypothermia

CHEST PAIN

Deep, Dull, Poorly Localized: Angina, variant angina, acute myocardial infarction, preinfarction angina, pericarditis, aortic aneurysm, pulmonary embolism, tumor, gastroesophageal reflux, hiatal hernia, esophagitis, gall bladder disease, anxiety

Sharp, Well Localized: Pulmonary embolism, pleurisy, pneumothorax, epidemic pleurodynia, herpes, aneurysm, breast lesions, variety of bony and soft tissue abnormalities (rib fractures, costochondritis, muscle damage), perforated ulcer, acute cholecystitis, pancreatitis

COMA

Use the mnemonic AEIOU TIPS: Alcohol, Encephalopathy (epilepsy, hemorrhage, encephalitis, mass), Insulin (hypoglycemia, hyperglycemia), Opiates (drugs), Uremia (and other metabolic conditions such as hepatic failure), Trauma, Infection, Psychiatric causes, Syncope (or decreased cardiac output)

DIARRHEA

Acute: Infections (bacterial, viral, fungal, protozoan, parasitic), toxicity (food poisoning, chemical), antibiotics and drugs, appendicitis, diverticular disease, gastrointestinal bleeding, ischemic colitis, food intolerance, fecal impaction (paradoxical diarrhea)

Chronic: After gastrectomy, after vagotomy, Zollinger-Ellison syndrome, regional enteritis, ulcerative colitis, malabsorption, diverticular disease, carcinoma, villous adenoma, functional bowel disorders (irritable colon, mucous colitis), pseudomembranous colitis, endocrine disease (carcinoid, hyperthyroidism), radiation eneritis, drugs

DYSPHAGIA

Loss of tongue function, pharyngeal dysfunction (myasthenia gravis), Zenker's diverticulum, tumor, stricture, esophageal web, Schatzki's ring, lower esophageal sphincter spasm, foreign body, aortic aneurysm, achalasia, scleroderma, diabetic neuropathy, amyloidosis, infection (especially candidiasis)

DYSPNEA (SHORTNESS OF BREATH)

Laryngeal and tracheal infections and foreign bodies, tumors (both intrinsic and extrinsic), COAD, allergies, pulmonary edema, congestive failure, acute myocardial infarction, pulmonary infiltrates (pneumonia, carcinoma, granuloma), atelectasis, pneumothorax, hemothorax, abdominal distention, pulmonary embolism, pulmonary infarction, anemia, carbon monoxide, any cause of pain from respiratory movements

DYSURIA

Urethral stricture, stones, blood clot, tumor, prostatic enlargement, infection (urethritis, cystitis), trauma, bladder spasm, dehydration

EDEMA

CHF, constrictive pericarditis, liver disease (cirrhosis), nephrotic syndrome, nephritic syndrome, hypoalbuminemia, malnutrition, myxedema, hemiplegia, volume overload, thrombophlebitis, lymphatic obstruction

FAILURE TO THRIVE

Environmental: Social deprivation, decreased food intake

Organic: Central nervous system disorder, intestinal malabsorption, cystic fibrosis, parasites, cleft palate, heart failure, endocrine diseases, hypercalcemia, Turner's syndrome, renal disease, chronic infection, malignancies

FLATULENCE

Aerophagia, food intolerance, disturbances in bowel motility (diabetes, uremia), lactose intolerance, gall bladder disease, peptic ulcers

FEVER OF UNKNOWN ORIGIN

Defined as a temperature of 101 F or greater for at least one week of hospitalization without any diagnosis. TB, fungal infection, endocarditis, abscess, neoplasm, connective tissue disease, drugs, pulmonary embolism, Crohn's disease, ulcerative colitis, hypothalamic injury

FREQUENCY

Infection (bladder, prostate), excessive fluid intake, use of diuretics (also coffee, tea, or colas), diabetes mellitus, diabetes insipidus, prostatic obstruction, bladder stones, bladder tumors, pregnancy, psychogenic spastic bladder syndrome, interstitial cystitis

HEADACHE

Includes cluster, tension, and migraine (classic or simple). Cranial arteritis, toxin exposure, intracranial mass, subarachnoid hemorrhage, meningitis, trauma, vascular (menstruation, hypertension), fever, sinusitis, eyestrain, lumbar puncture (spinal headache)

HEARTBURN (PYROSIS)

Gastroesophageal reflux, esophagitis, hiatal hernia, peptic ulcer, gallbladder disease, medications, tumors, scleroderma, food intolerance

HEMATEMESIS AND MELENA

Swallowed blood, esophageal varices, esophagitis, gastritis, Mallory-Weiss syndrome, peptic ulcer, hiatal hernia, carcinoma of the stomach, tumors (both small and large bowel), diverticulosis, excessive anticoagulation, bleeding diathesis, colitis (ischemic, pseudomembranous)

HEMATURIA

Rule out myoglobinuria, hemoglobinuria, porphyria. Tumors (malignant and benign), polycystic kidneys, trauma, infection (bladder, prostate, etc.), stones, prostatic hypertrophy, glomerulonephritis, renal infarction, renal vein thrombosis, excessive anticoagulation, bleeding diathesis

HEMOPTYSIS

Infection (pneumonia, bronchitis, fungal, TB), pulmonary embolus, pulmonary edema, cancer (usually bronchogenic), mitral stenosis, chronic obstructive pulmonary disease (COPD), granulomas, bronchiectasis, arteriovenous malformations, excessive anticoagulation, bleeding diathesis, pulmonary hemosiderosis, foreign body, trauma

HEPATOMEGALY

CHF, hepatitis, cirrhosis (alcoholic, etc.), tumor, amyloid, biliary obstruction

JAUNDICE

Hepatitis, Gilbert's disease, Crigler-Najjar syndrome, Dubin-Johnson syndrome, Wilson's disease, hepatotoxicity (drug, etc.), drug-induced cholestasis, gall bladder and biliary tract disease (including inflammation, infection, obstruction, and tumor—primary hepatic and metastatic), hemolysis, neonatal jaundice, cholestatic jaundice of pregnancy.

LYMPHADENOPATHY (SPLENOMEGALY)

Infection (bacterial, fungal, viral, parasitic), benign neoplasm (histiocytosis), malignant neoplasm (primary lymphoma, metastatic), sarcoid, connective tissue disease, dermopathy, drugs

MELENA

See hematemesis.

NAUSEA AND VOMITING

Appendicitis, acute cholecystitis, intestinal obstruction, peritonitis, ulcers, chronic gall bladder disease, food intolerance, acute systemic infections (especially in children), intestinal infection (bacterial, viral, parasitic), hepatitis, toxins (food poisoning), central nervous system disorders (increased intracranial pressure, tumor, anoxic damage, hydrocephalus, etc.), labrynthitis, Meniere's disease, migraine headaches, meningitis, acute myocardial infarction, CHF, endocrine disorders (diabetic acidosis, adrenal crisis), pregnancy, drugs (opiates, digitalis), psychogenic vomiting, uremia, gastritis (especially alcoholic), gastric distention (diabetic atony, pyloric obstruction), radiation therapy, chemotherapy

OLIGURIA AND ANURIA

Oliguria is <500 ml urine/24 hr; anuria is <100 ml urine/24 hr in adults.

Prerenal: Volume depletion, shock, heart failure, third spacing fluids, renal artery compromise

Renal: Glomerular disease, acute tubular necrosis, bilateral cortical necrosis, interstitial disease (acute and chronic interstitial nephritis, urate or hypercalcemic nephropathy), use of radiographic contrast media (especially in diabetics, dehydration, multiple myeloma), end-stage chronic renal disease

Postrenal: Bilateral ureteral obstruction, prostatic obstruction

(See also Chapter 8 under Urinary Indices.)

PLEURAL EFFUSION

Transudate: (Protein <3 gm/100 ml) CHF, cirrhosis, nephrotic syndrome

Exudate: (Protein >3 gm/100 ml) Bacterial or viral pneumonia, pulmonary infarction, TB, rheumatoid arthritis, SLE, malignancy, pancreatitis, pneumothorax, chest trauma, peritoneal dialysis

Chylothorax: Traumatic or postoperative complication

Empyema: Bacteria, fungi, TB, trauma, surgery

(See Chapter 4 under Thoracentesis for more details.)

SEIZURES

Idiopathic: No clear etiology. Grand mal, petit mal, pseudo (psychiatric problem)

Symptomatic: Demonstrable cause; includes auditory, olfactory, and focal motor (Jacksonian). Temporal lobe, psychomotor, dreamy state (dèjá vu), visual hallucination

SYNCOPE

Includes vasovagal (simple faint), orthostatic (volume depletion, sympathectomy, either functional or surgical) and hysterical. Cardiac syncope (Adams-Stokes attack), paroxysmal atrial tachycardia, sinoatrial or atrioventricular block, aortic stenosis, idiopathic hypertrophic subaortic stenosis (IHSS), cough syncope, hypoglycemia, seizure disorder, cerebrovascular accident, acute myocardial infarction

VERTIGO

External ear wax or foreign body, middle ear infection or injury, internal ear causes (infection, vascular compromise, Meniere's disease), motion sickness, eighth nerve trauma, tumor or infection, brainstem lesions (infection, trauma, multiple sclerosis, tumor, cerebrovascular accident)

WEIGHT LOSS

Normal or Increased Appetite: Diabetes, hyperthyroidism, anxiety, drugs (thyroid), carcinoid, sprue, pancreatic deficiency, parasites

Decreased Appetite: Depression, anorexia nervosa, gastrointestinal obstruction, neoplasm, liver disease, severe infection, severe cardiopulmonary disease, uremia, adrenal insufficiency, hypercalcemia, hypokalemia, intoxication (alcohol, lead), old age, drugs (amphetamines, digitalis)

WHEEZING

Large airway difficulty (laryngeal stridor, tracheal stenosis, foreign body), endobronchial tumor, asthma, bronchitis, emphysema, CHF, pulmonary embolus

6
Differential Diagnosis: Laboratory Values

The following is a list of the most commonly ordered lab tests with their normal values and a guide to the diagnosis of common abnormalities. If an increased or decreased value is not clinically useful, it is not listed. Since each laboratory has its own set of "normal" values, the normals given should only be used as a rough guide. For the differential diagnosis of CBC values, refer to Chapter 7 and for Urinalysis, refer to Chapter 8.

Acid Phosphatase
Albumin
Aldolase
Alkaline Phosphatase
Alpha-fetoprotein (AFP)
Ammonia
Amylase
ASO (Antistreptolysin O) Titer
B_{12} (Vitamin)
Base Deficit/Excess
Bicarbonate
Bilirubin
Bleeding Time

Blood Urea Nitrogen (BUN)
C Peptide
C-Reactive Protein (CRP)
Calcium
Carbon Dioxide
Carcinoembryonic Antigen (CEA)
Chloride
Cold Agglutinins
Complement C3
Complement C4
Complement CH50
Coombs' Test, Direct

Coombs' Test, Indirect
Cortisol
Creatinine
Creatinine Phosphokinase (CPK)
Fecal Fat
Fibrin Degradation Products (FDP)
Fibrinogen
Folic Acid
FTA-ABS (Fluorescent Treponemal Antibody-Absorbed)
Fungal Serologies
Glucose
Glycohemoglobin
HAA (Hepatitis-Associated Antigen)
Haptoglobin
Human Chorionic Gonadotropin (HCG)
Iron
Iron Binding Capacity
Lactate Dehydrogenase (LDH)
Lactic Acid
LAP (Leukocyte Alkaline Phosphatase) Score
Lee White Clotting Time
LE (Lupus Erythematosis) Preparation
Lipase
Magnesium
Monospot
5' Nucleotidase
Osmolality (Serum)
Oxygen

Partial Thromboplastin Time (PTT)
Phosphorus
Potassium
Protein
Prothrombin Time (PT)
Rheumatoid Factor (RA Latex Test)
Sedimentation Rate (ESR)
SGGT (Serum Gamma-Glutamyl Transpeptidase)
SGOT (Serum Glutamic-Oxaloacetic Transaminase)
SGPT (Serum Glutamic-Pyruvic Transaminase)
Sodium
Stool for Occult Blood
Stool for WBCs
Sweat Chloride
T_3 RIA (Radioimmunoassay)
T_3 RU (Resin Uptake)
T_4 RIA (Radioimmunoassay)
Thrombin Time
Thyroid Binding Globulin (TBG)
TORCH Battery
Transferrin
Triglycerides
TSH (Thyroid Stimulating Hormone)
Uric Acid
VDRL Test (RPR)

The range for normal values is given in parentheses. Check the ranges for each facility before interpreting results.

ACID PHOSPHATASE (1-9 U/liter or 0.5-2.0 Bodansky units)

Increased: Carcinoma of the prostate, prostatic surgery or trauma, excessive platelet destruction (idiopathic thrombocytopenic purpura), rarely in bone disease

ALBUMIN (3.5-5.5 gm/100 ml)

Decreased: Malnutrition, nephrotic syndrome, cystic fibrosis, multiple myeloma, Hodgkin's disease, leukemia, protein losing enteropathies, chronic glomerulonephritis, alcoholic cirrhosis, inflammatory bowel disease, collagen-vascular diseases, hyperthyroidism

ALDOLASE (1.5-8.1 mU/ml)

Increased: Myocardial infarction (MI), hepatitis, burns, muscular dystrophy, cancer (liver, prostate)

ALKALINE PHOSPHATASE (20-70 IU/liter or 2.0-4.5 Bodansky units)

NOTE: A fractionated alkaline phosphatase is often useful to differentiate between bone or liver origin of the enzyme. The heat stable fraction comes from liver, and the heat labile fraction comes from bone (remember "bone burns"). On a fractionated sample: if the heat stable fraction is <20%, suspect bone origin; if 25% to 55%, suspect liver origin.

Increased: Increased calcium deposition in bone (hyperparathyroidism), Paget's disease, osteoblastic bone tumors (metastatic or osteogenic sarcoma), osteomalacia, rickets, pregnancy, childhood, liver disease such as biliary obstruction (masses, drug therapy), hyperthyroidism

ALPHA-FETOPROTEIN (AFP) (<25 ng/ml)

Increased: Hepatoma, embryonal carcinoma, malignant teratoma, spina bifida (in mother's serum)

AMMONIA (<35 µmol/liter)

Increased: Liver failure, Reye's syndrome

AMYLASE (15–90 U/liter or 80–160 Somogyi units/100 ml)

Increased: Acute pancreatitis, pancreatic duct obstruction (stones, stricture, tumor, sphincter spasm secondary to drugs), alcoholic ingestion, mumps, parotiditis, renal disease, macro-amylasemia, cholecystitis, peptic ulcers, intestinal obstruction, mesenteric thrombosis, after surgery (upper abdominal)

Decreased: Pancreatic destruction (pancreatitis, cystic fibrosis), liver damage (hepatitis, cirrhosis)

ASO (ANTISTREPTOLYSIN O) TITER (<166 Todd units)

Increased: Streptococcal infections (pharyngitis, scarlet fever, rheumatic fever, poststreptococcal glomerulonephritis), rheumatoid arthritis, other collagen diseases

B$_{12}$ (VITAMIN B$_{12}$) (140–700 pg/ml)

Increased: Leukemia, polycythemia

Decreased: Pernicious anemia, malabsorption, pregnancy

BASE DEFICIT/EXCESS (−2 to +2) (See Chapter 10)

BICARBONATE (OR "TOTAL CO$_2$") (23–29 mmol/liter) (See Carbon Dioxide)

BILIRUBIN (Total, <0.2–1.0 mg/dl; direct, <0.2 mg/dl; indirect, <0.8 mg/dl)

Increased Total: Hepatic damage (hepatitis, toxins, cirrhosis), biliary obstruction (stone or tumor), hemolysis, fasting

Increased Direct (Conjugated): Excretory obstruction (gallstone, tumor, stricture), drug-induced cholestasis, Dubin-Johnson and Rotor's syndromes

Increased Indirect (Unconjugated): So-called "hemolytic jaundice" caused by any type of hemolytic anemia (transfusion reaction, sickle cell, etc.), Gilbert's disease, physiological jaundice of the newborn, Crigler-Najjar syndrome

BLEEDING TIME (Duke, Ivy <5 min; Template <10 min)

Increased: Thrombocytopenia, thrombocytopenic purpura, von Willebrand's disease, defective platelet function

BLOOD UREA NITROGEN (BUN) (10–20 mg/100 ml)

Increased: Renal (decreased function), prerenal azotemia (decreased perfusion secondary to CHF, shock, volume depletion), postrenal (obstruction), GI bleeding, stress, drugs (especially aminoglycosides)

Decreased: Starvation, liver failure (hepatitis, drugs), pregnancy, infancy, nephrotic syndrome, overhydration

C PEPTIDE (Fasting, 1.5–5.5 ng/ml)

Decreased: Diabetes (decreased endogenous insulin), factitious insulin administration

C-REACTIVE PROTEIN (CRP) (None detected)

Increased: Infection, inflammation, rheumatic fever, myocardial infarction

CALCIUM (4.2-5.3 mEq/liter or 8.5-10.5 mg/dl; ionized, 2.24-2.46 mEq/liter or 4.48-4.92 mg/dl)

NOTE: When interpreting a calcium value, the total protein and albumin must be known. If these are not within normal limits, a corrected calcium must be calculated by the following formula. Values for ionized calcium need no special corrections.

Corrected Ca =
0.8 (normal albumin − measured albumin) + reported Ca

Increased: Primary hyperthyroidism, parathyroid hormone (PTH) secreting tumors, vitamin D excess, metastatic bone tumors, osteoporosis, immobilization, milk-alkali syndrome, Paget's disease, idiopathic hypercalcemia of infants, infantile hypophosphatasia, thiazide drugs, chronic renal failure, sarcoidosis, multiple myeloma

Decreased: Hypoparathyroidism (surgical, idiopathic), pseudohypoparathyroidism, insufficient vitamin D, calcium and phosphorus ingestion (pregnancy, osteomalacia, rickets), hypoalbuminemia (cachexia, nephrotic syndrome, cystic fibrosis), chronic renal failure (phosphate retention), acute pancreatitis, factitious decrease because of low protein and albumin

CARBON DIOXIDE ("TOTAL CO$_2$" OR BICARBONATE) (23-29 mmol/liter) (See Chapter 10 for pCO$_2$ values)

Increased: Metabolic alkalosis, respiratory acidosis, emphysema, severe vomiting, primary aldosteronism

Decreased: Metabolic acidosis, severe diarrhea, respiratory alkalosis, starvation, diabetic ketoacidosis, renal failure, drugs (thiazide, salicylates, acetazolamide), dehydration, adrenal insufficiency

CARCINOEMBRYONIC ANTIGEN (CEA) (<2.5 mg/ml)

Increased: Carcinoma (colon, pancreas, lung, stomach), smokers

CHLORIDE (98–106 mEq/liter)

Increased: Hyperchloremic acidosis, respiratory alkalosis, dehydration, diabetes insipidus, medications (acetazolamide, ammonium chloride), renal tubular acidosis

Decreased: Metabolic alkalosis (vomiting, pyloric obstruction), respiratory acidosis, emphysema, adrenal cortical insufficiency (Addison's disease), primary aldosteronism, thiazide diuretics, diarrhea

CHOLESTEROL (140–250 mg/dl)

Increased: Idiopathic hypercholesterolemia, biliary obstruction, nephrosis, hypothyroidism, pancreatic disease (diabetes), pregnancy, hyperlipoproteinemia (type IIa, IIb, III, V)

Decreased: Liver disease (hepatitis, etc.), hyperthyroidism, malnutrition (cancer, starvation), chronic anemias, steroid therapy, lipoproteinemias

COLD AGGLUTININS (<1:32)

Increased: Atypical pneumonia (mycoplasmal pneumonia), other viral infections (especially mononucleosis, measles, mumps), cirrhosis, some parasites

COMPLEMENT C3 (80–170 mg/dl)

Decreased: Poststreptococcal glomerulonephritis (marked decrease), SLE nephritis (marked decrease), infectious endocarditis

COMPLEMENT C4   (15–45 mg/dl)

Decreased: Acute poststreptococcal gomerulonephritis (mild decrease), SLE nephritis (marked decrease)

COMPLEMENT CH50   (33–61 mg/ml)

Increased: Acute phase reactants (i.e., acute infections, tissue injury)

Decreased: Hereditary complement deficiencies

COOMBS' TEST, DIRECT   (Normal = negative; uses erythrocytes already coated with antibody)

Positive: Autoimmune hemolytic anemia (leukemia, lymphoma, collagen-vascular diseases), hemolytic transfusion reaction, some drug sensitizations (methyldopa, levodopa, cephalothin), hemolytic disease of the newborn (erythroblastosis fetalis)

COOMBS' TEST, INDIRECT   (Normal = negative; uses serum that contains antibody)

Positive: Isoimmunization from previous transfusion, incompatible blood due to improper crossmatching

CORTISOL   (8 A.M., 6.0–23.0 mg/dl; 4 P.M., 4.0–15.0 mg/dl)

Increased: Adrenal adenoma, adrenal carcinoma, Cushing's disease, steroid therapy

Decreased: Addison's disease, congenital adrenal hyperplasia, Waterhouse-Friderichsen syndrome

CREATININE PHOSPHOKINASE (CPK) (25–145 mU/ml)

Increased: Muscle damage (acute myocardial infarction, myocarditis, muscular dystrophy, muscle trauma [injection], after surgery), brain infarction, defibrillation, cardiac catheterization

CPK Isoenzymes MM, MB, BB: MB (normal <5%) increased in acute myocardial infarctions (begins in four to eight hours, peaks at 24 hours), muscular dystrophy, and cardiac surgery; MM increased in brain damage

CREATININE (0.4–1.5 mg/dl) (See also Chapter 8)

Increased: Prerenal and postrenal azotemia (see BUN), impaired renal function, gigantism, acromegaly, ingestion of roasted meat, aminoglycosides and other drugs

FECAL FAT (<6 mg/24 hrs)

Increased: Steatorrhea (pancreatic insufficiency)

FIBRIN DEGRADATION PRODUCTS (FDP) (<5 mg/ml)

Increased: Any thromboembolic condition (deep venous thrombosis, myocardial infarction, pulmonary embolus) disseminated intravascular coagulation

FIBRINOGEN (150–450 mg/dl)

Decreased: Congenital, disseminated intravascular coagulation due to multiple obstetrical problems (amniotic fluid embolism, abruptio placenta), surgery (prostate, open heart), neoplastic and hematological conditions, acute severe bleeding, burns

FOLIC ACID (SERUM FOLATE)   (1.8–9.0 mg/ml)

Increased: Folic acid administration

Decreased: Massive cellular growth (cancer), hemolytic anemia, megaloblastic anemia, malabsorption

FTA-ABS (FLUORESCENT TREPONEMAL ANTIBODY ABSORBED)

Positive: Syphilis (test of choice to confirm diagnosis)

FUNGAL SEROLOGIES   (Negative <1:8)

NOTE: This is a complement-fixation fungal antigen screen that usually includes antigens from *Histoplasma, Blastomyces, Aspergillus,* and *Coccidioides.*

GLUCOSE   (Fasting, 65–110 mg/dl)

Increased: Diabetes mellitus, Cushing's syndrome, acromegaly, increased epinephrine (injection, pheochromocytoma, stress, burns, etc.) acute pancreatitis, adrenocorticotropic hormone (ACTH) administration, spurious increase caused by drawing blood from a site above an IV line containing dextrose

Decreased: Pancreatic disorders (pancreatitis, islet cell tumors), extrapancreatic tumors (carcinoma of the adrenals, stomach), hepatic disease (hepatitis, cirrhosis, tumors), endocrine disorders (early diabetes, hypothyroidism, hypopituitarism), functional disorders (after gastrectomy), pediatric problems (prematurity, infant of a diabetic mother, ketotic hypoglycemia, enzyme diseases), exogenous insulin, oral hypoglycemics, malnutrition

GLYCOHEMOGLOBIN   (4.6%–8.0%)

Increased: Diabetes

HAA (HEPATITIS-ASSOCIATED ANTIGEN) OR HB$_S$Ag (HEPATITIS B SURFACE ANTIGEN)
(Negative)

Positive: Hepatitis B infection

HAPTOGLOBIN (Male, <2 mg/ml; female, <10 mg/ml)

Increased: Obstructive liver disease, any cause of increased erythrocyte sedimentation rate (ESR)

Decreased: Any type of hemolysis, liver disease

HUMAN CHORIONIC GONADOTROPIN (HCG BETA SUBUNIT) (Normal, nondetectable; 10 days post-conception, 5 mIU/ml; 30 days, 100 mIU/ml; 40 days, 2,000 mIU/ml; 14 weeks, 10,000–20,000 mIU/ml; thereafter, levels slowly decline)

Increased: Pregnancy, trophoblastic disease (hydatidiform mole, choriocarcinoma levels usually >100,000 mIU/ml)

IRON (Males, 80–160 μg/100 ml; females, 50–150 μg/100 ml)

Increased: Hemochromatosis, hemosiderosis caused by excessive iron intake, excess destruction or decreased production of erythrocytes, liver necrosis

Decreased: Iron deficiency anemia, nephrosis (loss of iron binding proteins), normochromic anemia of chronic diseases and infections

IRON BINDING CAPACITY (TOTAL) (TIBC)
(250–400 μg/dl)

NOTE: The normal iron/TIBC ratio is 25%–40%; <15% is almost diagnostic of iron deficiency anemia; 15%–20% suggests anemia of chronic disease.

Increased: Acute and chronic blood loss, iron deficiency anemia, hepatitis

Decreased: Anemia of infection and chronic diseases, cirrhosis, nephrosis, hemochromatosis

LACTATE DEHYDROGENASE (LDH) (110–250 mU/ml)

Increased: Acute myocardial infarction, cardiac surgery, prosthetic valve, hepatitis, pernicious anemia, malignant tumors, pulmonary embolus, hemolysis (anemias or factitious)

LDH Isoenzymes (LDH 1 to LDH 5): Normally, the ratio LDH 1/LDH 2 is <1. If the ratio becomes >1, suspect a recent myocardial infarction. With an acute myocardial infarction, the LDH will begin to rise at 10 to 12 hours and peak at 48 to 72 hours. LDH 5 is increased in hepatitis.

LACTIC ACID (LACTATE) (0.5–2.2 mmol/liter)

Increased: Lactic acidosis due to hypoxia, hemorrhage, circulatory collapse, sepsis, cirrhosis, exercise, others

LAP (LEUKOCYTE ALKALINE PHOSPHATASE) SCORE (70–140)

Increased: Leukemoid reaction, acute inflammation, Hodgkin's disease, pregnancy, liver disease

Decreased: Chronic myelogenous leukemia, nephrotic syndrome

LEE WHITE CLOTTING TIME (6–7 minutes)

Increased: Heparin therapy, plasma clotting factor deficiency (except Factors VII and XIII)

LE (LUPUS ERYTHEMATOSIS) PREPARATION
(No cells seen is normal)

Positive: SLE, scleroderma, rheumatoid arthritis, drug-induced lupus (procainamide hydrochloride, etc.)

LIPASE   (0–10 U/ml)

Increased: Acute pancreatitis, pancreatic duct obstruction (stone, stricture, tumor, drug-induced spasm), fat embolus syndrome, (increase usually normal in mumps)

MAGNESIUM   (1.4–3.2 mg/dl)

Increased: Renal failure, hypothyroidism, magnesium-containing antacids, Addison's disease, diabetic coma

Decreased: Malabsorption, steatorrhea, alcoholism and cirrhosis, hyperthyroidism, aldosteronism, diuretics, acute pancreatitis, hypoparathyroidism, hyperparathyroidism, hyperalimentation

MONOSPOT   (Negative)

Positive: Mononucleosis

5' NUCLEOTIDASE   (<1.6 units)

Increased: Obstructive liver disease

OSMOLALITY (SERUM)   (280–300 mOsm/kg)

NOTE: A rough estimation of osmolality is [2 (sodium) + BUN/2.8 + glucose/10].

Increased: Hyperglycemia, alcohol ingestion, increased sodium because of water loss (diabetes, hypercalcemia, diuresis)

Decreased: Low serum sodium, diuretics, Addison's disease, inappropriate antidiuretic hormone (ADH) (syndrome of inappropriate ADH [SIADH], seen in bronchogenic carcinoma, hypothyroidism), iatrogenic causes (poor fluid balance)

OXYGEN (ARTERIAL) (80–100 mm Hg) (See Chapter 10)

PARTIAL THROMBOPLASTIN TIME (PTT) (27–38 seconds)

Increased: Heparin and any defect in the intrinsic clotting mechanism (includes Factors I, II, V, VIII, IX, X, XI, and XII), prolonged use of a tourniquet before drawing a blood sample

PHOSPHORUS (2.5–4.5 mg/dl)

Increased: Hypoparathyroidism (surgical, pseudohypoparathyroidism), excess vitamin D, secondary hyperparathyroidism, renal failure, bone disease (healing fractures), Addison's disease, childhood, factitious increase (hemolysis of specimen)

Decreased: Alcoholism, diabetes, hyperalimentation, acidosis, alkalosis, gout, salycilate poisoning, IV steroid, glucose or insulin administration, hyperparathyroidism, hypokalemia, hypomagnesemia, diuretics, vitamin D deficiency, phosphate-binding antacids

POTASSIUM (3.5–5.3 mEq/liter)

Increased: Factitious increase (hemolysis in venipuncture, thrombocytosis), renal failure (acute or chronic), Addison's disease, acidosis, spironolactone, triamterene, dehydration, hemolysis, massive tissue damage, excess intake (oral or IV), potassium-containing medications

Decreased: Diuretics, decreased intake, vomiting, nasogastric suctioning, villous adenoma, diarrhea, Zollinger-Ellison syndrome, metabolic acidosis (chronic pyelonephritis, renal tubular acidosis), metabolic alkalosis (primary aldosteronism, Cushing's syndrome), after obstructive diuresis, diuretic phase of acute tubular necrosis

PROTEIN (6.0–8.0 gm/100 ml)

Increased: Multiple myeloma, macroglobulinemia, sarcoidosis

Decreased: Malnutrition, inflammatory bowel disease, Hodgkin's disease, leukemias

PROTHROMBIN TIME (PT) (10.0–13.5 seconds)

Increased: Drugs (sodium warfarin [Coumadin]), decreased vitamin K, poor fat absorption, liver disease (PT evaluates the extrinsic clotting mechanism that includes Factors I, II, V, VII, and X), prolonged use of a tourniquet before drawing a blood sample

RHEUMATOID FACTOR (RA LATEX TEST) (<1:40)

Increased: Rheumatoid arthritis, SLE, syphilis, chronic inflammation

SEDIMENTATION RATE (ESR) (Males, 0–9 mm/hr; females, 0–20 mm/hr) or (ZETA scale: 40%–54%, normal; 55%–59%, mildly elevated; 60%–64%, moderately elevated; >65%, markedly elevated)

Increased: Any type of infection, inflammation, rheumatic fever, endocarditis, metastasis, neoplasm, acute myocardial infarction

SGGT (SERUM GAMMA-GLUTAMYL TRANSPEPTIDASE) (8–50 U/liter)

Increased: Liver disease (hepatitis, cirrhosis, obstructive jaundice), pancreatitis, myocardial infarction

SGOT (SERUM GLUTAMIC-OXALOACETIC TRANSAMINASE) OR (SERUM ASPARTATE AMINOTRANSAMINASE) (10–20 mU/ml)

Increased: Acute myocardial infarction, liver disease, Reye's syndrome, muscle trauma and injection, pancreatitis, intestinal injury or surgery, factitious increase (erythromycin, opiates), burns, cardiac catheterization, brain damage

Decreased: Beriberi, severe diabetes with ketoacidosis, liver disease

SGPT (SERUM GLUTAMIC-PYRUVIC TRANSAMINASE) OR (SERUM ALANINE AMINOTRANSAMINASE) (5–20 U/liter)

Increased: Liver disease, liver metastasis, biliary obstruction, pancreatitis, liver congestion (SGPT is more elevated than SGOT in liver necrosis and hepatitis.)

SODIUM (135–145 mEq/liter)

Increased: Excess water loss (sweating or vomiting), diuresis (diabetes mellitus and insipidus, postobstructive diuresis, diuretic drugs, etc.), iatrogenic increase (improper fluid management)

Decreased: CHF, nephrosis, cirrhosis, sodium depletion (vomiting, diarrhea, diuretics), adrenal cortical insufficiency, inappropriate secretion of ADH (SIADH with COPD, tumors, etc.), factitious increase (hyperlipidemia, hyperglycemia)

STOOL FOR OCCULT BLOOD (HEMOCCULT TEST) (Normal = negative)

Positive: Swallowed blood, ingestion of rare meat, any GI tract ulcerated lesion (ulcer, carcinoma, polyp), large doses of vitamin C

STOOL FOR WBC   (Occasional WBC normal)

Increased (Usually Polys):   *Shigella, Salmonella,* enteropathogenic *Escherichia coli,* ulcerative colitis

SWEAT CHLORIDE   (<60 mmol/liter)

Increased: Cystic fibrosis

T_3 RIA (TRIIODOTHYRONINE)   (Male, 105–175 ng/dl; female, 108–205 ng/dl)

Increased: Hyperthyroidism, T_3 thyrotoxicosis, oral estrogen, pregnancy, exogenous T_4

T_3 RU (RESIN UPTAKE)   (26%–35%)

Increased: Hyperthyroidism, medications (phenytoin [Dilantin], steroids, heparin, aspirin, others)

Decreased: Hypothyroidism, pregnancy, medications (estrogens, iodine, propylthiouracil, others)

T_4 RIA (THYROXINE)   (5–12 µg/dl)

Increased: Hyperthyroidism, exogenous thyroid hormone, estrogens, pregnancy

Decreased: Hypothyroidism, testosterone, steroids, phenytoin

THROMBIN TIME (10–14 seconds)

Increased: Systemic heparin, disseminated intravascular coagulation, congenitally abnormal fibrinogen molecules

THYROID BINDING GLOBULIN (TBG) (15–34 µg/ml)

Increased: Hypothyroidism, pregnancy, oral contraceptives, estrogens, viral hepatitis, acute porphyria

Decreased: Thyrotoxicosis, androgens, anabolic steroids, prednisone, nephrotic syndrome, severe illness, surgical stress, phenytoin

TORCH BATTERY

NOTE: Test includes titers for antigens associated with toxoplasmosis, rubella, cytomegalovirus and herpes viruses. Syphilis is sometimes included.

TRANSFERRIN (200–400 mg/dl)

Increased: Iron deficiency

Decreased: Poor nutritional status, chronic and acute inflammation

TRIGLYCERIDES (Male, 40–160 mg/dl; female, 35–135 mg/dl)

Increased: Hyperlipoproteinemias (type I, IIb, III, IV, V), hypothyroidism, liver diseases, alcoholism, pancreatitis, acute myocardial infarction, nephrotic syndrome, familial increase

Decreased: Malnutrition

TSH (THYROID STIMULATING HORMONE)
(2–8 μU/ml)

Increased: Hypothyroidism

Decreased: Hyperthyroidism

URIC ACID   (4.0–8.0 mg/dl)

Increased: Gout, renal failure, destruction of massive amounts of nucleoproteins (leukemia, anemia, chemotherapy, toxemia of pregnancy), drugs (especially diuretics), hypothyroidism, polycystic kidney disease, hyperparathyroidism, hypoparathyroidism

Decreased: Uricosuric drugs (salycilates, probenecid, allopurinol), Wilson's disease, Fanconi's syndrome

VDRL TEST (RPR) (VENEREAL DISEASE RESEARCH LABORATORY)

Positive (Reactive): Syphilis (good for routine screening)

7
The CBC (Complete Blood Count)

RECORDING THE CBC

The following diagram shows a simple method for recording the results of a CBC.

	Hgb	Segs/Bands/Lymphs/Monos/Basos/Eos
WBC	———	MCV-MCH-MCHC
	HCT	platelet count

Example

	10.1	40S, 20B, 30L, 6M, 1B, 3E
11,000	———	80/27/32
	30.5	285,000

NORMAL VALUES (ADULT)

When you order a CBC, the lab will include all the following data except for the platelets and differential. These two must be ordered separately. A "Hemogram" is sometimes available that includes the CBC, differential, and platelets.

WBC (White Blood Cells): 4,800–10,800/mm^3

RBC (Red Blood Cells)

Male: 4,700,000–6,100,000/mm^3

Female: 4,200,000–5,400,000/mm^3

Hgb (Hemoglobin)

Male: 14.0–18.0 gm/dl

Female: 12.0–16.0 gm/dl

HCT (Hematocrit)

Male: 42% to 52%

Female: 37% to 47%

Differential

- Lymphocytes: 20% to 40%
- Polymorphonuclear "segs": 40% to 60%
- Polymorphonuclear "stabs" or "bands": 0 to 5%
- Monocytes: 4% to 8%
- Eosinophils: 1% to 3%
- Basophils: 0 to 1%
- Atypical lymphocytes: 0

Platelet Count: 130,000–400,000/mm^3

RBC Indices

MCV (Mean Cell Volume): HCT/#RBC = 80 to 94 μ^3

MCH (Mean Cell Hemoglobin):   Hgb/#RBC = 27 to 31 ng

MCHC (Mean Cell Hemoglobin Concentration):   Hgb/HCT = 32% to 36%

RDW (Red Cell Distribution Width):   8.5 to 11.5

BLOOD COLLECTION

The best sample is venous blood drawn with at least a 22 or larger gauge needle. If a capillary finger stick or heelstick is used, the hematocrit may be falsely low. If the finger needs to be "milked," "sludging" of the RBCs can create a falsely high hematocrit. Venous blood needs to be placed in a special hematology lab tube that has a special anticoagulant (EDTA) and mixed gently. Blood for a CBC should be fresh, less than three hours old. On the wards, you can draw the blood up in a capillary tube, seal an end with clay, and spin a tube on the crit spinner for two to three minutes and rapidly determine a hematocrit. A Wright stain can also be done and viewed as outlined in the next section. (See also Chapter 4 under Venipuncture.)

BLOOD SMEARS

Making the Blood Smear

1. Place a small drop of blood from the anticoagulated lab sample tube (usually purple topped) in the center of a clean glass slide, about 1 to 2 cm from the end.

2. Place the spreading slide (a glass slide with a perfectly smooth edge) at a 45 degree angle on the slide with the blood sample and slowly move it back to make contact with the drop. The drop should spread out quickly along the line of contact between the two slides. The moment this occurs, spread the film by a rapid, smooth forward movement of the spreader (Fig. 7-1).

3. The drop of blood should be a size that results in a film about 3 cm long. The faster a film is spread, the more

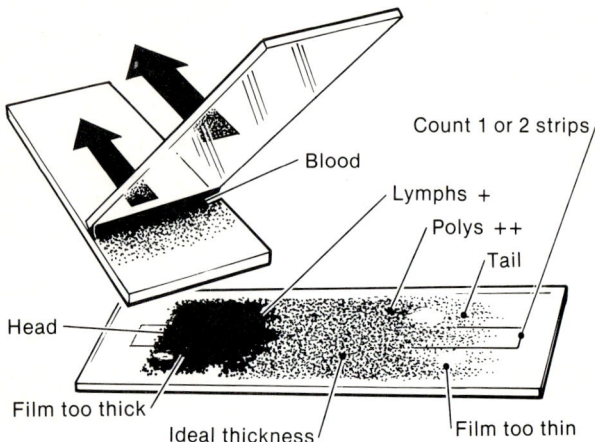

Fig. 7-1 Technique for preparing a blood smear and the distribution of white cells on a stained smear..

even it will be and the better the slide will be. The ideal thickness will show some overlap of the RBCs throughout much of the film's length with separation and lack of distortion toward the tail of the film. Leukocytes should be easily recognizable throughout the length of the film.

Staining the Blood Smear (Wright's Stain)

Make sure that all reagents used are fresh or the slide may not turn out properly.

1. Let the slide air dry and mark the patient's name and date in pencil on the blood film itself. It will not be removed by staining. An alternative method is to bring the slide to the hematology lab where there are machines that automatically stain the slides.

2. Fix the slide in methanol for one minute.

3. Shake off excess methanol from the slide, but do not rinse or dry it.

4. Flood the slide with Wright's stain and allow the slide to stand for three to five minutes (this time can vary with the batch of stain).

5. Flood the slide with Wright's buffer (pH 6.4) until about 50% of the Wright's stain is washed off. Blow air gently over the top of the slide to mix the fluids, and look for a greenish-copper sheen that appears on the surface. Let the slide stand for about eight minutes.

6. Rinse the slide with tap water, wipe the back of the slide with methanol, and air dry it.

Viewing the Film — The Differential WBC

1. The film should not be so thick that the leukocytes in the body of the film are shrunken.

2. If the film is too thin or if a rough-edged spreader is used, up to 50% of the WBCs may accumulate in the edges and tail.

3. WBCs are NOT randomly dispersed even in a well-made smear. Polys and monos predominate at the margins and tail and lymphs in the middle of the film. To overcome this problem, use the "high dry" or oil immersion objective and count cells in a strip running the whole length of the film. Avoid the lateral edges of the film.

4. If fewer than 200 cells are counted in a strip, count another strip until at least 200 are seen. The special white cell counter found in most labs is ideal for this purpose.

5. In smears of blood from patients with very high white counts, such as leukemics, count the cells in any well-spread area where the different cell types are easy to identify.
   The following table shows the correlation between the number of cells in a smear and the estimated white cell count.

Estimated WBC Based on Cells Counted in a Blood Smear

WBC per High Power Field (High dry or 40X)	Estimated WBC (per mm^3)
2–4	4,000– 7,000
4–6	7,000–10,000
6–10	10,000–13,000
10–20	13,000–18,000

NORMAL VARIATIONS

Hemoglobin and hematocrit are highest at birth (20 gm/100 ml and 62% respectively). There is a steep fall to a minimum at 3 months (9.5 gm/100 ml and 32%). There is a slow rise to near adult levels at puberty, and thereafter both values are higher in males. A normal decrease occurs in pregnancy.

The number of WBCs is highest at birth ($25,000/mm^3$), and there is a slow fall to adult levels by puberty. Lymphs predominate (up to 60%) from the second week of life until age 5 to 7 years when polys begin to predominate.

RETICULOCYTE COUNT

The reticulocyte count is not a part of the routine CBC. Reticulocytes are juvenile RBCs with remnants of cytoplasmic basophilic ribonucleic acid (RNA). These are not seen on Wright's stains; a special reticulocyte stain must be ordered. The result comes as a percentage, and you should calculate the corrected reticulocyte count for interpretation of the results (reticutocyte count = reported count × patient's HCT/normal HCT). This count is an excellent indicator of erythropoietic activity. The normal corrected count is <1% to 1½%.

Normal bone marrow responds to a decrease in erythrocytes (shown by a decreased hematocrit) with an increase in the production of reticulocytes. This increase is associated with blood loss and hemolytic anemias. Lack of increase of a reticulocyte count in an anemic patient suggests a chronic disease, a deficiency disease, marrow replacement, or marrow failure.

THE HEMATOCRIT

The hematocrit is a simple screening test for anemia and is performed on the floor as described previously. Always remember that since an equal amount of plasma and red cells are lost in acute blood loss, the hematocrit will not reflect the loss until sometime later (sometimes two to three hours). If an anemia is present, the red cell indices and reticulocyte count should be checked.

THE "LEFT SHIFT"

The degree of nuclear lobulation of polymorphonuclear neutrophils (PMNs) is thought to give some indication of cell age. A predominance of immature cells with only one or two nuclear lobes is called a "shift to the left." Conversely, a predominance of cells with four nuclear lobes is called a "shift to the right." (For historical information, left and right designations come from the formerly used manual lab counters, where the keys for entering the stabs were located on the left of the keyboard.)

As a general rule, 40% to 50% of PMNs have three lobes, 20% to 40% have two lobes, and 15% to 25% have four lobes. More than 20 five-lobed cells/100 WBC suggests incipient megaloblastic anemia, and a six-lobed or seven-lobed poly is virtually diagnostic.

"Bands" or "stabs," the more immature forms of PMNs (the more mature are called "segs"), are identified by the fact that the connections between ends or lobes of a nucleus are greater than one-half the width of the hypothetical round nucleus. In bands or stabs, the connection between the lobes of the nucleus is by a thick band; in segs, by a thin filament. A band is defined as a connecting strip wide enough to reveal two distinct margins with nuclear material in between. A filament is so narrow that there is no intervening nuclear material. When in doubt, call a cell a seg.

For practical purposes, a left shift is present in the CBC when more than 20% bands are seen or when the total PMN count (segs plus bands) is greater than 80%.

Left Shift: Infection, toxemia, hemorrhage

Right Shift: Liver disease, megaloblastic anemia, iron deficiency anemia

DIFFERENTIAL DIAGNOSIS

Basophils

Increased: Chronic myeloid leukemia, rarely in recovery from infection and from hypothyroidism

Decreased: Acute rheumatic fever, lobar pneumonia, after steroid therapy, thyrotoxicosis, stress

Eosinophils

Increased: Allergy, parasites, skin diseases, malignancy, drugs, asthma, Addison's disease, collagen-vascular diseases (handy mnemonic NAACP: Neoplasm, Allergy, Addison's disease, Collagen-vascular diseases, Parasites)

Decreased: After steroids, ACTH, after stress (infection, trauma, burns), Cushing's syndrome

Hematocrit

Decreased: Anemias (megaloblastic, iron deficiency, sickle cell, etc.), acute or chronic blood loss

Increased: Polycythemia, both primary and secondary (reduced fluid intake or excess fluid loss); congenital and acquired heart disease; lung disease; high altitudes; heavy smokers

Lymphocytes

Increased: Measles, German measles, mumps, whooping cough, smallpox, chicken pox, influenza, hepatitis, infectious mononucleosis, acute infectious lymphocytosis in children, virtually any viral infection, acute and chronic lymphocytic leukemias

Decreased: After stress, burns, trauma, normal finding in 22% of population, uremia, some viral infections

Atypical Lymphs

>20%: Infectious mononucleosis, cytomegalovirus (CMV) infection, infectious hepatitis, toxoplasmosis

<20%: Viral infections, rickettsial infections, TB

MCH

Increased: Macrocytosis (megaloblastic anemias, high reticulocyte counts)

Decreased: Microcytosis (iron deficiency)

MCHC

Increased: Very severe, prolonged dehydration; spherocytosis

Decreased: Iron deficiency anemia, overhydration, thalassemia, sideroblastic anemia

MCV

Increased: Megaloblastic anemia (B_{12}, folate deficiency) macrocytic (normoblastic) anemia, reticulocytosis, Down's syndrome, chronic liver disease

Decreased: Iron deficiency, thalassemia, some cases of lead poisoning

Monocytes

Increased: Bacterial infection (TB, subacute bacterial endocarditis [SBE], brucellosis, typhoid, recovery from an acute infection), protozoal infections, infectious mononucleosis, leukemia, Hodgkin's disease, ulcerative colitis, regional enteritis

Platelets

Increased: Sudden exercise, after trauma, bone fracture, after asphyxia, after surgery (especially splenectomy), acute hemorrhage, polycythemia, leukemias, after childbirth

Decreased: Idiopathic thrombocytopenic purpura, congenital disease, marrow suppressants (thiazide diuretics, alcohol, estrogens, x-rays), burns, snake and insect bites, leukemias, aplastic anemias, hypersplenism, thrombotic thrombocytopenic purpura, infectious mononucleosis, viral infections, cirrhosis (55% of cases), massive transfusions, eclampsia and preeclampsia, more than 30 different drugs

PMNs

(See also the "Left Shift.")

Increased

PHYSIOLOGICAL (NORMAL): Severe exercise, last months of pregnancy, labor, surgery, in newborns

PATHOLOGICAL: Infections (especially cocci), noninfective tissue damage (myocardial infarction, pulmonary infarction, crush injury, burn injury), metabolic disorders (eclampsia, diabetic ketoacidosis, uremia, acute gout), leukemias

Decreased: Pancytopenia, aplastic anemia, PMN depression (a mild decrease is referred to as neutropenia, severe is called agranulocytosis), marrow damage (x-rays, poisoning with benzene or antitumor drugs), severe overwhelming infections (disseminated TB, septicemia), acute malaria, severe osteomyelitis, infectious mononucleosis, atypical pneumonias, some viral infections, marrow obliteration (osteosclerosis, myelofibrosis, malignant infiltrate), drugs (more than 70, including chloramphenicol, phenylbutazone, chlorpromazine, quinine), B_{12} and folate deficiencies, hypoadrenalism, hypopituitarism, dialysis, familial decrease, idiopathic causes

RBC MORPHOLOGY

The following lists some erythrocyte abnormalities and the associated conditions.

General Terms

Poikilocytosis: Irregular RBC shape (sickle, Burr, etc.)

Anisocytosis: Irregular RBC size (microcytes, macrocytes)

Basophilic Stippling: Lead, heavy metal poisoning, thalassemia

Howell-Jolly Bodies: After a splenectomy, some severe anemias

Sickling: Sickle cell disease and trait

Nucleated RBCs: Severe bone marrow stress (hemorrhage, hemolysis, etc.)

Target Cells (Leptocytes): Thalassemia, hemoglobinopathies, liver disease

Spherocytes: Hereditary spherocytosis, immune OR microangiopathic hemolysis

Helmet Cells (Schistocytes): Microangiopathic hemolysis, other severe anemias

Burr Cells (Acanthocytes): Severe liver disease; high levels of bile, fatty acids, or toxins

Polychromasia: On routine Wright's stain suggests reticulocytes

WBC MORPHOLOGY

The following gives conditions associated with certain changes from the normal morphology of WBCs.

Auer Rod: Myelogenous leukemia

Döhle Bodies: Severe infection, burns, malignancy, pregnancy

Hypersegmentation: Megaloblastic anemia

Toxic Granulation: Severe illness (sepsis, burn, high temperature)

8
Urinalysis

NORMAL VALUES

Normal values for a urinalysis are as follows:

- pH: 4.6–8.0
- Specific Gravity
    - Neonate: 1.012
    - Infant: 1.002–1.006
    - After infancy: 1.001–1.035
- Negative For: Bilirubin, blood, acetone, glucose, protein, nitrite
- RBC: 0–3/High Power Field (HPF)
- WBC: 0–5/HPF
- Epithelial Cells: Occasional
- Hyaline Casts: Occasional
- Bacteria: None

FALSE-POSITIVES AND FALSE-NEGATIVES

Certain chemicals and conditions may lead to false-positives or false-negatives.

Bilirubin

False +: Thorazine

False −: Excess vitamin C, long standing sample

Blood

False +: Hypochlorite, microbial peroxidases, myoglobin

False −: Excess vitamin C, nitrites

Glucose

False +: None known

False −: Tetracycline, excess vitamin C

Ketones

False +: Bromosulphalein, phenylketones, L-dopa metabolites

False −: None significant

Proteins

False +: Alkaline urine, quaternary ammonium compounds

False −: Proteins other than albumin (e.g., Bence Jones) (Dipstick checks only albumin.)

PROCEDURE

For a routine screening urinalysis, a fresh (< one hour old), clean-catch urine is acceptable. (See Chapter 4 under Urinary Tract Procedures.)

1. Pour about 5 to 10 ml of well-mixed urine into a centrifuge tube.

2. Check for color, turbidity, and odor.

3. Perform the dipstick evaluation using the dipstick (Labstix, Chemstrip, or whatever other brand) supplied by your lab. Read the results according to the color chart and instructions on the bottle. Record glucose, ketones, blood, protein, pH, and nitrite, if available. BE SURE TO RECAP THE BOTTLE TIGHTLY AFTER USE.

4. Spin the sample at 3000 rpm for three minutes. Check the specific gravity with a urinometer or optic refractory urinometer.

5. Decant and discard the supernatant. Mix the remaining sediment well and pipette it onto a slide; cover it with a coverslip. If a urine sample looks very grossly cloudy, it is sometimes advisable to examine an unspun sample. If an unspun sample is used, note so on the report.

6. Examine 10 low power fields (10X objective) for epithelial cells, casts, crystals, and mucus. Casts are usually reported per low power field.

7. Examine 10 high power fields (45X objective) to look for casts, crystals, RBCs, WBCs, bacteria, and parasites (trichomonads). RBCs, WBCs, and bacteria are usually reported per high power field. Two reporting systems are used:

SYSTEM ONE
- Rare = <2 per field
- Occasional = 3–5 per field
- Frequent = 5–9 per field
- Many = "large number" per field
- TNTC = too numerous to count

SYSTEM TWO
- Trace = <¼ of field
- 1+ = ¼ of field

- 2+ = ½ of field
- 3+ = ¾ of field
- 4+ = field is full

DIFFERENTIAL DIAGNOSIS FOR ROUTINE URINALYSIS

pH

Acid: High protein diet, ammonium chloride, mandelic acid and other medications, acidosis, ketoacidosis (starvation, diabetic), COPD

Basic: UTI, renal tubular acidosis, diet (high vegetable, milk, immediately after meals), sodium bicarbonate therapy, vomiting, metabolic alkalosis

Specific Gravity

Increased: Volume depletion; CHF; adrenal insufficiency; diabetes mellitus; inappropriate ADH; increased proteins (nephrosis); if markedly increased (1.040 to 1.050), suspect artifact or excretion of radiographic contrast media.

Decreased: Diabetes insipidus, pyelonephritis, glomerulonephritis, water load with normal renal function

Bilirubin

Positive: Obstructive jaundice, hepatitis, cirrhosis, gallstones (especially common duct), CHF with hepatic congestion

Blood

Positive: Stones, trauma, tumors (benign and malignant, anywhere in the urinary tract), coagulopathy, infection, menses (contamination), polycystic kidneys, interstitial nephritis, hemolytic anemia, transfusion reaction, burns

If the dipstick is positive for blood, but no red cells are seen, there may be free hemoglobin from trauma or a transfusion reaction or from lysis of RBCs (RBCs will lyse if the pH is <5 or >8) or there is myoglobin present because of a crush injury, burn, or tissue ischemia.

Glucose

Positive: Diabetes mellitus, pancreatitis, pheochromocytoma, shock, pain, steroids, hyperthyroidism, renal tubular disease, iatrogenic causes

Ketones

Positive: Starvation, high fat diet, diabetic ketoacidosis, vomiting, diarrhea, hyperthyroidism, pregnancy, febrile states

Nitrite

Positive: Infection

Protein

Positive: Pyelonephritis, glomerulonephritis, nephrosis, Kimmelsteil-Wilson disease (diabetes), nephrotic syndrome, myeloma, postural causes, preeclampsia, inflammation and malignancies of the lower tract, functional causes (fever, stress, exercise), malignant hypertension, CHF

Reducing Substance

Positive: Glucose, fructose, galactose, contaminants (vitamin C, antibiotics, etc.)

Urobilinogen

Positive: Bile duct obstruction, suppression of gut flora with antibiotics

Sediment

RBCs: Trauma, pyelonephritis, genitourinary (GU) TB, cystitis, prostatitis, stones, tumors (malignant and benign), coagulopathy, and any cause of blood on dipstick (see previous section on blood)

WBCs: Infection anywhere in the urinary tract, anaerobic infections, TB, renal tumors, acute glomerulonephritis, radiation, interstitial nephritis (analgesic abuse)

Epithelial Cells: Acute tubular necrosis, necrotizing papillitis

Parasites: *Trichomonas vaginalis, Schistosoma hematobrium*

Yeast: *Candida albicans* (especially in diabetics, immunosuppressed patients, or if a vaginal infection is present)

Spermatozoa: Normal if after intercourse or nocturnal emission

Crystals

ABNORMAL: Cystine, sulfonamide, leucine, tyrosine, cholesterol

NORMAL

In Acid Urine: Calcium oxalate, urate

In Alkaline Urine: Calcium carbonate, phosphate

Contaminants: Cotton threads, hair, wood fibers, amorphous substances (all unimportant)

Mucus: Large amounts suggest urethral disease.

Glitter Cells: WBCs in hypotonic solution

Casts: The presence of casts in a urine localizes some or all of the disease process to the kidney itself.

HYALINE: (Acceptable unless they are "numerous"), benign hypertension, nephrotic syndrome

RBC: Acute glomerulonephritis, lupus nephritis, SBE, Goodpasture's disease, after a streptococcal infection, vasculitis, malignant hypertension

EPITHELIAL: Tubular damage, nephrotoxin, virus

GRANULAR: Breakdown of cellular casts, lead to waxy casts

WAXY: (End-stage of a granular cast), severe chronic renal disease, amyloidosis

FATTY: Nephrotic syndrome, diabetes mellitus, damaged renal tubular epithelial cells

BROAD: Chronic renal disease

Fig. 8-1 is a pictorial representation of materials found in urine sediments.

URINE CULTURE REPORTS

When a clean-catch urine sample is cultured for microorganisms, a colony count greater than 100,000 is considered significant for a urinary tract infection. If there is ever any doubt about an infection, urine collected by catheterization or, in children, by suprapubic aspiration should be cultured. Most consider ANY growth significant on a urine specimen collected by catheterization, but it is generally accepted that, in the presence of WBCs, a colony count greater than 10,000 is diagnostic for a urinary tract infection.

SPOT OR RANDOM URINE

Urine for electrolytes, the so-called "spot urine," is often ordered to aid in diagnosing various conditions. The usefulness of this assay is limited, however, because of large

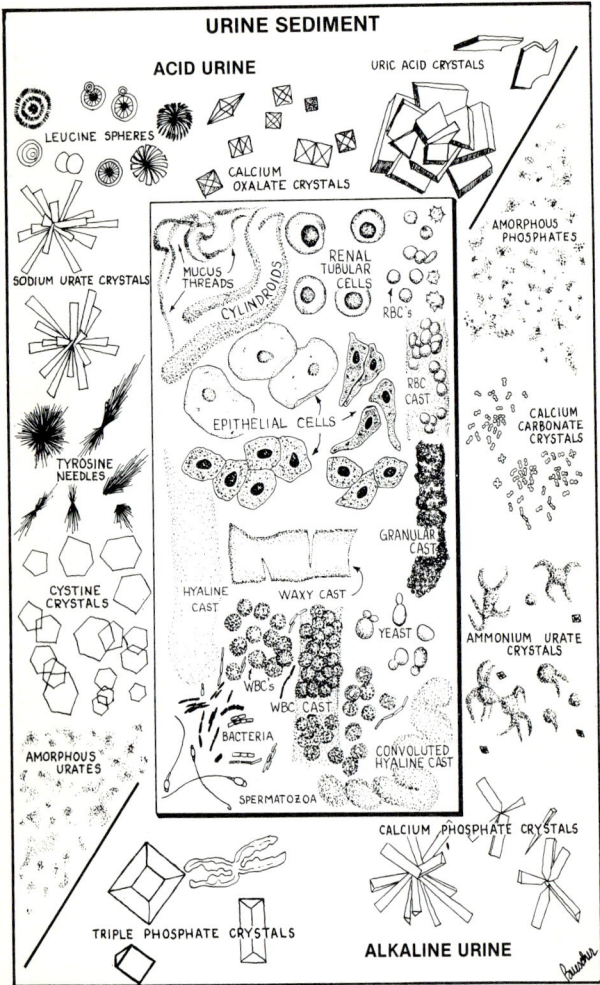

Fig. 8-1 Urine sediment chart. *(From Biller JA, Yeager AM, [eds]: The Harriet Lane Handbook: A Manual for Pediatric House Officers, ed 9. Chicago, Yearbook Medical Publishers Inc, 1981. Reproduced with permission of Johns Hopkins Hospital.)*

variations in daily fluid and salt intake. In addition, the results are usually indeterminate if a diuretic has been given.

Differential Diagnosis

Sodium <10 mEq/liter: Volume depletion, hyponatremic states, prerenal azotemia (CHF, shock, etc.)

Chloride <10 mEq/liter: Chloride-sensitive metabolic alkalosis

Potassium <10 mEq/liter: Hypokalemia, potassium depletion, extrarenal loss

Potassium >10 mEq/liter: Renal potassium wasting (brisk diuresis, etc.)

Protein: Normal is <10 mg/dl or <20 mg/dl for a sample taken in the early A.M. (See the earlier section for the differential diagnosis of protein in the urine.)

Osmolality: 500–1200 mOsm/liter (varies with water intake)

CREATININE CLEARANCE

Creatinine clearance (see the next section on 24 Hour Urine Studies for normal values and differential diagnosis) is one of the most sensitive indicators of early renal insufficiency. Clearances are ordered on patients with suspected renal disease and are useful for following patients who are taking nephrotoxic medications such as gentamicin.

To determine a creatinine clearance, you need to order a serum creatinine and a 24 hour urine for creatinine. A shorter time interval can be used, for example 12 hours, but remember that the formula must be corrected for this change and that a 24 hour sample is less prone to collection error.

Example

Calculation of the creatinine clearance from a 24 hour urine sample with a volume of 1000 ml, a urine creatinine of 108 mg/100 ml, and a serum creatinine of 1 mg/100 ml.

Creatinine clearance =

$$\frac{\text{Urine creatinine} \times \text{Total urine volume}}{\text{Plasma creatinine} \times \text{Time (1440 minutes for 24 hours)}}$$

Creatinine clearance =

$$\frac{(108 \text{ mg}/100 \text{ ml}) (1000 \text{ ml})}{(1 \text{ mg}/100 \text{ ml}) (1440 \text{ min})} = 75 \text{ ml/min}$$

Some people advocate a preliminary determination to see if the urine sample is valid by determining first if the sample contains at least 18–25 mg/kg/24 hr of creatinine for adult males or 12–20 mg/kg/24 hr for adult females. This preliminary test is not a requirement.

If the patient is an adult (150 lb = body surface area of 1.73 m^2), adjustment of the clearance for body size is not routinely done. Adjustment for pediatric patients is a necessity. If the values in the previous example were for a 10-year-old boy who weighed 70 lb (1.1 m^2; see Chapter 11 for the conversion formula), then the clearance would be

$$75 \text{ ml/min} \times \frac{1.73 \text{ m}^2}{1.1 \text{ m}^2} = 118 \text{ ml/min}$$

24 HOUR URINE STUDIES

A wide variety of diseases, most of them endocrine, can be diagnosed by assays of 24 hour urine samples. The following material gives the normal values for certain agents and the conditions associated with changes in these values.

Catecholamines

Normal: Epinephrine <15 µg/24 hr, norepinephrine <100 µg/24 hr

Increased: Pheochromocytoma, neuroblastoma, epinephrine administration, drugs (methyldopa, tetracyclines are false increases)

Chloride

Normal: 110–250 mEq/24 hr

Creatinine and Creatinine Clearance

Normal: 1.0–1.5 gm/24 hr or 18–25 mg/kg/24 hr in males and 12–20 mg/kg/24 hr in females and clearance of 80–140 ml/min

Decreased: A decreased creatinine clearance results in an increase in serum creatinine. See Chapter 6 for differential diagnosis and the previous section in this chapter on Creatinine Clearance for more details.

5-HIAA (5-hydroxyindoleacetic Acid)

Normal: 2–10 mg/24 hr

Increased: Carcinoid   syndrome,   medications (phenothiazines)

Metanephrines

Normal: <1.0 mg/24 hr

Increased: Pheochromocytoma, neuroblastoma (neural crest tumors)

Protein

Normal: 50–100 mg/24 hr (See the section on Differential Diagnosis in this chapter.)

17-Ketosteroids

Normal: 5–25 mg/24 hr

Increased: Adrenal cortex abnormalities (hyperplasia [Cushing's syndrome], adenoma, carcinoma, adrenogenital syndrome), severe stress, ACTH or pituitary tumor, testicular interstitial tumor and arrhenoblastoma (both produce testosterone)

Decreased: Panhypopituitarism, Addison's disease, castration in men

17-Ketogenic Steroids (Corticosteroids)

Normal: 5–20 mg/24 hr

Increased: Adrenal hyperplasia

Decreased: Panhypopituitarism, Addison's disease, acute steroid withdrawal

Sodium

Normal: 40–220 mEq/24 hr (varies with diet)

Vanillymandelic Acid (VMA)

Normal: <7 mg/24 hr

Increased: Pheochromocytoma, neural crest tumors (pheochromocytoma, ganglioneuroma), factitious increase (chocolate, coffee, tea, monoamine oxidase [MAO] inhibitors, methyldopa)

NOTE: VMA is the urinary product of both epinephrine and norepinephrine.

URINE OUTPUT

Although clinical situations vary greatly, the usual, minimal acceptable urine output for a patient is 0.5–1.0 ml/kg/hr.

AMYLASE/CREATININE CLEARANCE RATIO

The normal amylase/creatinine clearance ratio is <5%. A ratio >5% is virtually diagnostic of pancreatitis. Order urine and serum amylase and creatinine levels. The urine can be either a "spot urine" or a two hour collection.

$$\text{Ratio} = \frac{(\text{Urine amylase} \times \text{Volume})/(\text{Plasma amylase})}{(\text{Urine creatinine} \times \text{Volume})/(\text{Plasma creatinine})}$$

$$= \frac{\text{Urine amylase} \times \text{Plasma creatinine}}{\text{Urine creatinine} \times \text{Plasma amylase}} \times 100$$

URINARY INDICES IN RENAL FAILURE

Use the following table to help differentiate the causes (renal or prerenal) of oliguria.

(See also Chapter 5 under Anuria.)

Differential Diagnosis of Oliguria

Index	Prerenal	Renal
Urine Osmolality	>500	<350
Urinary Sodium	<20	>40
Urine/Plasma Creatinine	>40	<20
Fractional Excreted Sodium*	<1	>1

$$\text{*Fractional excreted sodium} = \frac{\text{Urine/Plasma Sodium}}{\text{Urine/Plasma Creatinine}} \times 100$$

9
Clinical Microbiology

GRAM STAIN

For gram-positive and gram-negative bacteria

Procedure

1. Smear the specimen on a glass slide in a fairly thin coat. If time permits, allow the specimen to air dry. The smear may also be fixed under VERY LOW HEAT (excessive heat can cause artifacts). If a bunsen burner is not available, a handy, instant heat source can be an alcohol swab set on fire with a match or cigarette lighter. Heat the slide until it is warm, but not hot, when touched to the back of the hand.

2. Timing for the stain is not critical, but at least 10 seconds should be allowed for each set of reagents.

3. Apply the crystal violet (Gram's stain), rinse the slide with tap water, apply iodine solution, and rinse with water.

4. Decolorize the slide carefully with the acetone-alcohol solution until the blue color is barely visible in the runoff. (This is the step where most gram stains are ruined.)

5. Counterstain with a few drops of safranin, rinse the slide with water, and blot it dry with lint-free bibulous or filter paper.

6. Use both the high dry and oil immersion lenses on the microscope to examine the slide. If the gram stain is satisfactory, any polys on the slide should be pink with light blue nuclei. On a gram stain of sputum, an excessive number of epithelial cells means the sample was more saliva than sputum.

GRAM STAIN CHARACTERISTICS OF COMMON PATHOGENS

Gram-Positive Cocci: *Staphylococcus, Streptococcus, Diplococcus, Micrococcus, Peptococcus* (anaerobic), and *Peptostreptococcus* (anaerobic) species

Gram-Positive Rods: *Clostridium* (anaerobic), *Corynebacterium, Listeria, Eubacterium* (anaerobic), and *Bacillus* species

Gram-Negative Cocci: *Neisseria* species

Gram-Negative Coccoid Rods: *Hemophilus, Pasteurella, Brucella,* and *Bordatella* species

Gram-Negative Straight Rods: *Escherichia, Salmonella, Shigella, Proteus, Enterobacter, Klebsiella, Serratia, Pseudomonas, Bacteroides* (anaerobic), *Fusobacterium* (anaerobic), and *Campylobacter* (comma shaped) species

ACID-FAST STAIN (KINYON STAIN) (AFB SMEAR)

1. Spread the smear on a slide, allow it to air dry, and then gently heat fix it.

2. Stain the smear for three to five minutes with tergitol in carbolfuchsin red solution.

3. Rinse the slide with tap water.

4. Decolorize with acid-alcohol solution for no longer than 30 seconds.

5. Rinse with tap water.

6. Counterstain with methylene blue for one minute.

7. Rinse the slide with tap water and allow it to air dry.

8. Examine the smear with high dry and oil immersion lenses; search for the "Red Snappers" (acid-fast bacilli like tubercle bacilli).

WAYSON'S STAIN

Wayson's stain is a good, quick scout stain that will color most bacteria.

1. Spread the smear on a slide and air or heat dry it.

2. Pour freshly filtered Wayson's stain onto the slide and allow it to stand for 10 to 20 seconds (timing is not critical).

3. Rinse the slide gently with tap water and dry it with filter paper.

4. Use the high dry and oil immersion lenses to examine the slide.

KOH PREPARATION (POTASSIUM HYDROXIDE)

KOH preps are used for diagnosis of fungal infections.

1. Apply the specimen (vaginal secretion, sputum, skin scrapings) to a slide.

2. Add 1 to 2 drops of KOH solution (10% to 40%) and mix. Gentle heating is helpful.

3. Put a coverslip over the specimen and examine the slide for branching hyphae and blastospores. KOH should destroy all elements other than the fungus.

INDIA INK PREPARATION

India ink is used primarily on cerebrospinal fluids to identify fungal organisms (especially cryptococci).

1. Add a drop of dilute India ink to the fluid on a slide and mix well.

2. Cover with a coverslip and examine the fluid for round, refractile organisms.

SCHLICTER TEST

The Schlicter test (serum cidal level) is used to determine the antibacterial level of the serum or CSF of patients who are receiving antibiotic therapy. The test uses eight serial dilutions of the patient's serum (1:1 through 1:128) to determine what dilution of the serum is bactericidal to the infecting organism. The test is usually coordinated by the infectious disease and microbiology services. One set of blood or CSF cultures must be negative for the infecting organism before the test is performed.

Opinion varies greatly as to interpretation of the results. Optimal killing of the organism occurs at dilutions ranging anywhere from 1:2 to 1:8. That is, a result such as "Staph aureus bactericidal level = 1:8″ means the infecting organism was killed at a serum dilution of 1:8. Some feel higher titers (1:32) are needed to treat bacterial endocarditis.

DIFFERENTIAL DIAGNOSIS OF INFECTIONS

The table beginning on p 154 gives the etiological agents of various types of infection.

Differential Diagnosis of Infections

Type of Infection	Etiological Agents		
	COMMON	RELATIVELY COMMON	UNUSUAL BUT IMPORTANT
Skin and subcutaneous tissue	Staphylococcus aureus	Streptococcus pyogenes, Candida, and superficial fungi	Gram-negative bacilli (burns, wounds)
Sinusitis	Streptococcus pneumoniae S. aureus	S. pyogenes, Hemophilus influenzae	Mucorales
Pharyngitis	Respiratory viruses, S. pyogenes	Gonococcus	Corynebacterium diphtheriae
Epiglottitis	H. influenzae		
Otitis, mastoiditis	S. pneumoniae, H. influenzae (children)	S. aureus, S. pyogenes	Pseudomonas, Proteus
Pneumonitis	S. pneumoniae, Mycoplasma pneumoniae, Mycobacterium tuberculosis	S. aureus, Klebsiella-Enterobacter, respiratory viruses, Legionella pneumophilia	S. pyogenes, gram-negative enteric bacilli, psittacosis, systemic fungi, Pneumocystis, H. influenzae, Pasteurella multocida

Differential Diagnosis of Infections (Continued)

Type of Infection	Etiological Agents		
	COMMON	RELATIVELY COMMON	UNUSUAL BUT IMPORTANT
Empyema and lung abscess	S. aureus, anaerobic streptococcus, Bacteroides, Fusobacterium	Klebsiella (abscess)	
Bacterial endocarditis	Streptococcus viridans, S. aureus, enterococcus	S. pneumoniae, anaerobic streptococci	Pseudomonas, Candida, Staphylococcus epidermidis
Gastroenteritis	Salmonella, Shigella, enteric viruses	S. aureus, Escherichia coli (enterotoxic), clostridia, Giardia	Pseudomonas, Entamoeba histolytica, Vibrio cholerae, Vibrio parahemolyticus
Peritonitis, cholangitis, intraabdominal abscess	E. coli, enterococcus, Bacteroides, anaerobic streptococcus, Fusobacterium	Klebsiella-Enterobacter, Proteus species	Clostridia, S. aureus
Urinary infection (cystitis, pyelonephritis)	E. coli, Klebsiella-Enterobacter, paracolon, Proteus, enterococcus	Pseudomonas	S. aureus
Urethritis	Gonococcus, ?Mycoplasma, Chlamydia, ?Acinetobacter (Mima-herellea)	Treponema pallidum	

Differential Diagnosis of Infections (Continued)

Type of Infection	Etiological Agents		
	COMMON	RELATIVELY COMMON	UNUSUAL BUT IMPORTANT
Pelvic inflammatory disease	Gonococcus, E. coli, Bacteroides, anaerobic streptococci, Chlamydia	Klebsiella-Enterobacter, enterococcus, Fusobacterium	Clostridia, S. aureus
Bones (osteomyelitis)	S. aureus	Salmonella	S. pyogenes
Joints	S. aureus, gonococcus, S. pneumoniae, H. influenzae	S. pyogenes, Neisseria meningitidis	
Meninges	S. pneumoniae, H. influenzae, N. meningitidis	E. coli, Klebsiella-Enterobacter, Proteus, Pseudomonas	S. pyogenes, M. tuberculosis, Cryptococcus, S. aureus, Listeria monocytogenes

From Isselbacher KJ, et al (eds): Harrison's Principles of Internal Medicine, ed 9. New York, Mc-Graw Hill Co, 1980. Used with permission.

10

Blood Gases and Acid-Base Disorders

NORMAL BLOOD GAS VALUES

The following table gives the normal values of a blood gas analysis.

PROCEDURE AND INTERPRETATION

Procedure

1. Obtain an arterial blood gas (see Chapter 4) and if desired, a simultaneous SMA-6 (for HCO_3) on blood from a peripheral or central vein.

Normal Blood Gas Values

Measurement	Arterial Blood	Mixed Venous Blood*
pH	7.40 (7.38–7.42)	7.36 (7.31–7.41)
pO_2	80–100 mm Hg	35–40 mm Hg (decreases with age)
pCO_2	35–45 mm Hg	41–51 mm Hg
O_2 Saturation	>95%	60%–80% (decreases with age)
HCO_3	22–26 mEq/liter	22–26 mEq/liter
Base Difference (Deficit/Excess)	−2 to +2	−2 to +2

*From right atrium.

2. (Optional) Check the numbers obtained in the Henderson-Hasselbach (H/H) equation. This is an extra step, but sometimes very important to rule out lab error.

H/H Equation

$$pH = pKa + \log \frac{HCO_3 \text{ (metabolic/renal compensation)}}{pCO_2 \text{ (respiratory/lung compensation)}}$$

Modified H/H Equation: More convenient to use

$$pCO_2 = \frac{(H) \times (HCO_3)}{24}$$

(For a rough estimate of H, subtract decimal digits of pH from 80; e.g., if pH = 7.48, 80 − 48 = 32, therefore H = 32.)

If the calculated HCO_3 from the H/H equation is within 3 to 4 of the HCO_3 on the SMA-6, you can proceed with the evaluation. If a discrepancy exists, a lab error has occurred, and all values should be repeated.

Interpretation

THE FOLLOWING RULES FOR ACUTE ACID-BASE DIS-
TURBANCES SHOULD BE COMMITTED TO MEMORY:

RULE I: A change in pCO_2 down or up 10 mm Hg is associated with an increase or decrease in pH of 0.08 units. (As the
pCO_2 decreases, the pH increases; as the pCO_2 increases, the
pH decreases.)

RULE II: A pH change of 0.15 = a base change of 10 mEq/
liter. (A decrease in base [sodium bicarbonate] is termed BASE
DEFICIT, and an increase in base is termed BASE EXCESS.)

RULE III: The dose of bicarbonate (in mEq) required to
correct a metabolic acidosis =

$$\frac{\text{Base Deficit (mEq/liter)} \times \text{Patient Weight (kg)}}{4}$$

RULE IV: If the alveolar ventilation increases, CO_2 will
decrease; if alveolar ventilation decreases, CO_2 will increase.

Although not needed for the interpretation of acid-base disturbances, oxygen saturation is a useful parameter to follow
how well the blood and lungs are able to deliver oxygen to the
tissues. Various conditions can shift the oxyhemoglobin
dissociation curve to the right or left (Fig. 10-1).

To analyze an acid-base disturbance, do the following:

1. First look at the pCO_2, and determine its difference from
    normal (normal pCO_2 is 40).

2. Calculate what the pH should be based on RULE I.

3. Is this calculated pH the same as the measured pH?

4. If the calculated and measured pHs are reasonably close,
    then all the changes seen in the pH are respiratory
    (caused by increased or decreased pCO_2).

O$_2$ dissociation curve of blood at 37 C

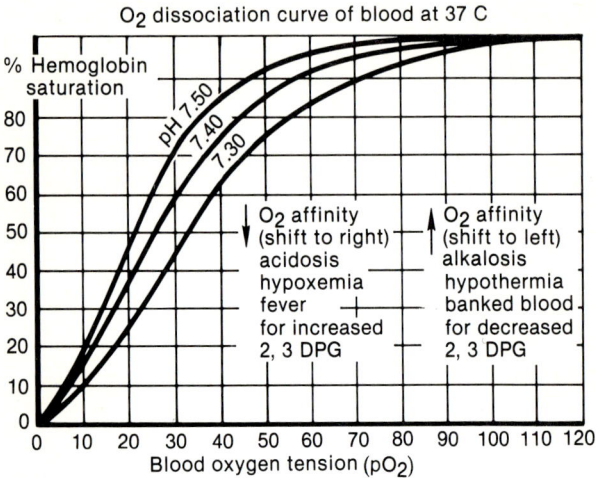

Fig. 10-1 Dissociation curve for oxyhemoglobin

5. If, on the other hand, the measured pH is LESS than the calculated pH, this disturbance must be a metabolic acidosis. Likewise, if the measured pH is GREATER than the calculated pH, this change represents a component of metabolic alkalosis.

6. If the calculated pH and measured pH are not close, subtract the calculated pH from the measured pH (measured minus calculated).

7. A negative number (when the measured pH is less than the calculated pH) represents a base deficit or metabolic acidosis.

8. A positive number (when the measured pH is greater than the calculated pH) represents a base excess or metabolic alkalosis.

9. Use this difference between the measured and calculated pH and RULE II to determine the exact base change.

10. For a metabolic acidosis, use RULE III to calculate the dose of bicarbonate to correct the acidosis.

The preceding blood gas analysis is modified from *ACLS Providers Manual.* Chicago, American Heart Association, 1975.

SAMPLE ACID-BASE PROBLEMS

Patient 1: pCO_2 52 and pH 7.30

- pCO_2 increased by 12; therefore, there is a RESPIRATORY ACIDOSIS from HYPOVENTILATION
- Calculated pH = 7.30 (use RULE I)
- Measured pH = 7.30
- pH difference = 0
- Therefore, there is no metabolic component—RESPIRATORY ACIDOSIS ONLY

Patient 2: pCO_2 40 and pH 7.25, weight 70 kg

- pCO_2 is normal; therefore, no respiratory component present
- Calculated pH = 7.40
- Measured pH = 7.25
- pH difference = minus 0.15; therefore, there is a METABOLIC ACIDOSIS
- Base deficit (use RULE II) = negative 10 mEq/liter
- Therefore, there is no respiratory component—a METABOLIC ACIDOSIS ONLY
- According to RULE III, the dose of bicarbonate required to FULLY correct this metabolic acidosis is 175 mEq.

Patient 3: pCO_2 50 and pH 7.26

- pCO_2 increased by 10; therefore, there is a RESPIRATORY ACIDOSIS
- Calculated pH = 7.32 (use RULE I)
- Measured pH = 7.26
- pH difference = (measured − calculated) = minus 0.06
- Base deficit = minus 4 mEq/liter (use RULE II)
- Therefore, a mixed disturbance—RESPIRATORY AND METABOLIC ACIDOSIS

DEFINITION OF ACID-BASE DISORDERS

The following table shows the changes in pH, HCO_3, and pCO_2 associated with acid-base disorders.

Acid-Base Disorders (Partial Compensation)

Disorder	Changes in Normal Values*		
	pH	HCO_3	pCO_2
Metabolic Acidosis	<	<<	<
Metabolic Alkalosis	>	>>	>
Respiratory Acidosis	<	>	>>
Respiratory Alkalosis	>	<	<<

*< = decreased, > = increased, << or >> = primary disturbance

DIFFERENTIAL DIAGNOSIS OF ACID-BASE DISORDERS

Metabolic Acidosis

Causes
- Addition of strong acid
- Loss of HCO_3 via GI tract or kidney

Anion Gap: To distinguish between acid gain and HCO_3 loss, calculate the anion gap.

$$\text{Anion Gap} = (Na + K) - (Cl + HCO_3)$$
$$\text{Normal Gap} = 12\text{--}16 \text{ mEq/liter}$$

ANION GAP ACIDOSIS: Gap >16 mEq/liter; caused by a decrease in HCO_3 balanced by an increase in unmeasured acid ions, not by an increase in chloride (so-called normo-chloremic acidosis)

NON-ANION GAP ACIDOSIS: Gap is between 12–16 mEq/liter; caused by a decrease in HCO_3 balanced by an increase in chloride (hyperchloremic acidosis)

Differential Diagnosis

GAP (NORMOCHLOREMIC)
- Increased acid production: Ketoacidosis (diabetic, alcoholic), lactic acidosis, starvation, nonketotic hyperosmolar coma
- Toxic ingestion: Salicylates, paraldehyde, methanol, ethylene glycol
- Failure of acid excretion: Chronic and acute renal failure

NONGAP (HYPERCHLOREMIC)
- GI loss of HCO_3: Diarrhea, small bowel or pancreatic fistula, ileal loop obstruction, anion exchange resins
- Renal HCO_3 loss: Carbonic anhydrase inhibitors, renal tubular acidosis
- Miscellaneous: Dilutional, addition of HCl with drugs, hyperalimentation

Treatment: Correct underlying disorder.

- If acute, correct with sodium bicarbonate (use RULE III described previously). Treat only one-half the deficit initially and then reassess the problem.

Metabolic Alkalosis

Causes
- Loss of H from extracellular fluid
- Addition of HCO_3 or its precursors (lactate, citrate, acetate) to extracellular fluid
- Loss of extracellular fluid containing Cl in greater proportions than HCO_3.

Generation Versus Maintenance: The kidneys can usually correct increased HCO_3 fairly rapidly, so renal function usually has to be interrupted for alkalosis to be maintained.

GENERATION
- Net H loss: GI tract (NG suction, emesis), renal (hyperaldosteronism), via intracellular shifts

- Net HCO_3 addition: Rapid HCO_3 precursor administration (lactate, citrate, acetate)
- Cl loss $>>$ HCO_3 loss: GI (villous adenoma), diuretics (Lasix), posthypercapnic (COPD)

MAINTENANCE
- Cl deficiency: Either HCO_3 or Cl required for Na reabsorption
- Volume depletion
- K depletion: Intracellular H shift results in increased renal H secretion

Classification

CHLORIDE RESPONSIVE: NaCl and extracellular fluid depletion; LOW URINARY CHLORIDE (Urinary Cl <10 mEq/liter)

CHLORIDE UNRESPONSIVE: Increased mineralocorticoid effect; NORMAL URINARY CHLORIDE (Urinary Cl >10 mEq/liter)

Differential Diagnosis

NaCl RESPONSIVE
- GI disorders: Emesis, NG suction, villous adenoma
- Diuretic therapy
- Rapid correction of chronic pCO_2 elevation
- Cystic fibrosis

NaCl RESISTANT
- Excess mineralocorticoid: Hyperaldosteronism, Cushing's syndrome, Bartter's syndrome
- Profound K depletion
- Miscellaneous: Alkali administration, milk-alkali syndrome, nonparathyroid hypercalcemia

Treatment: Correct underlying disorder.

- Replace volume with NaCl if depleted.
- Correct hypokalemia if present.
- NH_4Cl and HCl should be reserved for extreme cases.

Respiratory Acidosis

Differential Diagnosis

NEUROMUSCULAR ABNORMALITIES
- Primary neuromuscular disease
- Secondary neuromuscular disease: Sedatives, analgesics, tranquilizers

AIRWAY OBSTRUCTION
- Chronic (COPD)
- Acute (asthma)

THORACIC-PULMONARY DISORDERS
- Bony thoracic cage: Flail chest, rib fractures
- Parenchymal lesions: Pneumothorax, noncardiac pulmonary edema, severe pneumonia

VASCULAR DISEASE
- Massive pulmonary embolus with respiratory failure

Treatment

- Improve ventilation: Intubate and place on ventilator, increase ventilator rate, etc.

Respiratory Alkalosis

Differential Diagnosis

CENTRAL STIMULATION
- Anxiety
- Hyperventilation syndrome
- Pain
- Head trauma: Central neurogenic hyperventilation
- Cerebrovascular accident (CVA)
- Tumors
- Salicylates: Early toxicity
- Fever
- Early sepsis

PERIPHERAL STIMULATION
- Pulmonary embolus
- CHF
- Interstitial lung disease
- Pneumonia
- Altitude
- Hypoxemia: Any cause (See the following section.)

MISCELLANEOUS
- Gram-negative sepsis
- Hepatic insufficiency
- Pregnancy
- Iatrogenic overventilation

Treatment: Correct the underlying disorder.

- Hyperventilation syndrome: Best treated by having the patient rebreathe into a bag to increase pCO_2.

HYPOXIA

Differential Diagnosis

VENTILATION-PERFUSION (V/Q) ABNORMALITIES
- COPD: Asthma, emphysema
- Atelectasis
- Pneumonia
- Pulmonary embolus
- Adult respiratory distress syndrome
- Pneumothorax
- TB
- Pneumoconiosis
- Cystic fibrosis
- Obstructed airway

ALVEOLAR HYPOVENTILATION
- Skeletal abnormalities
- Neuromuscular disorders
- Pickwickian syndrome

DECREASED PULMONARY DIFFUSING CAPACITY
- Pneumoconiosis
- Pulmonary edema
- Pulmonary fibrosis

RIGHT TO LEFT SHUNT
- Congenital heart disease: Tetrology of Fallot, transposition, etc.

CAPILLARY BLOOD GASES

A capillary blood gas (CBG) is obtained from a highly vascularized capillary bed (the heel is the most commonly used site). CBGs are often used for pediatric patients. They are easier to obtain than arterial blood gases and are less traumatic (no risk of arterial thrombosis, hemorrhage). The procedure is fully described in Chapter 4 under Heelstick.

Interpretation

When interpreting a CBG, apply the following rules:

pH: Same as arterial or slightly lower (N = 7.35–7.40)

pCO$_2$:   Same as arterial or slightly higher (N = 40–45)

pO$_2$:   Lower than arterial (N = 45–60)

O$_2$ Saturation: >70% is acceptable. Saturation is probably more useful than the pO$_2$ itself.

11
Fluids and Electrolytes

PRINCIPLES OF FLUIDS AND ELECTROLYTES

Fluid Compartments: (70 kg male)

Total Body Water: 42,000 ml (60% of body weight [BW])

- Intracellular: 28,000 ml (40% BW)

- Extracellular: 14,000 ml (20% BW)
  Plasma: 3,500 ml (5% BW)
  Interstitial: 10,500 ml (15% BW)

Total Blood Volume: 5,600 ml (8% BW)

Water Requirements

For a 70 kg Male

- 2500 ml/day (about 35 ml/kg/day)
- Lost as urine: 800–1500 ml
- Lost in stool: 250 ml
- Insensible loss: 600–900 ml (increases 10% for each degree of fever and decreases if a patient is on a ventilator)

If Not a 70 kg Male: You can calculate the water requirement according to the following:

- For the first 10 kg of body weight: 100 ml/kg/day PLUS
- For the second 10 kg of body weight: 50 ml/kg/day PLUS
- For weight above 20 kg: 20 ml/kg/day

Electrolyte Requirements: (For a 70 kg adult, unless specified)

Sodium (as NaCl)

50–90 mEq (3–5 gm) per day (for pediatric patients, 3–4 mEq/kg/24 hr)

Potassium

50–100 mEq/day (for pediatric patients, 2–3 mEq/kg/24 hr). In the absence of hypokalemia and with normal renal function, most of this is excreted in the urine. Of the total amount of potassium, 98% is intracellular, and 2% is extracellular. Thus, assuming the serum potassium level is normal, about 4.5 mEq/liter, the total extracellular pool of K = 4.5 × 14 liter = 63 mEq. There is an easy interchange of potassium between intracellular and extracellular stores under certain conditions such as acidosis. Potassium demands increase with diuresis and building of new body tissues (anabolic states).

Calcium

1–3 gm/day, most of which is secreted by the GI tract. Routine administration is not needed in the absence of specific indications.

Magnesium

20 mEq/day. Routine administration not needed in the absence of specific indications such as parenteral hyperalimentation, massive diuresis, or preeclampsia.

Glucose Requirements

During starvation, caloric needs are supplied by body fat and protein; the majority of protein comes from the skeletal muscles. Every gram of nitrogen in the urine represents 6.25 gm of protein broken down.

Protein-Sparing Effect: The goal of basic IV therapy. The administration of at least 100 gm of glucose/day reduces protein loss by more than half. Virtually all IV fluid solutions supply glucose as dextrose (pure dextrorotary glucose). Pediatric patients require about 100–200 mg/kg/hr.

COMPOSITION OF PARENTERAL FLUIDS

Colloids: (See Chapter 22 for a description of each.)

- Albumin
- Plasma protein fraction
- Hetastarch (Hespan)

Blood Products: (See Chapter 14.)

- Packed red cells
- Fresh frozen plasma

Crystalloids

The following table gives the number of calories and the amount of crystalloids present in common parenteral fluids.

Composition of Parenteral Fluids

Fluid	Glucose (gm/100 ml)	Na	Cl	K	Ca	HCO$_3$	Calories (per liter)
				(mEq/liter)			
D 5% Water (D5W)	5	—	—	—	—	—	170
D 5% ¼ NS* (0.25%)	5	34	34	—	—	—	170
D 5% ½ NS* (0.45%)	5	77	77	—	—	—	170
D 5% NS* (0.9%)	5	154	154	—	—	—	170
D 5% Lactated Ringer's (D5LR)	5	130	110	4	3	27	180
Lactated Ringer's	—	130	110	4	3	27	<10
D 10% Water	10	—	—	—	—	—	340

*NS = normal saline

COMPOSITION OF BODY FLUIDS

The following table gives the average daily production and the amount of some major electrolytes present in various body fluids.

Composition and Daily Production of Body Fluids

Fluid	Electrolytes				Average Daily Production* (in ml)
	Na	Cl	K	HCO$_3$	
	mEq/liter				
Saliva	10	10	26	30	1500
Gastric juice	60–100	100	10	0	1500–2000
Duodenum	130	90	5	0–10	300–2000
Bile	145	100	5	15–35	100–800
Pancreatic juice	140	75	5	70–115	100–800
Ileum	140	100	5	15–30	2000–3000
Diarrhea	50	40	35	45	—

*In adults

ORDERING IV FLUIDS

One of the most difficult tasks to master is choosing appropriate IV therapy for a patient. The patient's underlying illness, vital signs, serum electrolytes, and a host of other variables all must be considered. The following are general guidelines for IV therapy. Specific requirements for each patient can vary tremendously from these guidelines.

Maintenance Fluids: (These amounts provide the minimum requirements for routine daily needs.)

70 kg Male: D5¼NS with 20 mEq KCl/liter at 125 ml/hr (This will deliver about 3 liters of free water.)

Other Patients: Also use D5¼NS with 20 mEq KCl/liter. Determine their 24 hour water requirement by the following formula, called the "Kg Method," and divide by 24 hours to determine the hourly rate.

Kg METHOD:

- For the first 10 kg body weight: 100 ml/kg/day PLUS
- For the second 10 kg body weight: 50 ml/kg/day PLUS
- For weight above 20 kg: 20 ml/kg/day

Pediatric Patients: Use the same solution, but determine the daily fluid requirements by either of the following:

Kg METHOD: As outlined before

METER SQUARED METHOD: Maintenance fluids are 1500 ml/m^2/day. Divide by 24 to get the flow rate per hour. To calculate the surface area, use the following handy table. Formal body surface area charts are in the Appendix.

Specific Replacement Fluids

Gastric (NG Tube, Emesis): D5½NS with 20 mEq/liter KCl ml for ml

Rule of Sixes Normogram

Weight (in lb)	Body Surface Area (in m^2)
3	0.1
6	0.2
12	0.3
18	0.4
24	0.5
30	0.6
36	0.7
42	0.8
48	0.9
60	1.0

- After 60 lb, add 0.1 for each additional 10 lb.
- Over 100 lb, can be treated as an adult.

Diarrhea: D5LR with 15 mEq/liter KCl. Use body weight as a replacement guide (1 liter for each 1 kg or 2.2 lb lost).

Bile: D5LR with 25 mEq/liter of HCO_3 ml for ml

Pancreatic: D5LR with 50 mEq/liter HCO_3 ml for ml

ELECTROLYTE ABNORMALITIES

In all of the following situations, the primary goal should be to correct the underlying condition. Unless specified, all dosages are for adults.

Hypernatremia

Symptoms

- Confusion, stupor, coma
- Muscle tremors, seizures
- Pulmonary and peripheral edema

Treatment

- Give D5W SLOWLY (24 to 48 hours).
- Check the serum sodium levels frequently.
- Avoid medications that contain excessive sodium.
- Calculate the total water (as D5W) needed to correct; use the following equation.

$$\text{Liters of water} = \frac{60\% \text{ weight (kg)} \times (140 - \text{serum Na})}{140}$$

Hyponatremia: (Na usually <125 mEq/liter)

Symptoms

- Lethargy, confusion, coma
- Muscle twitches and irritability, convulsions
- Nausea, vomiting, ileus

Treatment

IF DILUTIONAL: (SIADH, water intoxication)
- Restrict fluids (1000–1500 ml/day)
- Consider diuretics

IF DEHYDRATED
- Give D5NS

Hyperkalemia

Symptoms

- Weakness, flaccid paralysis, hyperactive deep tendon reflexes (DTR)
- ECG: Peaked T waves, wide QRS, asystole
- K = 7–8 mEq/liter yields ventricular fibrillation in 5% of patients
- K = 10 mEq/liter yields ventricular fibrillation in 90% of patients

Treatment

RAPID
- 50 ml D50, IV push, with 10–25 units regular insulin, IV push
- Alkalinize with 50 mEq (1 ampule) sodium bicarbonate
- Calcium chloride, 500 mg, slow IV push (only protects heart from effect)

SLOW
- Sodium polystyrene sulfonate (Kayexalate) 20–40 gm given orally (po) with 100 to 200 ml of 20% sorbitol or 40 gm Kayexalate with 40 gm sorbitol in 100 ml water given as an enema. Repeat doses four times a day (qid) as needed.
- Dialysis (hemodialysis or peritoneal)

Hypokalemia

Symptoms

- Muscle weakness, cramps
- Nausea, vomiting, ileus, polyuria, polydypsia
- ECG: Flattening of T waves, "U" wave becomes obvious (U wave is the upward deflection after the T wave.)

Treatment: Replace with KCl.

RAPID CORRECTION: Give KCl IV.
- Patient <40 kg: 0.25 mEq/kg/hr × 2 hr
- Patient >40 kg
  - K <3.7: Give 10 mEq/hr × 2 hr
  - K 3.7–4.0: Give 5 mEq/hr × 2 hr
- IN ALL CASES CHECK A STAT K FOLLOWING EACH 2 HOUR DOSE.

SLOW CORRECTION: Give KCl orally.
- Adult: 20–40 mEq two to three times a day (bid or tid)
- Pediatric patients: 1–2 mEq/kg/day in divided doses

Hypercalcemia

Symptoms

- Anorexia, nausea, vomiting, constipation, renal stones ("stones, bones, and abdominal groans")
- Fatigue, hypotonia, lethargy, coma
- Shortening of the QT interval on ECG

Treatment: See Chapter 21.

Hypocalcemia

Symptoms

- Peripheral and perioral paresthesias
- Hyperactive DTRs, carpopedal spasm (Trousseau's sign)
- Abdominal pain and cramps
- Positive Chvostek's sign (facial nerve twitch)
- Lethargy and irritability (in infants)
- Prolonged QT interval on ECG
- Generalized seizures, tetany, laryngospasm

Treatment

ACUTE CASES
- Calcium gluconate or calcium chloride IV (see Chapter 22)

CHRONIC STATES (RENAL FAILURE, ETC.)
- Use vitamin D along with oral calcium and phosphate binders like aluminum hydroxide

Hypermagnesemia

Symptoms

- 3–5 mEq/liter: Nausea, vomiting, hypotension
- 7–10 mEq/liter: Hyporeflexia, weakness, drowsiness
- >12 mEq/liter: Coma, respiratory failure

Treatment

- Calcium gluconate: 500 mg given IV to reverse symptoms
- Dialysis for removal

Hypomagnesemia

Symptoms

- Weakness, muscle twitches
- Tremors, vertigo, convulsions
- Symptoms of hypocalcemia (hypomagnesemia and hypocalcemia often coexist)

Treatment

SEVERE CASES
- Magnesium sulfate: 1 gm given intramuscularly (IM) every four to six hours or 1 gm of a 10% solution IV over 15 minutes followed by doses IM

MILD CASES
- Magnesium oxide: 10 gm (1 to 2 tablets) given orally every day (qd)

Hyperphosphatemia

Symptoms

- Metastatic calcifications

Treatment

- Low phosphate diet
- Phosphate binders like aluminum hydroxide gel (Amphojel) or basic aluminum carbonate gel (Basagel) po

Hypophosphatemia

Symptoms

- <1 mg/100 ml: Weakness, rhabdomyolysis, cardiac failure
- Paresthesias, hemolysis, platelet abnormalities

Treatment

MODERATE CASES

- Potassium phosphate (Neutraphos): Two tablets po, bid or tid
- Phosphosoda: 5 ml po, bid or tid

SEVERE CASES

- Potassium phosphate: 2.5–5.0 mg/kg given IV over eight hours

Burn Patients

Parkland Formula: Total fluid required during the first 24 hours = (% body burn) × (body weight in kg) × 4 ml. Replace with lactated Ringer's solution over 24 hours. Use

- ½ total over first eight hours (from time of burn)
- ¼ total over second eight hours
- ¼ total over third eight hours

Rules of Nines: (for estimating % body burned in adults)

- Head: 9%
- Chest and abdomen: 9% each
- Upper and lower back: 9% each
- Arms: 9% each
- Upper leg: 9% each
- Lower leg: 9% each
- Perineum: 1%

DETERMINING AN IV RATE

For a MAXI Drip: Use 10 drops/ml, thus

- 10 drops/min = 60 ml/hr or
- 16 drops/min = 100 ml/hr

For a MINI Drip: Use 60 drops/ml, thus

- 60 drops/min = 60 ml/hr or
- 100 drops/min = 100 ml/hr

12
Total Parenteral Nutrition (TPN)

INDICATIONS

TPN, also known as INF (intravenous nutritional fluids), is a technique of supplying protein, carbohydrates, and lipids via the parenteral route. This technique is used when the GI tract cannot be used as a route to provide nutrition to the patient. Indications can be categorized into four patient populations.

Categories

- Patients who are unable to ingest any food, orally or by nasogastric tube (regional enteritis, paralytic ileus, bowel anastamosis breakdown)
- Patients who can ingest food, but not enough to maintain an anabolic state (malabsorption syndromes, short-bowel syndrome, ulcerative colitis)
- Patients who are able to ingest food, but refuse to do so (anorexia nervosa, chronic depression, geriatric post-operative patients)

- Patients who should not be fed orally or by nasogastric tube (acute pancreatitis, enterocutaneous fistula)

These four populations can be broken down further depending upon their nutritional status at the time TPN is initiated.

Nondepleted Patients: Those in a mild catabolic state (after minor surgery)

Depleted Patients: Those definitely in a catabolic state (preoperative malnourished)

Hypermetabolic Patients: Those in a severely stressed catabolic state (trauma, burn, sepsis)

Nutritional assessment to determine the need for TPN should be based on a perceptive history, physical, and laboratory evaluation in addition to a good knowledge of the indications presented here. Absolute indications for when to begin TPN are difficult to define, but indications of nutritional status include nitrogen balance, total lymphocyte count, transferrin levels, anergy screening with skin tests, total protein, and albumin. These latter indications are each discussed in Chapter 13 under Nutritional Assessment, and nitrogen balance is presented in the third section of this chapter.

NUTRITIONAL PRINCIPLES

To initiate TPN therapy, an understanding of the daily energy and protein requirements is needed. The Basal Energy Expenditure/requirement (BEE) can be determined by an equation which takes into account sex, height, age, and weight.

BEE

Male = $66 + (13.7 \times W) + (5 \times H) - (6.8 \times A)$

Female = $65.5 + (9.6 \times W) + (1.8 \times H) - (4.7 \times A)$
- W = actual or, if >10% loss, usual weight in kilograms
- H = height in centimeters
- A = age in years

BEE can be estimated as approximately 1400–1800 cal/day in adults (30 cal/kg/day) and can increase to more than 3000 cal/day in stressed patients.

Requirements for both energy and protein (measured as nitrogen) vary according to the nutritional status of the patient. To help determine these initial needs the following guidelines are used.

Nondepleted Patients

GOAL: Prevent excessive loss of lean tissue

REQUIREMENTS: 0.8–1.0 gm protein/kg/day total daily calories of 20% above BEE

Depleted Patients

GOAL: Restoration of lean tissues with concommitant restoration of fat reserves

REQUIREMENTS: 1.5–1.8 gm protein/kg/day total daily calories of 50% above BEE

Hypermetabolic Patients

GOAL: Prevent worsening of catabolic state and subsequently cause a reversal towards an anabolic state

REQUIREMENTS: 2.0 gm protein/kg/day total daily calories or twice BEE

NOTE: In TPN, protein or amino acid intake is measured as the amount of nitrogen supplied to the patient. 1 gm nitrogen = 6.25 gm protein (amino acids).

NITROGEN BALANCE

The overall goal in TPN is to establish or maintain the patient in an anabolic state and to reverse or prevent a catabolic state. One method to determine if the therapy is achieving this goal is to measure nitrogen balance.

Definition: NITROGEN BALANCE = nitrogen input minus nitrogen output

Positive (+) Nitrogen Balance: Indicates an anabolic state (protein sparing or replacement)

Negative (−) Nitrogen Balance: Indicates a catabolic state (protein breakdown)

Determination

Input: Calculate the total nitrogen intake from both oral and IV routes.

Output: Order a 24 hour urine for urinary urea nitrogen (UUN) in mg/dl. Determine the total UUN based on the 24 hour volume, and add a rough correction of 4.0 to account for nitrogen losses in stool, etc.

Example: Patient is receiving 2 liters INF/24 hr with 27.5 gm protein/liter.

1. 27.5 gm protein/liter × 2 liters = 55 gm protein/24 hr

2. Recall that 1 gm nitrogen = 6.25 gm protein

3. $$\text{Nitrogen input} = \frac{55 \text{ gm protein}}{6.25 \text{ gm protein/gm N}} = 8.8 \text{ gm}$$

4. Patient voided 22.5 dl urine/24 hr with UUN 66 mg/dl

5. Nitrogen lost in urine = 22.5 dl × 66 mg/dl = 1485 mg or about 1.5 gm

6. Add 4.0 gm for other losses

7. Nitrogen output = 1.5 gm + 4.0 gm = 5.5 gm

8. Nitrogen balance = input minus output = 8.8 − 5.5 = positive (+) 3.3 gm nitrogen

INF SOLUTIONS AND ADDITIVES

Several companies currently manufacture different INF solutions. All solutions will provide amino acids, dextrose, and electrolytes. The amino acids are supplied as crystalline (CAA) or synthetic amino acids (SAA) in 2.75%, 3.25%, or 4.25% concentrations depending on the company. The dextrose is usually D 25% and the electrolytes vary with the product selected. Most hospital pharmacies can custom mix a TPN solution for specific patient needs. Remember to provide enough calories to utilize the protein provided. The following table gives the composition of a generally used INF solution produced by the Travenol company. An INF solution is hypertonic and damaging to veins; therefore, it needs to be given via a deep line. If a deep line is contraindicated, you can give a peripheral solution of 2.75% SAA and D12.5 maximum with little damage to veins.

Typical INF Solution for Adults*

Amount Provided†			
Kilocalories		Na	50
(nonprotein)	850	Cl	50
Protein	27.5	K	50
Fat	0	Ca	6
CHO‡	250	PO_4	30
Gluconate	6	Mg	6
		SO_4	1

*2.75% SAA, D25W
†Protein, fat, and CHO given in gm/liter. Gluconate and other electrolytes in mEq/liter.
‡CHO = complex carbohydrates

Nephramine is a special INF solution designed for patients with renal failure. It contains essential amino acids (EAA) with NO electrolytes. This solution is designed to provide a minimum protein load; theoretically, endogenous BUN is utilized as an adjunct protein source. Controversy presently exists as to how effectively Nephramine lowers the BUN of patients with renal failure. Some clinicians suggest the use of regular TPN solutions as long as the patient is on dialysis. Regular solutions also contain arginine, an amino acid which allows the metabolism and prevention of elevated NH_3 levels seen with patients receiving Nephramine.

Additives

Vitamins and Minerals

It is necessary to supplement the TPN patient with vitamins and minerals. To do this, 1 ml of multivitamin injection (MVI) can be added per liter to the TPN solution. Typical values for 1 ml of MVI:

- Folate: 0.5 mg
- Vitamin B_1 (Thiamine): 10 mg
- Vitamin B_2 (Riboflavin): 2 mg
- Niacinamide: 20 mg
- Vitamin C: 100 mg
- Vitamin A: 2000 units
- Vitamin D: 200 units
- Vitamin E: 1 unit
- Dexapanthenol: 5 mg
- Vitamin B_6 (Pyridoxine): 3 mg

In addition, other vitamins not compatible with TPN solution must be given routinely. These include vitamins K and B_{12}.

- Vitamin K (phytonadione): 10 mg given IM weekly
- Vitamin B_{12} (cyanocobalamin): 100 μg given IM weekly OR 1000 μg given IM monthly

Trace Elements

Trace elements normally supplied in the diet must be added to the TPN regimen. Until recently there was no product commercially available, and each hospital pharmacy developed its own formulation. Abbott Laboratories has marketed a trace element solution; each 5 ml of this solution contains the following:

- Zinc: 4 mg
- Copper: 1 mg

- Chromium: 10 mg
- Manganese: 0.8 mg

At the present time there are no recommended daily allowances for trace elements. However, trace element deficiencies have been identified in patients who received TPN solutions in which these elements were absent. To prevent these deficiencies, it is recommended that you supply 5 ml of the Abbott formulation (or equivalent) in the TPN solution per day.

Supplements

The following supplements are added as needed:

- Iron (iron dextran):   Given IV or IM
- Insulin (regular):   Either sliding scale (see the following table) or added to the bottle (10–30 units/bottle is usual)

Sliding Scale for Insulin Orders

Urine Glucose	Regular Insulin Dose (units given SQ*)
0–1 +	0
2 +	5
3 +	10
4 +	15
Any Acetone: Call house officer	

*SQ = subcutaneously

Fat Emulsion

There are presently two indications for the use of a fat emulsion in TPN therapy.

- To correct or prevent essential fatty acid deficiency (EFAD):   Includes dry skin and hair loss
- To provide an additional or alternative source of calories

The emulsions commercially available are listed in the following table.

Fat Emulsions Commercially Available

Emulsion	Source	Calories/ml
Intralipid: 10%	Soybean	1.1
Liposyn: 10%	Safflower	1.1
Intralipid: 20%	Soybean	2.0
Liposyn: 20%	Safflower	2.0

Since the particle size of these emulsions closely approximates that of naturally occurring chylomicrons, parenteral infusion is possible. In addition, the emulsions are cleared from the bloodstream in a similar manner and rate as chylomicrons. The clearance rate is 2.0–4.0 gm/kg/day; this can increase if the patient is in stress.

Most clinicians agree that the provision of 500 ml of a 10% fat emulsion every other day (qod) to twice weekly can correct or prevent EFAD. The use of fat emulsions as an additional or alternative caloric source is a recent proposal. However, the optimal amount of calories provided by the emulsion has not been established. Between 30% and 60% of the calories supplied by glucose may be replaced with the lipid emulsion (not to exceed 2.0–2.5 gm fat/kg/day). Remember that approximately 300–400 calories/day must be provided as glucose to enable the body to utilize the fat emulsion for energy via the Krebs cycle. The major advantage of using a fat emulsion in this manner is its concentrated caloric source as compared to glucose. The 20% emulsions are a very concentrated caloric source when fluid restriction is a main adjunct to the overall care of the patient.

Fat emulsions should be infused at an initial rate of 1 ml/min for the first 15 minutes. This first 15 ml serves as a test dose for acute hypersensitivity reactions:

- Dypsnea
- Chills
- Sudden tightness of chest
- Palpitations
- Wheezing

The remainder of the first bottle and subsequent infusions can be administered at a rate of 50–100 ml/hr.

OTHER COMPLICATIONS: (Primarily associated with the rate of infusion)
- Nausea
- Headache
- Fever
- Chills
- Wheezing
- Tachypnea
- Palpitations

Fat emulsions can be administered via a peripheral vein although loss of the IV site usually occurs in two to three days. For this reason, it is recommended that the emulsions be infused into the central line under strict aseptic technique via a sterile "Y" connector.

CONTRAINDICATIONS
- Pathological hyperlipidemia
- Lipoid nephrosis
- Severe hepatic failure
- Acute pancreatitis with hyperlipidemia
- Allergies to eggs or egg products

STARTING A PATIENT ON INF

Placement of a deep line must be done aseptically. Infection is one of the most common complications of TPN and can be avoided with careful insertion of the deep line and careful dressing changes every 24 hours.

Procedure

1. Check a set of baseline laboratory tests:

- CBC with differential
- Platelets
- PT and PTT
- SMA-6 (Na, K, Cl, HCO_3, glucose, BUN)

- SMA-12 (Total protein, albumin, Ca, PO_4, cholesterol, creatinine, bilirubin, alkaline phosphatase, CPK, LDH, SGOT, uric acid)
- Osmolality
- Ammonia (arterial)
- Magnesium
- Iron, iron binding capacity
- Transferrin
- Urinalysis
- Arterial blood gas
- 24 hour urine for creatinine, UUN
- Baseline weight

2. Order the type of TPN desired along with the additives and supplements. A 22 micron filter is usually placed in the IV tubing. Fat must be infused BELOW the filter.

3. Order the labs for the coming week that need to be followed:

- Urinary S&A (sugar and acetone), every 6 hours (q6h)
- SMA-6 daily and then qod when stable
- SMA-12 or equivalent, serum osmolality, magnesium, ammonia, and blood gases twice weekly
- CBC with differential, PT, and PTT twice weekly
- 24 hour urines for urea nitrogen and creatinine twice weekly initially, then once a week when stable
- Body weight at least qod

4. Begin the INF at 50 ml/hr × 6 hours, then check SMA-6 and urine S&A (sugar and acetone). If the patient is tolerating this rate fairly well, increase to 75 ml/hr for 6 to 12 hours, recheck the labs, and then advance to 100 ml/hr and then to 125 ml/hr. Check the labs each time. The maximum should be <175 ml/hr. Remember, this is a large sugar load, and many patients will be unable to tolerate it. Urine S&A should be kept <2+ and serum glucose <180–200 mg/100 ml. If the values rise above these levels, slow down the rate if you are just starting INF or consider adding insulin either according to a sliding scale

or directly to the bottle (10–30 units/bottle is usual). Often the insulin can be discontinued after one to seven days.

5. IV fat emulsion can be run into a peripheral vein or deep line via a sterile "Y" at 50–100 ml/hr.

6. TPN SHOULD NEVER BE STOPPED ACUTELY. Severe hypoglycemia may result. The patient should be weaned off the TPN in much the same way the therapy was begun. If needed acutely, D 10% can be used in place of TPN.

7. A customary order for routine adult TPN might read as follows:

   - Regular adult TPN solution (2.75% SAA, D 25%); begin infusion at 50 ml/hr per deep line
   - Add 1 ml MVI to each bottle
   - Add 10 units of regular insulin to each bottle
   - 5 ml trace elements, in TPN qd
   - Vitamin K 10 mg/week IM, vitamin B_{12} 1 mg/month IM
   - Intralipid 10%, 500 ml, IV over five hours qd
   - Urine S&A every six hours
   - SMA-6 in six hours
   - Weekly labs (as described before)
   - Sterile deep line dressing changes qd
   - 22 micron IV filter for INF solution

COMMON COMPLICATIONS

- Hyperosmolar nonketotic coma: Usually found in patients with an impaired insulin response. Caused by excessive glucose levels, usually corrected by insulin and rehydration.
- Infection with secondary sepsis: The care of the deep line site and tubing must be meticulous. If a patient suddenly does not tolerate TPN, i.e., becomes hyperglycemic, suspect sepsis. If the patient becomes septic, the deep line should be considered a possible source

and removed. The tip should be sent for routine C&S, but *Candida* is the most common isolate on the catheter. In addition, the TPN solution should be cultured as a potential source of infection.

- Hyperchloremic acidosis: Due to the large amount of amino acids being infused.
- EFAD (dry skin, hair loss):   From the administration of a fat-free parenteral diet.
- Hypophosphatemia: Secondary to the increased metabolic processes requiring phosphate.
- Trace element deficiency: Associated with an increased loss via fistulas or inadequate supplementation in the diet.
- Hyperglycemia: Due to the slow bodily compensation associated with an abrupt glucose load.
- Hypoglycemia: Secondary to the abrupt withdrawal of the increased glucose load associated with TPN solutions.
- Osmotic diuresis: Associated with the hypertonicity of the TPN solution.
- Elevated liver function tests: Caused by excessive glycogen formation and storage. Will usually see a transient rise in these tests initially followed by a decrease towards baseline values within two weeks.

13
Diets and Clinical Nutrition

Hospital Diets
Enteral Formulas
Nutritional Assessment

HOSPITAL DIETS

The most commonly ordered hospital diets and their indications are listed here. Part of every patient's orders should include diet instruction, if education is necessary. Most hospitals have excellent diet manuals as well as dieticians who are readily available for consultation.

Regular (General): Used for all adult patients with no dietary restrictions. The composition is based on recommended dietary allowances (RDAs).

Soft: Designed for patients unable to physically or psychologically tolerate a general diet. It may be used as a progression from full liquid to general diets.

Mechanical Soft: For patients without teeth or those having difficulty chewing or swallowing.

Clear Liquid: For the management of acute conditions (pre op or post op), useful in the transition from NPO to oral feedings, and a preparation for various lab tests. Of little or no nutritional benefit, it only relieves thirst and provides fluid and salts.

Full Liquid: Used in the transition from clear liquid to soft or general diet, especially in the post op patient or for those in whom GI function is moderately reduced.

Pediatric: Usually ordered as "diet for age."

Pureed (Blenderized): For the patient who is unable to chew or swallow solid foods.

Low Residue: Indicated for patients with colitis, ileitis, or diarrhea. Decreases fecal volume.

High Fiber: Useful for atonic constipation, diverticular disease, irritable bowel syndrome, and diabetes.

Reduction: Designed to achieve and maintain ideal body weight. Caloric level should be specified.

Diabetic: Used for patients with insulin-dependent diabetes (IDDM) or non-insulin-dependent diabetes (NIDDM). Increased complex carbohydrate and increased plant fiber should be required in addition to a specific caloric level (e.g., 1800 calorie, 55% CHO, increased complex CHO, high fiber).

Hyperlipidemia: Used for lipid abnormalities. Diet should be written as Type I, IIa, IIb, III, IV, or V.

Low Fat: Designed to limit fat to approximately 50 gm/day. Indicated for diseases of gall bladder, liver, or pancreas.

Protein Restricted: Useful in renal failure or hepatic disorders. May also require Na or K limitations (e.g., 60 gm protein diet).

Sodium Restricted: Used for the management of CHF, hypertension, or other forms of fluid retention. Must specify level of sodium desired (22, 44, 88 mEq). A general diet "without added salt" provides about 120 mEq sodium.

Potassium Restricted: Used in renal failure (e.g., 60 mEq potassium diet).

ENTERAL FORMULAS (TUBE FEEDINGS)

Enteral formulas are used as an adjunct to a patient's oral diet when there is inadequate intake or as tube feedings in patients who are unable to swallow. Tube-fed patients are often difficult to manage from the standpoint of fluids and electrolytes. Many develop an osmotic diarrhea that requires slowing down the rate of administration, the addition of water, or the addition of antidiarrheals such as calcium carbonate or diphenoxylate hydrochloride plus atropine (Lomotil). When starting a tube feeding, start slowly, use a dilute (one-half-strength) solution, and advance as tolerated.

Availability of enteral products varies with institutions; consult a diet manual before requesting them. The next two tables give the composition of enteral formulas and of nutrient modules.

Composition of Enteral Formulas*

Product	Kcal/ml	Pro (gm)	Fat (gm)	CHO (gm)	Na (mEq)	K (mEq)	mOsm/kg	Comments and/or Protein Source
MEAL REPLACEMENTS Requires normal proteolytic and lipolytic function. Contain lactose.								
Compleat B	1.00	4.00	4.00	12.0	5.20	3.40	390	Beef puree, nonfat dry milk
Formula 2	1.00	3.80	4.00	12.3	2.60	4.50	435–510	Nonfat dry milk, beef
PROTEIN ISOLATE Provides proximal absorption. Requires normal proteolytic and lipolytic function. Low residue.								
Ensure	1.06	3.70	3.70	14.5	3.10	3.30	450	Palatable oral supplement Ca-Na caseinates, soy protein isolate
Ensure Plus	1.50	5.50	5.30	19.7	4.60	4.90	600	Palatable oral supplement Ca-Na caseinate, soy protein isolates
Isocal	1.06	3.20	4.20	12.5	2.20	3.20	300	Ca-Na caseinates Soy protein isolate
Osmolite	1.06	3.70	3.80	14.4	2.30	2.60	300	Ca-Na caseinates Soy protein isolates
Precision Isotonic	0.96	2.90	3.00	14.4	3.50	2.50	300	Egg albumin, Na caseinates
Precision LR	1.08	2.40	0.08	24.0	3.00	2.20	500–545	Egg albumin
Precision HN	1.02	4.20	0.05	21.1	4.30	2.30	557	Egg albumin
Sustacal	1.00	6.10	2.30	13.8	4.00	5.30	625–697	Palatable oral supplement Ca-Na caseinates Soy protein isolate

Composition of Enteral Formulas* (Continued)

Product	Kcal/ ml	per 100 Kcal					mOsm/ kg	Comments and/or Protein Source
		Pro (gm)	Fat (gm)	CHO (gm)	Na (mEq)	K (mEq)		
DEFINED FORMULAS		Provides rapid, proximal absorption. Indicated for pancreatic-biliary dysfunction, selection malabsorption, fistulas, and short bowel syndrome (SBS). Low residue. Nutrients predigested.						
Vipep	1.00	2.50	2.40	17.0	3.26	2.18	520	Uses free amino acid (AA) peptide carrier system
Vital	1.00	4.20	1.00	18.5	1.70	3.00	450	Protein components: hydrolyzed whey, meat, and soy; free AA
Vivonex HN	1.00	4.17	1.08	21.0	2.30	3.00	844	Protein source: L-amino acids
Vivonex	1.00	2.04	0.15	22.6	2.00	3.00	500	Protein source: L-amino acids
SPECIAL METABOLIC		Requires vitamin-mineral supplement if used as principal source of nutrition.						
Amin-Aid	2.00	1.00	2.40	18.7	<1	<1	850	Contains essential AA; indicated for renal disease
Hepatic Aid	1.60	2.60	2.20	17.5	<1	<1	900	Highly branched chain amino acids (BCAA); indicated for liver disease

*Partial listing only.

Nutrient Modules* for Enteral Formulas

| Product | Amount to give 100 kcal | Composition per 100 kcal | | | | |
		Pro (gm)	Fat (gm)	CHO (gm)	Na (mEq)	K (mEq)
PROTEIN						
Casec (Calcium caseinate)	27.60 gm (dry wt)	23.5	0.54	0	1.8	tr
Promix (Acid whey)	29.50 gm (dry wt)	22.5	0	2.5	1.9	12.1
FAT						
MCT Oil (Fractionated coconut oil)	13.04 ml (liquid)	0	12.2	0	0	0
Microlipid (Safflower oil)	22.20 ml (liquid)	0	11.1	0	0	0
CARBOHYDRATE						
Controlyte (Maltodextrins)	19.80 gm (dry wt)	tr	4.75	14.3	0.13	0.02
Hycal (Dextrose)	14.16 ml (liquid)	tr	tr	25.0	0.15	tr
Polycose (Glucose polymers)	26.70 gm (dry wt)	0	0	25.0	1.30	0.27

*These are specific nutrients, not complete feedings. A complete enteral feeding will require addition of vitamins, mineral salts, and trace elements to core molecules (proteins, fat, and carbohydrates).

NUTRITIONAL ASSESSMENT

Nutritional assessment provides the medical staff with a tool to monitor the nutritional care of the hospitalized patient. Studies have shown that well-nourished patients have significantly shorter postoperative hospital stays and lower mortality rates than undernourished patients.

There exists no single procedure that can be used to assess a patient's nutritional status. The following table, "Guidelines for Nutritional Assessment," indicates which tests are needed,

Guidelines for Nutritional Assessment

Data	Relevance	Suggested Frequency of Measurement	Diagnosis of Nutritional Deficiencies		
			DEFICITS		
			SEVERE	MODERATE	MINIMAL
NUTRITION HISTORY	Indicates patient weight changes, food habits	Initially	—	—	—
SOMATIC PROTEIN					
Height/Weight Ratio (See Appendix)	Indicates skeletal muscle stores	Ht initially; wt daily	>30%	>15%–30%	>5%–15%
Midarm Muscle Circumference* (See Appendix)		Initially and weekly thereafter	>30%	>15%–30%	>5%–15%
TRICEPS SKINFOLD* (See Appendix)	Indicates fat stores	Initially and weekly thereafter	>30%	>15%–30%	>5%–15%
VISCERAL PROTEINS	Indicates visceral protein synthesis				
Serum Albumin		Initially and weekly thereafter	<2.3 gm/dl	2.3–<3.0	3.0–<3.5
Serum Transferrin or TIBC		Initially and every 2 weeks thereafter	<120 mg/dl	120–<175	175–<200

Guidelines for Nutritional Assessment (Continued)

Data	Relevance	Suggested Frequency of Measurement	Diagnosis of Nutritional Deficiencies DEFICITS		
			SEVERE	MODERATE	MINIMAL
Total Lymphocytes		Initially and weekly thereafter	<900	900–<1400	1400–<1800
SKIN TESTS (Candida, mumps, SKSD, PPD)	Indicates immune competence	Initially and every 3 weeks thereafter	0–<5 mm	5–<10 mm	10–15 mm
NITROGEN BALANCE (See Chapter 12)	Reflects adequacy of nutritional support	Weekly			

*Sequential anthropometric measurements should be performed by the same person; the patient's same arm should be used.

their relevance, how they are obtained, and suggested frequency of measurement. When the nutritional assessment is ordered, the physician should order tests as indicated by the guidelines. The dietitian evaluates the results and makes recommendations for nutritional care when laboratory results become available. Additional discussion on nutritional principles can be found in Chapter 12. Normal weights, triceps skin fold, midarm muscle circumference, and other useful nutritional tables can be found in the Appendix.

Formulas Used in Nutritional Assessment

Midarm Muscle Circumference (cm) = Midarm circumference (cm) − [0.314 × triceps skinfold (mm)]

Total Lymphocyte Count = White blood cells × percent lymphocytes

Nitrogen Balance: (See Chapter 12.)

$$\text{\% Weight Change} = \frac{\text{Usual Weight} - \text{Actual Weight}}{\text{Ideal Weight}} \times 100$$

$$\text{\% of Ideal Weight} = \frac{\text{Actual Weight}}{\text{Ideal Weight}} \times 100$$

Transferrin: Derived from total iron binding capacity (TIBC). Serum Transferrin = (0.8 × TIBC) − 43 (Can also be directly measured by the lab)

14
Blood Bank

BLOOD BANKING PROCEDURES AND PRODUCTS

Procedures

Type and Hold (T&H): The blood bank will type your patient's blood and screen it for irregular antibodies, but usually will not match the patient to specific units until you tell them to do so.

Type and Cross (T&C): The bank will type and screen the patient's blood and match the patient with specific donor units.

Stat: The bank will set up blood immediately and usually hold it for 12 hours.

Routine: The blood bank will set up blood at a date and time you specify and usually hold it for 36 hours.

Products

The following table describes blood bank products and gives common indications for their use.

Blood Bank Products

Product	Description	Common Indications
Whole Blood	No elements removed 1 unit = 500 ml	Neonatal total exchange Acute, massive bleeding Open heart surgery Not for routine use
Packed Red Cells (PRBC)	Most plasma removed 1 unit = 250 ml 1 unit should raise HCT 3% in an adult	Replacement in chronic and acute blood loss especially after GI bleeding or surgery
Platelets	1 "pack" should raise count by 6,000 "6-pack" means a pack of platelets from 6 units of blood	Platelets <20,000 in nonbleeding, <60,000 in pre op patient, <50,000 in bleeding patient Nondestructive thrombocytopenia (Not in idiopathic thrombocytopenic purpura [ITP] or thrombotic thrombocytopenic purpura [TTP])
Leukocyte Poor Red Cells	Most WBC removed to make it less antigenic	Potential renal transplant patients Previous febrile transfusion reactions Patients requiring multiple transfusions (leukemia, etc.)
Washed RBCs	Like leukocyte poor red cells, but WBC almost completely removed	As for leukocyte poor red cells, but very expensive

Blood Bank Products (Continued)

Product	Description	Common Indications
Cryoprecipitated Antihemophilic Factor (Cryo)	Contains Factor VIII, Factor XIII, von Willebrand's factor, and fibrinogen	Hemophilia A (Factor VIII deficiency), von Willebrand's disease, and fibrinogen deficiency
Fresh Frozen Plasma (FFP)	Contains Factors II, VII, IX, X, XI, XII, XIII and heat labile V and VIII About 1 hr to thaw	Undiagnosed bleeding disease with active bleeding When transfusing >10 units of blood Patient with liver disease Reversal of Coumadin
Single Donor Plasma	Like FFP, but lacks Factors V and VIII About 1 hr to thaw	Plasma replacement (cheaper than FFP) Stable clotting factor replacement
Rho Gam	Antibody against Rh factor	Rh − mother with Rh + baby, within 72 hr of delivery

All of the aforementioned items usually require a "clot tube" to be sent for typing. The following products are usually dispensed by most hospital pharmacies and are ordered just like a medication.

Product	Description	Common Indications
Factor VIII (Purified Antihemophilic Factor)	From pooled plasma, pure Factor VIII Increased hepatitis risk	Routine for hemophilia A (Factor VIII deficiency)
Factor IX Concentrate (Prothrombin Complex)	Increased hepatitis risk Factors II, VII, IX, and X Equivalent to 2 units of plasma	Active bleeding in Christmas disease (Factor IX deficiency) Emergency Coumadin reversal

Blood Bank Products (Continued)

Product	Description	Common Indications
Immune Serum Globulin	Precipitate from plasma "Gamma globulin"	Immune globulin deficiency Disease prophylaxis (hepatitis A, measles, etc.)
5% Albumin or 5% Plasma Protein Fraction	Precipitate from plasma (see Chapter 22)	Plasma volume expanders in acute blood loss
25% Albumin	Precipitate from plasma Draws extravascular fluid into circulation	Hypoalbuminemia, volume expander, burns

TRANSFUSION PROCEDURE

1. Draw a clot tube (red top), and sign the lab slips to verify it is the sample from the correct patient.

2. When the blood products become available, make sure that the patient has a good venous access for the transfusion (18 gauge or larger is preferred).

3. Remember to verify the information with another person, such as a nurse, on the request slip, blood bag, and with the patient's identification (ID) bracelet. (Many hospitals have defined protocols for this procedure.)

4. Blood products MUST be transfused with isosmotic solutions only (such as normal saline or Ringer's solution). Using hypotonic products such as D5W may result in hemolysis of the blood in the tubing.

5. When transfusing large volumes of blood (>6 to 8 units), it is necessary to also transfuse platelets and FFP periodically. Also, a calcium replacement is needed since the preservative used in the blood is a calcium binder and hypocalcemia can result after large amounts of blood are transfused.

TRANSFUSION REACTIONS

Signs and Symptons

- Sudden fever (most common)
- Headache
- Backache
- Chills
- Diaphoresis
- Tachycardia
- Hypotension
- Shock
- Hypersensitivity reaction: Hives, wheezing, pruritis
- Exacerbation of congestive heart failure

Detection

1. Spin a hematocrit to look for a pink plasma layer (indicates hemolysis).

2. Order serum for free hemoglobin and serum haptoglobin (haptoglobin decreased with a reaction) and urine for hemosiderin.

Treatment

1. Stop the blood product immediately.

2. Keep the IV line open and monitor the patient's vital signs carefully.

3. Save the blood bag and have the lab verify the type and crossmatch.

4. Try to prevent acute renal failure. Monitor the urine output closely and maintain a brisk diuresis with plain D5W and mannitol as needed. Consider alkalinization of the urine with bicarbonate. Beware of disseminated intravascular coagulation (DIC).

5. Support pressure as needed (fluids, vasopressors such as dopamine).

HEPATITIS RISKS

Incidence of posttransfusion hepatitis is 0.3–0.9 cases/1000 units transfused. Anicteric hepatitis is much more common than hepatitis with jaundice. The greatest risk is with pooled factor products such as concentrates of Factors II, VII, and VIII (up to 30% after one dosage). Use of albumin and globulins involves no risk of hepatitis.

BLOOD GROUPS

The following table gives information on the four major blood groups.

Major Blood Groups

Type	% Population	Can Receive Blood From
AB	7	AB, A, B, O
A	40	A, O
B	10	B, O
O	43	O

TRANSFUSION FORMULA

To determine the volume of whole blood or packed red cells needed to raise a hematocrit to a known amount, use the following formula:

$$\text{Volume of Cells} = \frac{\text{Total blood volume of patient} \times (\text{Desired HCT} - \text{Actual HCT})}{\text{Hematocrit of transfusion product}}$$

- Total blood volume = 70 ml/kg in adults, 80 ml/kg in children
- Hematocrit, packed cells = approximately 70
- Hematocrit, whole blood = approximately 40

Example: What volume of packed cells is needed to raise the hematocrit of a 50 kg adult from 20 to 30?

$$\text{Volume PRBC} = \frac{50 \text{ kg } (70 \text{ ml/kg}) \times (30 - 20)}{70} = 500 \text{ ml}$$

15
Radiology, Nuclear Scans, and Ultrasound

X-Ray Preparations
Common X-Ray Studies
How to Read a Chest
   X-Ray Film

Nuclear Scans
Ultrasound

X-RAY PREPARATIONS

In general, plain films before dye, dye before barium.

Examinations That Require No Preparation

- Routine chest x-rays: Posteroanterior (PA) and lateral

- Kidney, ureter, bladder (KUB): Flat and upright abdominal

- Chest or cardiac fluoroscopy or cinefluorography

- Esophagram or cine-esophagram: Study of swallowing

- T-tube cholangiogram

- Laminograms

Examinations That Require Special Preparations

Hospital x-ray departments may have their own special preps.

Oral Cholecystogram (OCG, Gallbladder Series)

PREP
- Begins two days before study
- 6 iopanoic acid (Telepaque) tabs one hour after evening meal two nights before
- 6 Telepaque tabs one hour after evening meal night before
- Then NPO until after study
- If a patient is already in the hospital, it may be wise to give only 1 dose and repeat the dose if the gallbladder is not visualized.

Intravenous Cholangiogram (IVC)

PREP
- Regular diet day before exam
- 3 5-mg Ducolax tablets at bedtime
- Then NPO past midnight

Barium Enema (BE), Air-Contrast Barium Enema

PREP
- Minimal residue diet for two days
- Then clear liquid for one day
- Day before exam, force fluids: 1 glass of water every hour, then 2 oz castor oil at 6 P.M. (may take this with clear juice)
- 2000 ml tap water enema in A.M. one hour before exam (If patient is still full of stool, may need a more vigorous prep with more enemas or magnesium citrate.)

Upper GI Series (UGI): Includes stomach, esophagus, and duodenum

PREP • STRICT NPO past midnight (no chewing gum, brushing teeth, etc.)

Small Bowel Series (Small Bowel Follow-Through, SBFT)

PREP • Done with a UGI, same prep as for UGI

Intravenous Pyelogram (IVP): Both standard and hypertensive

PREP • 2 oz castor oil one-half hour after lunch the day before
• Force fluids to hydrate well, liquid evening meal
• NPO past midnight
• Beware of history of allergy to dye, multiple myeloma, diabetes, renal failure, and dehydration.

IVP and BE Same Day

PREP • Same as for BE

OCG and UGI Same Day

PREP • Same as for OCG

Retrograde Pyelogram

PREP • Usually specified by the urologist

Voiding Cystourethrogram (VCUG, Cystogram)

PREP • Indwelling Foley catheter

Ultrasonography: Remember that gas, stool, barium, and bones interfere with a good ultrasound study. For this reason, some ultrasonographers also include an anti-gas prep like simethicone (Mylicon).

PREP FOR UPPER ABDOMINAL STUDY
- NPO past midnight
- Clean GI tract (no barium)

PREP FOR PELVIC STUDY: Including pregnant females
- Bladder as full as possible
- No voiding two hours before test

COMMON X-RAY STUDIES

Plain

PA and Lateral Chest: The standard x-ray studies.

Portable Chest and Anteroposterior (AP) Films: Cannot be used to accurately evaluate heart size.

Lordotic Chest: Allows better visualization of apices and some lesions of the right upper lobe (RUL) and left upper lobe (LUL).

Expiratory Chest: Used to help visualize a small pneumothorax.

Lateral Decubitus Chest: Allows small amounts of pleural effusion or suspected subpulmonic effusion to layer out and permits diagnosis of as little as 100 to 200 ml of pleural fluid.

KUB, Supine and Erect: Also known as "flat and upright abdominal." Useful when the patient complains of abdominal pain, distention, or change of bowel habits and for an initial evaluation of the GU tract (80% of stones will be apparent).
   To read a flat plate, look for calcifications, foreign bodies, the gas pattern, psoas shadows, renal and liver shadows, flank stripes, the vertebras, and pelvic bones. On the upright, look for air-fluid levels of an ileus or obstruction and for free air under the diaphragm which suggests a perforated viscus or recent surgery.

Acute Abdominal Series (AAS):   Includes a flat and upright abdominal and a chest x-ray. Good for initial evaluation of an acute abdomen.

Abdominal Decubitus: Used in debilitated patients instead of an upright abdominal. The left side should be down. Used to find free air.

Cross Table Lateral Abdominal: Used in debilitated patients to look for free air and for an aortic aneurysm.

Contrast

Barium Swallow (Esophagram):   Used to evaluate the swallowing mechanism and to investigate esophageal lesions or abnormal peristalsis.

UGI: Includes the esophagram plus the stomach and duodenum. Useful for ulcers, masses, hiatal hernias and in the evaluation of heme-positive stools and upper abdominal pain.

SBFT: Done after a UGI series. A delayed film that shows the jejunum and ileum. Used in the work-up for diarrhea, for cramps, malabsorption, and upper GI bleeding.

BE: Used to exam the colon and rectum. Indications are diarrhea, crampy abdominal pain, blood in the stool, and unexplained weight loss.

Air-Contrast BE: Done with the "double contrast" technique (air and barium) to better delineate the mucosa. More likely to show polyps.

IVP or Excretory Urogram: Dye study of the kidneys and ureters. Limited usefulness for bladder abnormalities. Indications are flank pain, kidney stones, hematuria, work-up for hypertension, recurrent UTIs, and work-up for malignancy. A "hypertensive IVP" means that the films are shot in very rapid sequence to detect subtle differences in right (R) and left (L) kidney function; however, these films are often uninformative.

Retrograde Pyelogram: Contrast material is injected into the ureters via a cystoscope, usually by a urologist. Indications are a kidney or ureter that cannot be visualized on an IVP, renal pelvic mass, and ureteral obstruction.

Retrograde Urethrogram (RUG): Used to demonstrate traumatic disruption, urethral stenosis, strictures, and posterior urethral valves.

VCUG: Used for diagnosis of ureteral reflux and urethral valves.

Cystourethrogram: Used to evaluate bladder (tumor, diverticulum, laceration) and urethral abnormalities.

Sinogram (Fistulogram): Injection of contrast media into any wound or body opening to determine the connection of the wound or opening with other structures.

OCG: Used to visualize the gall bladder. Patient is given oral contrast pills. Serum bilirubin should be <2 mg/100 ml.

IVC: Used to visualize the gallbladder and common bile duct when an OCG cannot be done. Bilirubin for an IVC must be <3 mg/100 ml.

T-Tube Cholangiogram: Some patients who have gallbladder and common bile duct surgery need to have a T-tube placed in the common bile duct for drainage until the swelling resolves. The cholangiogram is used to evaluate the degree of swelling and to look for residual stones.

Percutaneous Transhepatic Cholangiogram (PTHC): Used to visualize the biliary tree in a patient who is unable to concentrate the contrast media (bilirubin >3 mg/100 ml). A percutaneous needle is inserted into a dilated biliary duct. Usually done under ultrasound.

HOW TO READ A CHEST X-RAY FILM

PA Films

Remember, the film is on the patient's chest and the x-rays are passing from back (posterior) to front (anterior). The structures described in the following material are shown in Fig. 15-1, A.

Soft Tissues: Check for symmetry, swelling, loss of tissue planes, and subcutaneous air.

Skeletal Structures: Examine the clavicles, scapulas, vertebras, sternum, and ribs. Look for symmetry. In a good x-ray, the clavicles will be symmetrical. Are there osteolytic or osteoblastic lesions, fractures, or arthritic changes? Is rib notching present?

Diaphragm: Sides should be equal and slightly rounded, although the left may be slightly lower. Costophrenic angles should be clear and sharp. Blunting suggests scarring or fluid. It takes about 300 to 500 ml of pleural fluid to cause blunting. Check below the diaphragm for the gas pattern and free air. A unilateral high diaphragm suggests paralysis (either from nerve damage, trauma, or an abscess) or loss of volume on that side because of atelectasis or pneumothorax. A flat diaphragm suggests COPD.

Mediastinum and Heart: The aortic knob should be visible and distinct. The trachea should be in a straight line with a sharp carina. Tracheal deviation suggests a mass (tumor), unilateral loss of lung volume (collapse), or a tension pneumothorax. The heart should be less then one-half the width of the chest wall on a PA film (if greater than one-half, think of CHF or pericardial fluid).

Hilum: The left hilum should be up to 2 to 3 cm higher than the right. Vessels are seen here. Look for any masses, nodes, or calcifications.

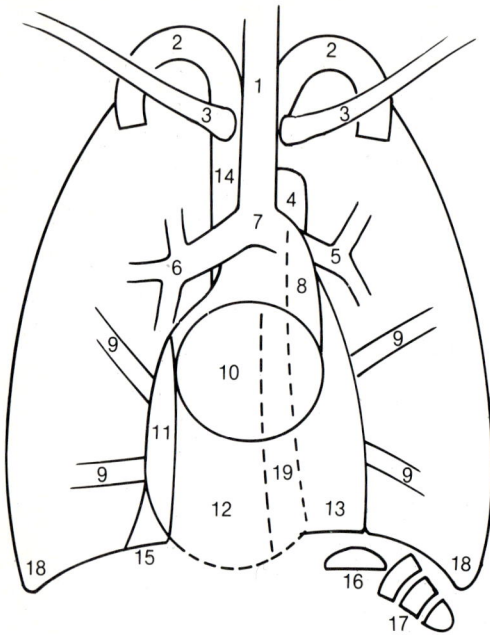

PA
CHEST X-RAY

1) Trachea
2) First rib
3) Clavicle
4) Aortic knob
5) Left pulmonary artery
6) Right pulmonary artery
7) Carina
8) Pulmonary trunk
9) Pulmonary veins
10) Left atrium
11) Right atrium
12) Right ventricle
13) Left ventricle
14) Superior vena cava
15) Inferior vena cava
16) Gastric air bubble
17) Splenic flexure air
18) Costophrenic angles
19) Descending aorta

Fig. 15-1, A Chest x-ray films. Posteroanterior (PA).

Lung Fields: Note the presence of any shadows like deep lines, NG tubes, Swan-Ganz catheters, etc. The fields should be "clear" with normal "lung markings" all the way to the periphery. The vessels should taper to become almost invisible at the periphery.

Vessels in the lower lung should be larger than those in the upper lung. A reversal of this difference (called cephalization) suggests heart failure. Check the margins carefully; look for pleural thickening, masses, or pneumothorax.

To locate a lesion, don't forget to check a lateral film and remember the "silhouette sign." Obliteration of all or part of a heart border means the lesion is anterior in the chest and lies in the right middle lobe (RML), lingula, or anterior segment of the upper lobe. A radiopacity that overlaps the heart but does not obliterate the heart border is posterior and lies in the lower lobes.

Examine carefully for the following:

COIN LESIONS: Causes are granulomas (50%), usually calcified, (histoplasmosis 25%, TB 20%, coccidiomycosis 20%; varies with locale); primary carcinoma (25%); hamartoma (<10%); metastatic disease (<5%).

CAVITARY LESIONS: Causes are abscess, cancer, TB, coccidiomycosis.

INFILTRATES

Interstitial Pattern: Nodular or reticular or both, "honeycombing." Causes are granulomatous infections, miliary TB, coccidiomycosis, pneumoconiosis, sarcoidosis, CHF.

Alveolar Pattern: Diffuse, quick progression and regression. Can see either butterfly pattern or air bronchograms. Causes are pulmonary embolus, pneumonia, bleeding, CHF.

Lateral Films

Examine the structures shown in Fig. 15-1, B. Use this diagram to check for the three-dimensional location of

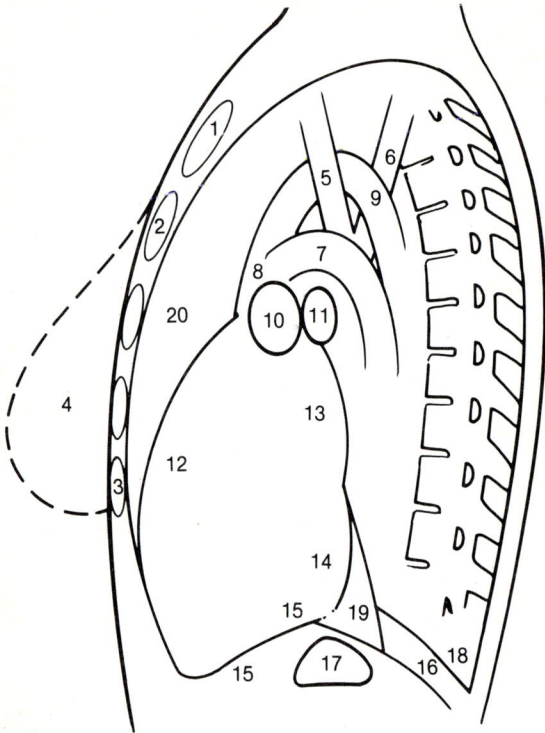

LATERAL
CHEST X-RAY

1) Manubrium
2) Body of sternum
3) Xiphoid process
4) Breast shadow
5) Trachea
6) Scapula
7) Left pulmonary artery
8) Ascending aorta
9) Aortic arch
10) Right pulmonary artery
11) Left mainstem bronchus
12) Right ventricle
13) Left atrium
14) Left ventricle
15) Right diaphragm
16) Left diaphragm
17) Gastric air bubble
18) Costophrenic angles
19) Inferior vena cava
20) Retrosternal clear space

Fig. 15-1, B Chest x-ray films. Lateral.

lesions. Pay attention to the retrosternal clear space, costo-phrenic angles, and the path of the aorta.

NUCLEAR SCANS

The following is a listing of some of the more commonly used nuclear scans and their purposes.

Bone Scan: Metastatic work-ups, evaluation of delayed union of fractures, osteomyelitis, avascular necrosis of the femoral head, evaluation of hip prosthesis, to distinguish pathological fractures from traumatic fractures

Brain Scan: Metastatic work-ups, determination of blood flow (in brain death or atherosclerotic disease), evaluation of space-occupying lesions (tumor, hematoma, abscess, arterio-venous [A-V] malformation)

Cardiac Scans: Diagnosis of myocardial infarction, stress testing, ejection fractions, measurements of cardiac output, diagnosis of ventricular aneurysms

Gallium Scans: Location of abscesses (5 to 10 days old), lymphoma, lung cancer, other neoplastic tissues

Hepatobiliary Scans (HIDA-Scan, BIDA-Scan): Differential diagnosis of biliary obstruction (when bilirubin >1.5 mg/100 ml), acute cholecystitis, diagnosis of biliary atresia; NOT good for stones unless cystic duct completely occluded and acute cholecystitis present

Liver-Lung Scan: Location of a subphrenic abscess

Liver-Spleen Scan: Estimation of organ size, parenchymal diseases (hepatitis, etc.), abscess, cysts, primary and secondary tumors

Lung Scan (Ventilation-Perfusion [V/Q] Scan): Evaluation for pulmonary emboli, resectability of tumors preoperatively, diagnosis of COPD

Renal Scans

PERFUSION (TECHNECIUM): Evaluation of renal transplants, renal arteries and veins; diagnosis of infarction and ischemia

FUNCTION (HIPPURAN): Detection of differences in right and left renal function, masses, hypertension, renal failure

Thyroid Scan: Evaluation of nodules (25% of cold nodules are cancerous), location of ectopic thyroid tissues (especially after thyroidectomy for cancer), identification of superior mediastinal masses

ULTRASOUND

The following are some commonly used ultrasound studies and their diagnostic abilities. Gas and barium interfere with these studies.

Abdominal: Gallbladder (stones, thickening), biliary tree (obstruction), pancreas (pseudocyst, tumor, pancreatitis), aorta (aneurysm), kidneys (obstruction, tumor, cyst), abscesses, ascites

Pelvis

PREGNANCY: Dating, twinning, biparietal diameters, other determinations of fetal well-being, localization of the placenta (previa, abruptio, etc.)

GYNECOLOGY: Ovarian and uterine masses (tumors, cysts, fibroids, etc.), ectopic pregnancy, abscesses

Echocardiograms

M-MODE: Valve motility, chamber size, pericardial effusions, septal size

TWO-DIMENSIONAL: Valvular vegetations, septal defects

16
Introduction to the Operating Room

Sterile Technique　　　　**Gowning and Gloving**
Entering the OR　　　　　**Draping the Patient**
The Surgical Hand Scrub　**Finding Your Place**
Preparing the Patient

The operating room (OR) can be the best or worst experience of the third year of medical school. Familiarity with it is one of the major determinants of how good a surgery or obstetrics rotation might be. "Cranky nurses, egotistical surgeons, and those stupid medical students" are unnecessary comments and can be avoided if one understands the "routine" of the OR. Just be alert, attentive, and above all, patient. Within a brief time, the routine should become second nature.

STERILE TECHNIQUE

Certain members of the OR team (surgeon, assistants, students, and scrub technician — the one who is responsible for passing the instruments) maintain a sterile field. The circulating nurse acts as a go-between, between the sterile and non-sterile areas.

What things are sterile? The front of the gown to the waist, the gloved hands and arms to the shoulder, the draped part of the patient down to table level, the covered part of the "Mayo stand" and the "back table" where additional instruments are kept. The sides of the back table are not considered sterile, and anything that falls below the level of the patient table is considered contaminated.

From the moment you enter the OR, everything is geared towards maintaining a sterile field. Try to remember not to change any patient dressings on the mornings prior to going to the OR. This procedure helps cut down on contamination.

ENTERING THE OR

The use of sterile technique begins in the locker room. Change into scrub clothing (remember to remove T-shirts and tuck the scrub shirt into the pants). Knee socks can be worn with scrub dresses if they have not been worn outside the OR. Scrub clothes can occasionally be worn on the wards, provided that they are covered by a clinic coat or some other form of gown.

Pass into the anteroom to get your cap, mask, and shoe covers. If required, put the black strap inside your shoe; it's for grounding purposes. The idea is to cover nose, mouth, and ALL hair. Full hoods are necessary for men with beards. If you wear glasses, it is often helpful to tape the mask to the bridge of your nose to prevent fogging during the case. Tape the glasses to your forehead if you think the glasses may be loose enough to fall onto the table during the case! Do not wear nail polish, and remove any loose jewelry, watches, and rings before scrubbing.

The mask does not need to be worn in the hall of the OR suite (but everything else does) at most hospitals. The mask must be worn in the OR itself, by scrub sinks, and in the sub-sterile rooms between ORs.

Find the room where the patient is located, and assist in transport, if necessary. Tell the resident or intern who you are, and try to get an idea of when to begin scrubbing (usually when the first surgeon starts to scrub).

THE SURGICAL HAND SCRUB

The purpose of a surgical hand scrub is to decrease the bacterial flora of the skin by mechanically cleansing the arms and hands before the operation. Key points to remember: (1) if contamination occurs during the scrub, it is necessary to start over and (2) in emergency situations there are exceptions to the time allowed for scrubbing (as in obstetrics [OB] when the baby is brought out from the delivery room and the student is STILL scrubbing!). Caps and masks should be properly positioned before the start of the scrub.

Betadine Hand Scrub

1. Perform a general prewash, with surgical soap and water, up to 2 inches above the elbows.

2. Use disposable brushes if available. Aseptically open one brush and place it on the ledge above the sink for the second half of the scrub. Open another brush and begin the scrub with Betadine. Use the nail cleaner to clean under all fingernails.

3. Scrub both arms during the first five minutes. Start at the fingertips and end 2 inches above the elbows; pay close attention to the fingernails and interdigital spaces. Discard the brush and rinse from fingertips to elbow.

4. Take the second brush and repeat step 3. Always start at the fingertips and work up to the elbow.

5. ALWAYS ALLOW WATER TO DRIP OFF THE ELBOWS BY KEEPING THE HANDS ABOVE THE LEVEL OF THE ELBOWS.

6. Move into the OR to dry your hands and arms (back into the room to push the door open).

7. Scrubbing times:
   - 10 minutes at the start of the day or with no previous scrub within the last 12 hours and on all orthopedic cases
   - Five minutes with a previous scrub or between cases if you have not been out of the OR working with other patients

Hibiclens Six-Minute Hand Scrub

1. Wet your hands and forearms to the elbow with water.

2. Dispense about 5 ml of Hibiclens into your cupped hands and spread it over both hands and arms to the elbow.

3. Scrub vigorously for three minutes without adding water. Use a sponge or a brush for scrubbing and pay particular attention to fingernails, cuticles, and interdigital spaces.

4. Rinse thoroughly with running water.

5. Dispense another 5 ml of Hibiclens into your cupped hands.

6. Wash for an additional three minutes. There is no need to use a brush or sponge at this point. Rinse thoroughly. Move into the OR back first to dry your hands.

PREPARING THE PATIENT

The exact technique may vary in different medical centers, but the patient prep involves mechanically cleansing the patient's skin in the region of the surgical site to reduce the bacterial flora. Ask the intern or resident to guide you through the procedure the first time, and then do it yourself thereafter.

Procedure

Materials: Usually there is a small "prep table" that contains
   - Gloves
   - Towels

- Betadine or Hibiclens scrub soap
- Betadine or Hibitane paint solution
- 4 x 4 gauze squares
- Ring forceps

Technique

1. Don a pair of gloves, and scrub the area designated by the intern or resident for four to six minutes. Use the 4 x 4s and the soap solution. This is usually done before putting on the sterile gown.

2. Drape the area with towels, and then gently pat the area dry. Taking care not to contaminate the area, gently peel off the towels.

3. Next, use 4 x 4s to paint the exposed area with the Betadine paint; use the proposed incision site as the center. Move circumferentially away from the incision site. NEVER bring the 4 x 4s back to the center after they have painted more peripheral areas.

GOWNING AND GLOVING

1. Back into the room to push the door open; keep your hands above your elbows.

2. Ask the scrub nurse for a towel. Don't be impatient as often the nurse will be very busy. Stick out one hand palm up and well away from the body. The nurse will drape the towel over your hand.

3. BEND at the waist to maintain sterility of the towel. It should never touch your clothing.

4. With one-half of the towel, dry one arm, beginning at the fingers; change hands and dry the other arm with the remaining half of the towel. NEVER go back to the forearm or hands after drying your elbows.

5. Drop the towel in the hamper. Again, remember to keep your hands above your elbows.

6. Ask for a gown and hold your arms out straight. The scrub nurse will place the gown on you, and the circulator will tie it back for you.

7. The nurse will hold out a right glove with the palm towards you. Push your hand through the glove.

8. Repeat the procedure with the left glove. It is easier if you use two fingers of your gloved right hand to help hold the left glove open.

9. Visually inspect the gloves for any holes.

10. Give the scrub nurse the long string of your front gown-tie. Hold the other string yourself and turn around in place. Tie the strings.

11. Ask the nurse for a damp sponge to clean the powder off the gloves (the powder has been implicated in some post op complications such as adhesions).

12. Now what to do? Wait patiently; stay out of the way, and keep your hands above your waist. Hold them together to prevent yourself from accidently dropping them or touching your mask. This is one of the most difficult things for the neophyte in the OR to remember. Be attentive. The only things that are sterile are your chest to your waist in the front and your hands to the shoulders. Your back is not sterile nor is your body below the waist. Avoid crossing your arms.

DRAPING THE PATIENT

Draping the patient is usually done by the surgeons. Watch how they do it, and consider helping at a later date. It is harder to keep sterile than it looks.

FINDING YOUR PLACE

The medical student is the low man on the totem pole and initially, usually stands on the side down by the patient's feet.

THE FIRST THING TO REMEMBER IS DON'T TOUCH ANYTHING THAT IS NOT STERILE. PUT YOUR HANDS ON THE STERILE FIELD AND DON'T MOVE ABOUT UNNECESSARILY. If you need to move to the head around someone else, pass back to back. When passing by a sterile field, try to face it. When passing a nonsterile field, pass it with your back towards it. If you are observing a case and are not scrubbed in, do not go between two sterile fields, and stay about 1 foot away from all sterile fields to avoid contamination (and condemnation!).

Do not drop your hands below your waist or table level. Do not grab at anything that falls off the side of the table — it's considered contaminated.

Do not reach for anything on the scrub nurse's small instrument stand (the Mayo stand). You may get your hand smashed with an instrument.

If someone says that you have contaminated a glove or anything else, do not move and do not complain or disagree. It is an unwritten rule that if anyone says, "You're contaminated," you accept the statement and change gloves, gown, or whatever is needed. If a glove alone is contaminated, hold the hand out away from the sterile field, fingers extended and palms up, and a circulating nurse will pull the glove off. The same is true if a needle sticks you or if a glove tears. Tell the surgeon and scrub nurse that you are contaminated and change gloves.

If you have to change your gown, step away from the table. The circulator will FIRST remove the gown and then the gloves. This procedure prevents the contaminated inside of the gown from passing over the hands. Regown and reglove without scrubbing again.

At the end of the case (once the dressing is on the wound), you may remove the gown and the gloves but not the mask, cap, or shoe covers. Assist in the transfer of the patient to the post op recovery room. Post op orders and a brief op note are written immediately. See Chapter 3 on how to write notes and orders.

17
Suturing Techniques

Suture Materials
Lacerations and Wound
   Care

Suturing Techniques
Suture Removal
Surgical Knots

SUTURE MATERIALS

Suture materials can be broadly defined as absorbable and nonabsorbable. Absorbable sutures can be thought of as "temporary"; these include plain gut, chromic gut, and synthetic materials such as polyglycolic acid (Dexon and Vicryl). Nonabsorbable sutures can be thought of as "permanent"; these include silk, cotton, stainless steel wire, Dacron, Prolene, and nylon.

The size of a suture is defined by the number of zeros. The more zeros in the number, the smaller the suture. For example, a 5-0 suture (00000) is much smaller than a 2-0 (00) suture.

LACERATIONS AND WOUND CARE

The following serves as a guide to the repair of lacerations in the emergency setting. Similar principles hold true for closure of wounds in the operating room.

The choice of appropriate suture material is based on many factors including location, extent of the laceration, strength of the tissues, and preference of the physician. In general, use 5-0 and 6-0 nylon where cosmetic concerns are important, such as on the face and neck. 3-0 and 4-0 nylon are general purpose sizes for the scalp and trunk. Use 3-0 or 4-0 absorbable sutures such as Dexon or Vicryl to approximate deep tissues. Skin is usually best closed by using interrupted sutures placed with good approximation with a minimum amount of tension. Suture techniques are discussed in the next section.

Procedure

1. Remove all foreign materials and devitalized tissues. Gently clean the wound with either plain saline or an antiseptic solution.

2. In general, do not suture infected or contaminated wounds, lacerations more than 8 to 12 hours old (24 hours on the face), and human or animal bites.

3. Anesthetize the wound by infiltrating it with an agent such as 1% lidocaine (Xylocaine). The maximum safe dosage is 4.5 mg/kg. Lidocaine is available with epinephrine (1:200,000) added to produce local vasoconstriction and prolong the anesthetic effect. EPINEPHRINE SHOULD NOT BE USED ON THE DIGITS, NOSE, EARS, OR PENIS.

4. Suture the wound. (See the section on suturing techniques.)

5. Cover the wound and keep it dry for at least 24 hours.

6. Finally, keep tetanus and antibacterial prophylaxis in mind, particularly for contaminated wounds.

Tetanus Prophylaxis

Previously Immunized: (within 10 years)
- Clean wound: None needed
- Clean wound and >10 years since booster or contaminated wound and >5 years since booster: 0.5 ml tetanus toxoid, IM

Nonimmunized
- Clean wound: 0.5 ml tetanus toxoid, IM
- Contaminated wound: 0.5 ml tetanus toxoid, plus 250 units tetanus immune globulin (TIG) IM

SUTURING TECHNIQUES

Opinions vary greatly on the ideal technique for skin closure. The following are the common techniques used for approximation of skin. Critical to any suturing technique is making certain the edges of the wound closely approximate without overlapping or inversion.

Simple Interrupted Suture: Bites are taken well through the thickness of the skin (Fig. 17-1).

Continuous Running Suture: Allows rapid closure, but depends on only two knots for security (Fig. 17-2).

Vertical Mattress Suture: Allows precise approximation of the skin edges with little tension. The needle is passed through the skin in a "far, far, near, near" sequence (Fig. 17-3).

Subcuticular Sutures: Utilizes intradermal absorbable suture, either Vicryl or Dexon (4-0 or 5-0), buried under the skin to help prevent "suture tracks." Most useful for clean, linear incisions, particularly on the face. Can be reinforced with Steri-Strips (Fig. 17-4).

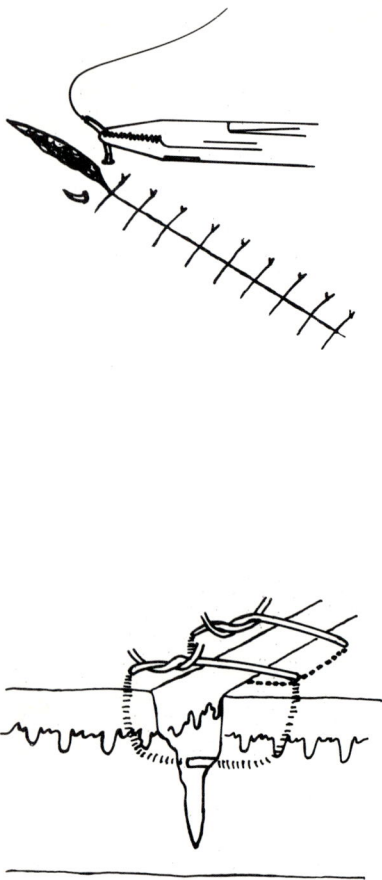

Fig. 17-1 Simple interrupted suture.

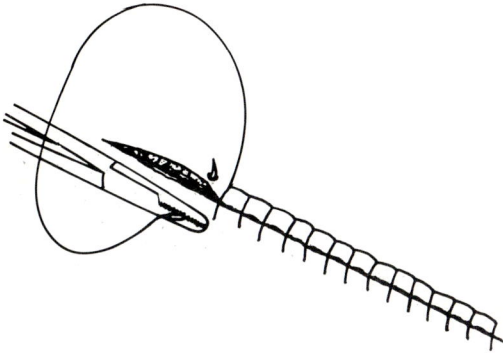

Fig. 17-2 Continuous running suture.

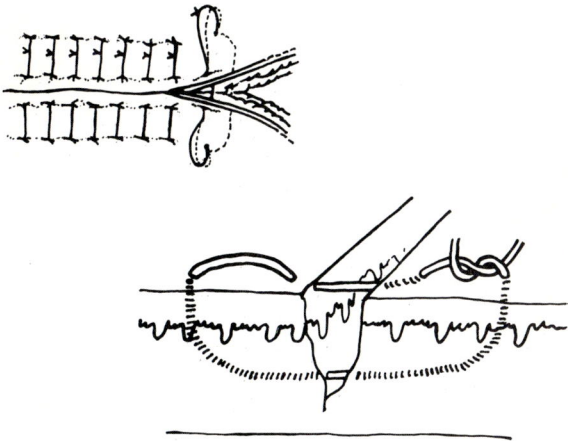

Fig. 17-3 Vertical mattress suture.

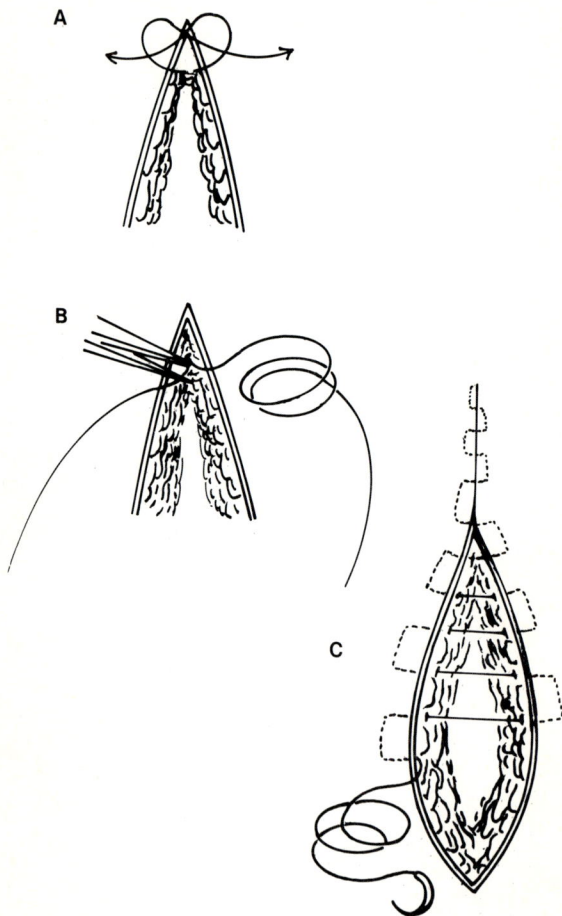

Fig. 17-4 The subcuticular suture. All stitches are under the skin.

SUTURE REMOVAL

The longer suture material is left in place, the more scarring it will produce. Sutures can be safely removed when a wound has developed sufficient tensile strength. Situations vary greatly, but general guidelines are face and neck, two to three days; scalp and body, five to seven days; and extremities, five to eight days (longer over joints). Any suture material or skin clip can be removed earlier if reinforced with materials such as Steri-Strips.

Procedure

1. Use hydrogen peroxide to clean the wound of all debris such as clotted blood and serum.

2. Use a forceps to elevate the knot off the skin.

3. Cut the suture as close to the skin as possible so that a minimal amount of "dirty suture" is dragged through the wound. When removing continuous sutures, cut and pull out each section individually (Fig. 17-5).

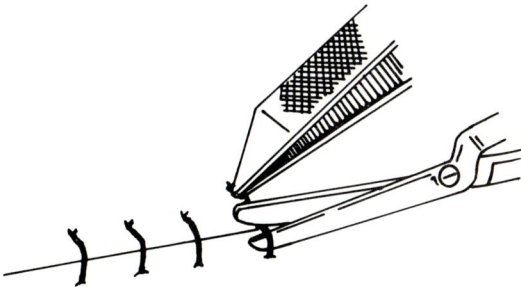

Fig. 17-5   Technique for suture removal.

4. The use of skin staples has become commonplace in the operating room because of the rapidity of closure and the nonreactive nature of the steel staples. Remove these at three to five days as shown in Fig. 17-6 and reinforce the incision with Steri-Strips.

5. Culture any pus that comes out of the suture tract.

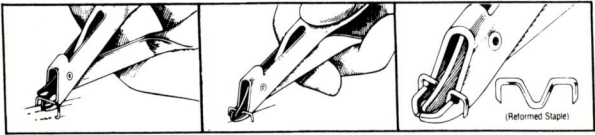

(Reformed Staple)

Fig. 17-6 Removal of skin staples. The staple removal instrument is passed beneath the staple and completely closed. The opened staple is then gently lifted out. *(Courtesy of Ethicon, Inc.)*

SURGICAL KNOTS

The following section outlines two basic knot-tying techniques: the two-hand tie and the instrument tie. These techniques are useful not only in the operating room but also in the repair of lacerations in the emergency department and for many invasive procedures including insertion of deep lines and cutdowns.

Two-Hand Square Knot: Figs. 17-7 and 17-8 show the technique for tying a two-hand square knot. This is the standard surgical knot.

Instrument Tie: Fig. 17-9 shows the technique for an instrument tie.

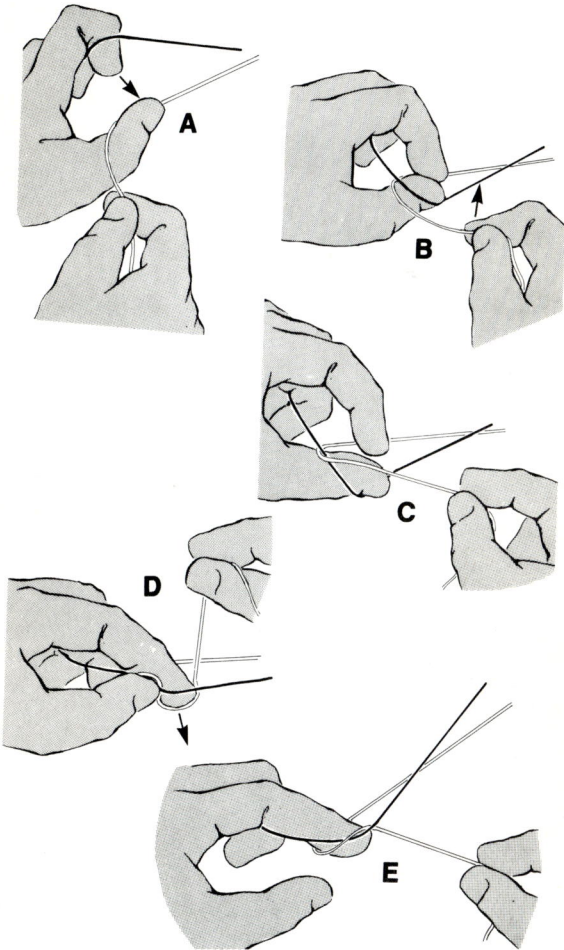

Fig. 17-7 Technique for the two-hand square knot. The suture ends are uncrossed as Step A begins. *(From Hill GJ: Outpatient Surgery, ed 2. Philadelphia, WB Saunders Co, 1980. Used with permission.)*

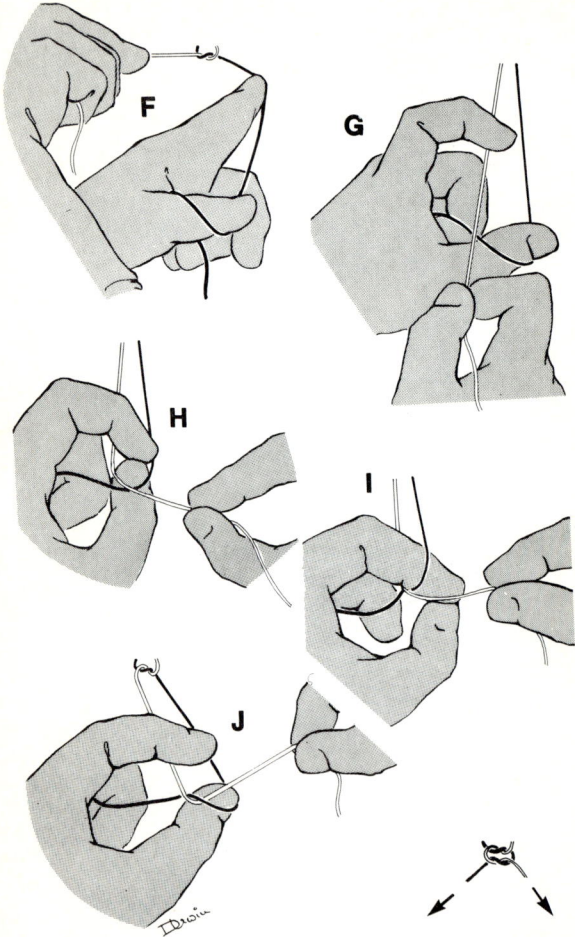

Fig. 17-8 The two-hand square knot, continued. Hands must cross at the end of the first loop tie (Step F) to produce a flat knot. The hands are not crossed at the end of the second loop tie (Step J). *(From Hill GH:* Outpatient Surgery, ed 2. *Philadelphia, WB Saunders Co, 1980. Used with permission.)*

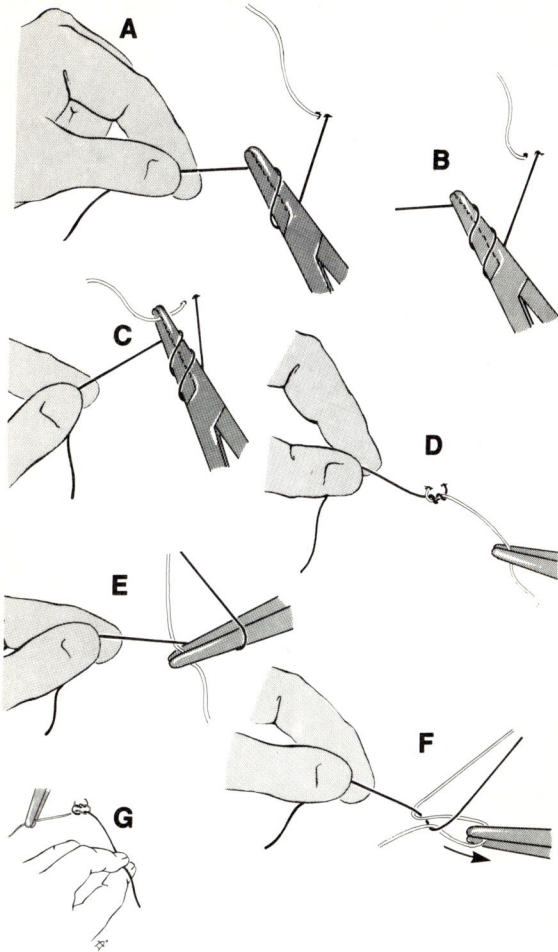

Fig. 17-9 The instrument tie begins with either a single or double (illustrated) looping of the lower end of the suture about the needle holder. The first loop is laid flat without crossing the hands. Hands must be crossed after the second loop tie (Step G) to produce a flat square knot. *(From Hill GJ: Outpatient Surgery, ed 2. Philadelphia, WB Saunders Co, 1980. Used with permission.)*

18
Respiratory System

Pulmonary Function Tests Oxygen Supplements
Differential Diagnosis of   Respiratory Therapy
    PFTs

PULMONARY FUNCTION TESTS

Pulmonary function tests (PFTs) are useful in diagnosing obstructive airway diseases such as asthma or emphysema, in determining their response to medical therapy, in diagnosing restrictive lung diseases, and in preoperative evaluation of patients. PFTs can be done before and after the administration of bronchodilators if they are not contraindicated (i.e., with severe heart disease). Ordering "routine spirometry with and without bronchodilators" will cover virtually all routine parameters of pulmonary function.

Normal PFT values vary tremendously with age, sex, and body size. Normals for a given patient are routinely provided by the pulmonary lab along with the results. ARTERIAL BLOOD GASES SHOULD BE INCLUDED IN ALL PFTs. Clinically useful pulmonary function tests are as follows:

Tidal Volume (TV):   Volume of air moved during normal, quiet respiration

Forced Vital Capacity (FVC):
Maximum volume of air that can be forcibly expired after a full inspiratory effort

Functional Residual Capacity (FRC):
Volume of air in lungs after a normal tidal expiration (FRC = reserve volume + expiratory reserve volume)

Total Lung Capacity (TLC):
Volume of air in the lungs after maximal inspiration

Forced Expired Volume in One Second (FEV_1):
Measured after maximum inspiration, the volume of air that can be expelled in one second

Maximal Mid Expiratory Flow (MMEF):
The flow rate of air expired over the middle 50% of the FVC

Maximum Voluntary Ventilation (MVV):
Maximum volume of gas that can be moved in and out of the lung per unit time during a voluntary effort

Vital Capacity (VC):
Maximum volume of air that can be exhaled from the lungs after a maximal inspiration

Residual Volume (RV):
The volume of air remaining in the lungs at the end of a maximal exhalation

Some lung volumes useful in interpreting PFTs are shown in Fig. 18-1.

DIFFERENTIAL DIAGNOSIS OF PFTs

When interpreting pulmonary function tests, remember that many patients have mixed restrictive and obstructive disease. The table on p. 246 gives the differential diagnosis of PFTs.

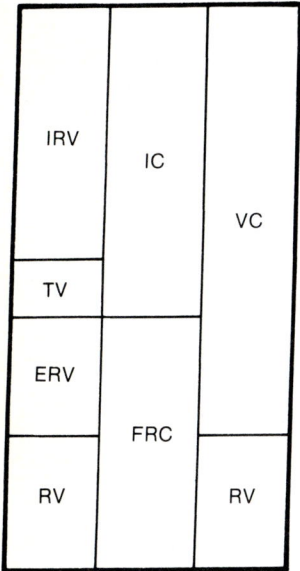

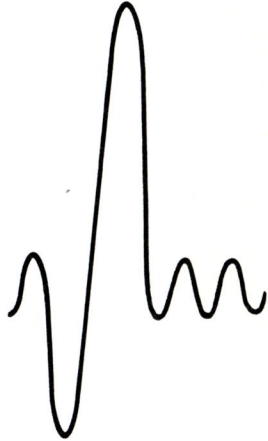

VC = vital capacity

RV = residual volume

FRC = functional residual capacity

TV = tidal volume

FRV = expiratory reserve volume

IRV = inspiratory reserve volume

IC = inspiratory capcity

Fig. 18-1 Lung volumes useful in the interpretation of pulmonary function tests.

Differential Diagnosis of Pulmonary Function Tests*

Test	Restrictive Disease	Obstructive Disease
FVC/VC	<	N or <
TLC	<	>
RV/FRC	<	>
FEV_1	N or >	<
MMEF	<	<
MVV	N or <	<

Obstructive Airways Disease (COPD)
(Asthma, emphysema, chronic bronchitis, mixed)

TEST	NORMAL	MILD	MODERATE	SEVERE	VERY SEVERE
VC (% of predicted)	>80	80	80	<	<
FEV_1 (% of VC)	>75	60–75	40–60	<40	<40
MVV (% of predicted)	>80	65–80	45–65	30–45	<30
RV (% of predicted)	80–120	120–150	150–175	>200	>200

Restrictive Lung Disease
(Pneumoconiosis, Wegener's granulomatosis, Goodpasture's disease, pulmonary hypertension)

TEST	NORMAL	MILD	MODERATE	SEVERE
VC (% of predicted)	>80	60–80	50–60	<50
FEV_1 (% of VC)	>75	>75	>75	>75
MVV (% of predicted)	>80	>80	70–80	<70
RV (% of predicted)	80–120	80–120	70–80	<70

*N = normal, < = decreased, > = increased

OXYGEN SUPPLEMENTS

The following table describes various methods of oxygen supplementation.

Oxygen Supplementation

Equipment	Flow Rate (liters/min)	Maximum FIO_2 Possible (%)
Nasal cannula	1–6	24–44
Nasal catheter	1–6	24–44
Face mask	5–8	25–45
Face mask with reservoir bag	6–10	60–90
Face tent	5–15	25–50
Venturi mask (Set to exact amount)	n.a.*	24, 28, 35, 40, 60, etc.
Intubation and Ventilator	n.a.*	Room air (21–100)

*n.a. = not applicable

RESPIRATORY THERAPY

Respiratory therapy is a vital component of health care. The objective is the treatment and care of all types of patients with cardiopulmonary diseases. Functions of the respiratory therapist include emergency care, ventilatory support, airway management, oxygen therapy, humidity and aerosol therapy, chest physiotherapy, physiological monitoring, and pulmonary diagnostics.

The following is a listing of the modalities available through the respiratory therapy or nursing services of all hospitals. All are designed to help patients with their bronchopulmonary hygiene, more commonly referred to as "pulmonary toilet." Their indications and expected outcome are based on guidelines from the National Association of Medical Directors for Respiratory Care.

Aerosol (Nebulizer) Therapy: Delivers aerosolized medications such as bronchodilators and mucolytic agents to patients able to coordinate their breathing patterns.

Indications

- Treatment of COPD, acute asthma, cystic fibrosis, and bronchiectasis
- Help in inducing sputum for diagnostic tests

Goals

- Relief of bronchospasm
- Help in decreasing the viscosity of secretions

To Order: Specify the following:

- Frequency
- Heated or cool mist
- Medications: In sterile water only
- FIO_2

EXAMPLE: Aerosol therapy, qid for 20 minutes with cool mist, 0.25 ml isoproterenol (Isuprel) 1:200 in 3 ml sterile water, FIO_2 28%

Intermittent Positive Pressure Breathing (IPPB):
Uses higher than ambient pressures to help forcibly inflate the lungs. Its usefulness is currently controversial.

Indications

- Treatment of atelectasis in a patient who on his own cannot or will not produce a tidal volume greater than that furnished by the machine
- Delivery of topical agents to a patient unable to co-ordinate his breathing pattern
- Management of acute exacerbations of COPD
- Help in inducing sputums for diagnostic tests

Goals

- Help in reinflating areas of atelectasis
- Relief of wheezing
- Help in clearing secretions

Complications

- Barotrauma such as pneumothorax and decreased cardiac output

To Order: Specify the following:

- Duration
- Medications: In normal saline or sterile water
- FIO_2

EXAMPLE: IPPB therapy qid for 15 minutes with 1 ml acetylcysteine (Mucomyst) 20% in 2 ml normal saline, FIO_2 28%

Chest Physiotherapy: Utilizes percussion and postural drainage (P&PD) along with assisted coughing and deep breathing exercises ("turn, cough, and deep breathe" or TC&DB) and nasotracheal suctioning (NT suctioning) to allow clearing of excessive secretions. P&PD is performed by positioning the patient so that the involved lobes of the lung are placed in a dependent drainage position and then using a cupped hand or vibrator to percuss the chest wall. Nasotracheal suctioning is quite uncomfortable to the patient and should be used only as a secondary mode of treatment. It involves passing a catheter through the nose and down the throat to evoke a coughing reflex.

Indications

- Treatment of pneumonia, atelectasis, and diseases resulting in weak or ineffective coughing

To Order

P&PD: Specify the following:
- Frequency
- Lobes involved

TC&DB, NT SUCTIONING: Ordered on a timed schedule or as needed

EXAMPLE: P&PD qid to RUL and RML or TC&DB every four hours (q4h)

Incentive Spirometry: Encourages patients to make a maximal and sustained inspiratory effort to help reinflate the lungs.

Indications

- Treatment of patients at risk for developing post op pulmonary complications
- Treatment and prevention of atelectasis

Goals: Set for the patient depending on the device available

- Lighting lights
- Moving ping-pong balls
- Moving colored fluids in "blow bottles"

To Order: Specify the following:

- Frequency
- Device (if you have a preference)

  EXAMPLE: Incentive spirometry q2h with blow bottle

Topical Medications: The following agents can be added to an IPPB or aerosol therapy order as needed. Remember, even though these are primarily topical agents, there can often be some systemic absorption.

Bronkosol or Bronkometer (Isoetharine and Phenylephrine Hydrochloride):   A bronchodilator with less cardiac effect than Isuprel

  USUAL ADULT DOSAGE: 0.5 ml in 1.5 ml normal saline

Mucomyst (Acetylcysteine):   A mucolytic agent useful for treating COPD, cystic fibrosis, and pneumonia

  USUAL DOSAGE: 1 ml of 20% acetylcysteine in 1 ml saline

Alupent (Metaproterenol Sulfate):   A bronchodilator with almost pure beta-1 activity

USUAL DOSAGE: 0.3 ml of a 5% solution in 2.5 ml saline bid–qid

Isuprel (Isoproterenol):   A potent bronchodilator good for acute bronchospasm; has both beta-1 and beta-2 actions (cardiac side effects)

USUAL DOSAGE: 0.5 ml of a 5% solution in 2 ml saline

Racemic Epinephrine: Contains both d-forms and l-forms of epinephrine; most useful for laryngotracheobronchitis and immediately after extubation in children

19
Basic ECG Reading

INTRODUCTION

The formal procedure for obtaining a readable ECG is given in Chapter 4.

Every electrocardiogram should be approached in a systematic stepwise fashion. Determine each of the following:

Standardization: With the ECG instrument set on 1 mv, there should be a 10 mm standardization mark (0.1 mv/mm) (Fig. 19-1).

Axis: If the QRS is upright in leads I and AVF, the axis is normal.

Intervals: Determine the PR and QRS intervals (Fig. 19-2). The PR should be >0.11 or <0.20 seconds and the QRS <0.12 seconds.

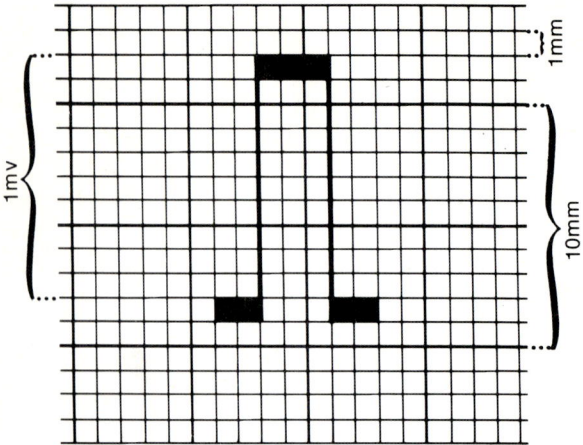

Fig. 19-1 A 10 mm standardization mark.

Rate: Count the number of QRS cycles in a six-second strip and multiply it by 10.

Rhythm: Determine if each QRS is preceded by a P wave, look for variation in the PR interval and RR interval (duration between 2 QRS cycles), and look for ectopic beats.

Hypertrophy: Calculate the sum of the S wave in V1 or V2 plus the R wave in V5 or V6. A sum greater than 35 indicates left ventricular hypertrophy.

Infarction or Ischemia: Check for the presence of Q waves, inverted T waves, poor R wave progression in the precordial leads, and ST segment elevation or depression.

A more detailed presentation of each of these categories is presented in the next six sections of this chapter.

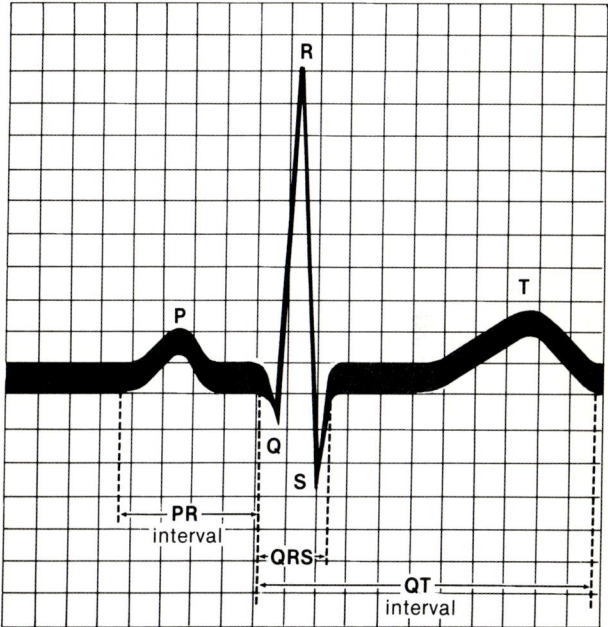

Fig. 19-2 Commonly measured intervals.

BASIC INFORMATION

Equipment

Bipolar Leads

- Lead I—left arm to right arm
- Lead II—left leg to right arm
- Lead III—left leg to left arm

Precordial Leads: V1 to V6 across the chest as shown in the section on Electrocardiograms in Chapter 4.

ECG Paper: With the ECG machine set at 25 mm/sec, each small box is 0.04 seconds and each large box is 0.2 seconds (Fig. 19-3).

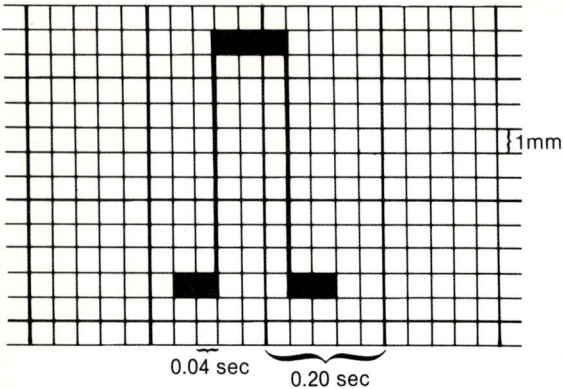

Fig. 19-3 Time marks on standard ECG paper running at 25 mm/sec.

Normal ECG Complex: (Fig. 19-4)

P Wave: Caused by depolarization of the atria.

QRS Complex: Represents ventricular depolarization.

Q Wave: The first negative deflection of the QRS complex (not always present).

R Wave: The first positive deflection (R′ is the positive deflection that sometimes occurs after the S wave).

S Wave: The negative deflection following the R wave.

T Wave: Caused by repolarization of the ventricles.

NOTE: If the wave amplitude is small, it is represented by a small letter; if it is large, by a capital letter. The pattern shown in Fig. 19-4 could also be noted as qRs.

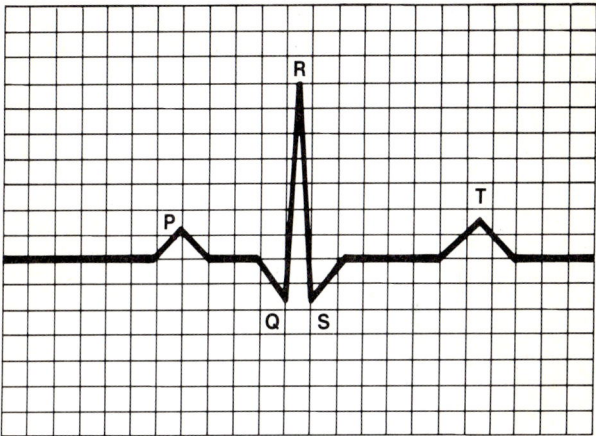

Fig. 19-4 Normal ECG complex.

AXIS DEVIATION

The term axis, which represents the sum of the vectors of the electrical depolarization of the ventricles, gives some idea of the orientation of the heart in the body. In a normal person, the axis is downward and to the left as shown in Fig. 19-5.

The QRS axis will be midway between two leads that have QRS complexes of equal amplitude OR the axis will be 90 degrees to the lead in which the QRS is isoelectric, i.e., biphasic (R wave = S wave).

Normal Axis: QRS positive in I and AVF (0–90 degrees)

Left Axis Deviation (LAD):   QRS positive in I and negative in AVF (S wave > R wave in lead II; 0 to −90 degrees)

Right Axis Deviation (RAD):   QRS negative in I and positive in AVF (QRS in lead III > QRS in lead I; +90 to +180 degrees)

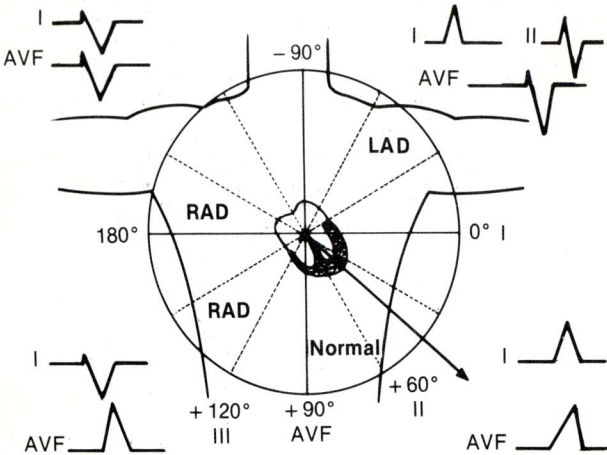

Fig. 19-5 Graphic representation of "axis deviation." Configurations of each type of axis are shown in each quadrant.

Extreme Right Axis Deviation: QRS negative in I and negative in AVF

CLINICAL CORRELATIONS

RAD: Seen with right ventricular hypertrophy (RVH), COPD, acute pulmonary embolism (sudden change in axis towards the right), normal individuals (occasionally).

LAD: Seen with left ventricular hypertrophy (LVH), left anterior hemiblock (< -45 degrees), left bundle branch block (LBBB), some normal individuals.

HEART RATE

Bradycardia: Heart rate <60 beats per minute (BPM).

Tachycardia: Heart rate >100 BPM.

Rate Determination: (See Fig. 19-6.)

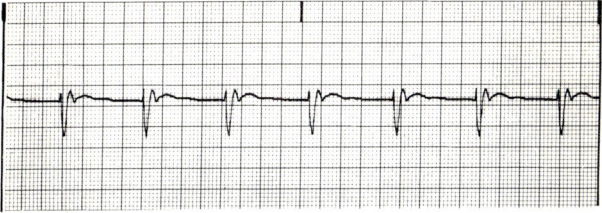

Fig. 19-6   Sample strip for rapid rate determination. Approximate rate is 70–75 BPM.

METHOD ONE: Note 3 second marks along top or bottom of ECG paper (15 large squares). The approximate rate = number of cycles (i.e., QRSs) in a six-second strip × 10.

Example: 7 cycles × 10 = 70 BPM.

ALTERNATIVE METHOD: (For regular rhythms) Count the number of large squares (0.2 second boxes) between two successive cycles. Rate = 300/number of squares.

Example: 300/4 = 75 BPM.

RHYTHM

Sinus Rhythms

Normal: Each QRS preceded by a P wave (which is positive in II and negative in AVR) with a regular PR and RR interval and a rate between 60–100 BPM (Fig. 19-7).

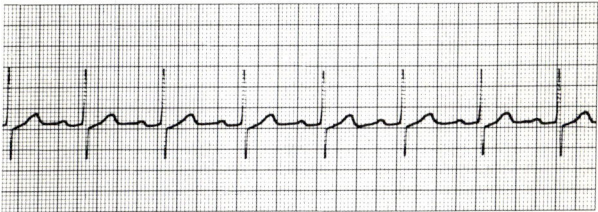

Fig. 19-7   Normal sinus rhythm. *(From Jones KM, Ochs GM: Interpretation of the Electrocardiogram: A Review for Health Professionals. Long Beach, Ca, Capistrano Press Ltd, 1982. Used with permission.)*

Sinus Tachycardia: Normal sinus rhythm with a heart rate >100 BPM and <180 BPM (Fig. 19-8).

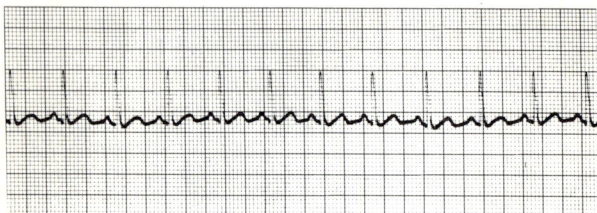

Fig. 19-8 Sinus tachycardia. *(From Jones KM, Ochs GM:* Interpretation of the Electrocardiogram: A Review for Health Professionals. *Long Beach, Ca, Capistrano Press Ltd, 1982. Used with permission.)*

CLINICAL CORRELATIONS: Anxiety, exertion, fever, hypotension, increased sympathetic tone (secondary to drugs with adrenergic effects [e.g., epinephrine], congestive heart failure), anticholinergic effect (e.g., atropine), pulmonary embolism, COPD, acute myocardial infarction, hyperthyroidism, and others.

Sinus Bradycardia: Normal sinus rhythm with a heart rate <60 BPM (Fig. 19-9).

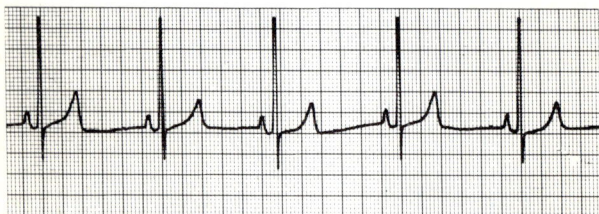

Fig. 19-9 Sinus bradycardia. *(From Jones KM, Ochs GM:* Interpretation of the Electrocardiogram: A Review for Health Professionals. *Long Beach, Ca, Capistrano Press Ltd, 1982. Used with permission.)*

CLINICAL CORRELATIONS: Well-trained athlete, normal variant, secondary to medications (e.g., propranolol [Inderal], digitalis), hypothyroidism, sick sinus syndrome (tachy-brady syndrome), and others.

TREATMENT
- If asymptomatic (good urine output, adequate BP and sensorium): No therapy needed
- If hypotensive or disoriented: See Chapter 21

Sinus Arrhythmia: Normal sinus rhythm with a somewhat irregular heart rate often associated with respiration. Inspiration causes a slight increase in rate; expiration decreases the rate.

Atrial Arrhythmias

Premature Atrial Contraction (PAC): Ectopic atrial focus firing prematurely followed by a normal QRS. Usually not of clinical significance; can be caused by stress, caffeine, and some myocardial diseases (Fig. 19-10).

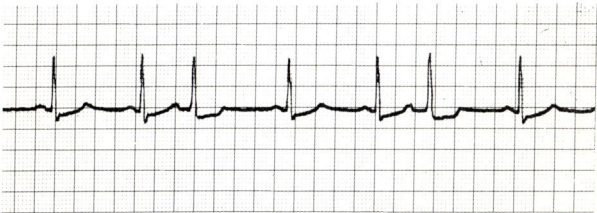

Fig. 19-10 Premature atrial contractions. *(From Jones KM, Ochs GM:* Interpretation of the Electrocardiogram: A Review for Health Professionals. *Long Beach, Ca, Capistrano Press Ltd, 1982. Used with permission.)*

Paroxysmal Atrial Tachycardia (PAT): A run of three or more consecutive PACs. Heart rate usually between 140–250 BPM. The P wave may not be visible, but the RR interval is very regular (Fig. 19-11).

CLINICAL CORRELATIONS: Can be seen in normal individuals but also occurs with a variety of heart diseases. Symptoms include palpitations, light-headedness, and syncope.

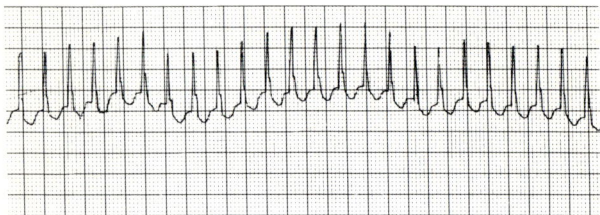

Fig. 19-11 Paroxysmal atrial tachycardia. *(From Jones KM, Ochs GM:* Interpretation of the Electrocardiogram: A Review for Health Professionals. *Long Beach, Ca, Capistrano Press Ltd, 1982. Used with permission.)*

TREATMENT
- Increase vagal tone: The Valsalva maneuver or carotid massage
- Medical treatment: Can include digoxin, edrophonium, propranolol, phenylephrine, quinidine, or verapamil (verapamil and propranolol should not be used at the same time—may cause asystole)
- Cardioversion with synchronized DC shock, particularly in the hemodynamically unstable patient

Atrial Fibrillation (AF): Irregularly irregular rhythm with no discernable P waves. The ventricular rate usually varies between 150–200 BPM (Fig. 19-12). (The ventricular response is slower with digoxin therapy.)

CLINICAL CORRELATIONS: Seen in some normal individuals, but commonly associated with organic heart disease (coronary artery disease, hypertensive heart disease, rheumatic fever), thyrotoxicosis, pericarditis, and pulmonary embolism.

TREATMENT
- Pharmacological therapy: Includes use of digoxin, quinidine, propranolol, or verapamil
- DC synchronized cardioversion: Indicated if associated with increased myocardial ischemia, hypotension, or CHF

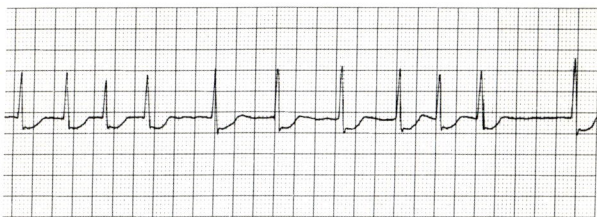

Fig. 19-12 Atrial fibrillation. *(From Jones KM, Ochs GM:* Interpretation of the Electrocardiogram: A Review for Health Professionals. *Long Beach, Ca, Capistrano Press Ltd, 1982. Used with permission.)*

Atrial Flutter: Characterized by sawtooth flutter waves with an atrial rate between 250–350 BPM and a variable ventricular rate depending on the number of atrial impulses conducted through the AV node (Fig. 19-13).

Example: 1 ventricular contraction (QRS) for every 2 flutter waves = a 2:1 flutter.

CLINICAL CORRELATIONS: Seen with valvular heart disease, ischemic heart disease, and pulmonary disease including pulmonary emboli.

TREATMENT
- Similar to treatment of atrial fibrillation

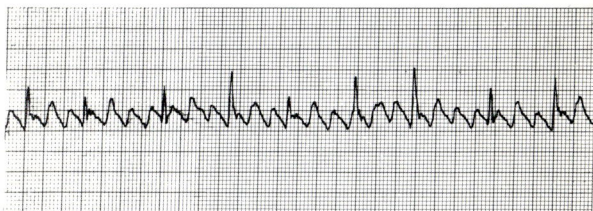

Fig. 19-13 Atrial flutter. *(From Jones KM, Ochs GM:* Interpretation of the Electrocardiogram: A Review for Health Professionals. *Long Beach, Ca, Capistrano Press Ltd, 1982. Used with permission.)*

Nodal Rhythm

AV Junctional or Nodal Rhythm: Originates in the AV node. Often associated with retrograde P waves which may precede or follow the QRS. If the P wave is present, it will be negative in lead II and positive in AVR (just the opposite of normal sinus rhythm). Three or more premature junctional beats in a row constitute a junctional tachycardia which has the same clinical significance as PAT.

Ventricular Arrhythmias

Premature Ventricular Contraction (PVC):   As implied by the name, a premature beat arising in the ventricle. P waves may be present but have no relation to the QRS of the PVC. The QRS will usually be >0.12 seconds with a left bundle branch pattern. There is a compensatory pause following a PVC that is usually longer than after a PAC (Fig. 19-14).

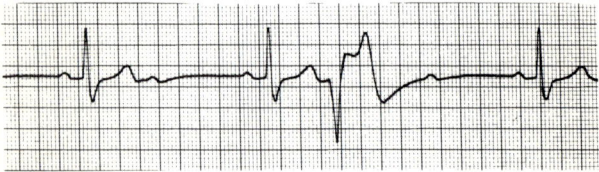

Fig. 19-14   Premature ventricular contraction. *(From Jones KM, Ochs GM:* Interpretation of the Electrocardiogram: A Review for Health Professionals. *Long Beach, Ca, Capistrano Press Ltd, 1982. Used with permission.)*

BIGEMINY: One normal sinus beat followed by one PVC in an alternating fashion (Fig. 19-15).

TRIGEMINY: Sequence of two normal beats followed by one PVC.

UNIFOCAL PVCs: Arise from one site in the ventricle. Each has the same configuration.

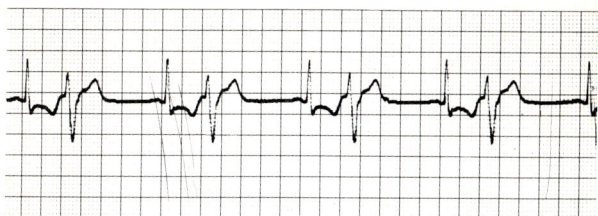

Fig. 19-15 Bigeminy. *(From Jones KM, Ochs GM:* Interpretation of the Electrocardiogram: A Review for Health Professionals. *Long Beach, Ca, Capistrano Press Ltd, 1982. Used with permission.)*

MULTIFOCAL PVCs: Arise from different sites, therefore have different shapes (Fig. 19-16).

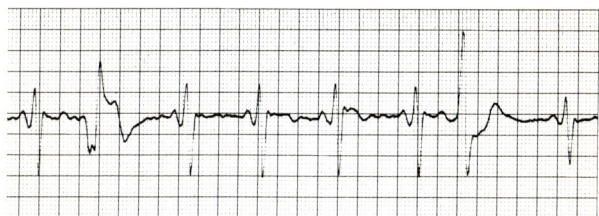

Fig. 19-16 Multifocal PVCs. *(From Jones KM, Ochs GM:* Interpretation of the Electrocardiogram: A Review for Health Professionals. *Long Beach, Ca, Capistrano Press Ltd, 1982. Used with permission.)*

CLINICAL CORRELATIONS: Occur in some normal persons, excessive caffeine ingestion, anxiety, with organic heart disease (ischemic, valvular, or hypertensive), secondary to toxicity (from digitalis, aminophylline, epinephrine, or isoproterenol), predisposing metabolic abnormalities (hypoxia, hypokalemia, acidosis, anemia).

CRITERIA FOR TREATMENT: (In the setting of an acute myocardial infarction)
- > five PVCs in one minute
- PVCs in couplets (two in a row)
- Numerous multifocal PVCs
- PVC that falls on the preceeding T wave (R on T)

TREATMENT
- Lidocaine: Most commonly used
- Other antiarrhythmics: Procainamide, quinidine, phenytoin, disopyramide
- See also Chapter 21
- Treatment of aggravating cause usually sufficient (e.g., treat hypoxia)

Ventricular Tachycardia: By definition, three or more PVCs in a row. Appears as a wide QRS usually with a LBBB pattern (as opposed to a narrow complex seen with supraventricular tachycardia). May occur as a short paroxysm or as a sustained run with a rate between 120–250 BPM. Can be life threatening because of hypotension and the tendency to degenerate into ventricular fibrillation (Fig. 19-17).

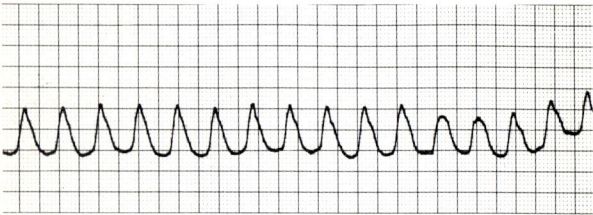

Fig. 19-17 Ventricular tachycardia. *(From Jones KM, Ochs GM: Interpretation of the Electrocardiogram: A Review for Health Professionals. Long Beach, Ca, Capistrano Press Ltd, 1982. Used with permission.)*

CLINICAL CORRELATIONS: See the previous section on PVCs. Patients with ventricular aneurysm are more susceptible to developing ventricular arrhythmias.

TREATMENT
- See Chapter 21

Ventricular Fibrillation: Erratic electrical activity from the ventricles which fibrillate or twitch asynchronously. There is no cardiac output with this rhythm (Fig. 19-18).

CLINICAL CORRELATIONS: One of two patterns seen with cardiac arrest (the other would be asystole or flatline).

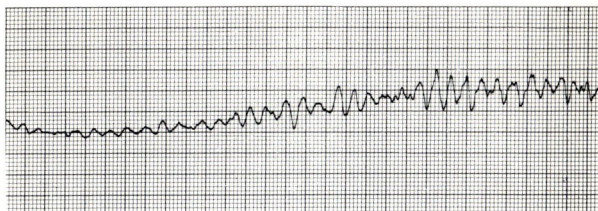

Fig. 19-18 Ventricular fibrillation. *(From Jones KM, Ochs GM: Interpretation of the Electrocardiogram: A Review for Health Professionals. Long Beach, Ca, Capistrano Press Ltd, 1982. Used with permission.)*

TREATMENT
- See Chapter 21

Heart Blocks

First-Degree Block: PR interval >0.2 seconds (or five small boxes). Usually not clinically significant. Can be caused by increased vagal tone or toxic levels of drugs such as digoxin (Fig. 19-19).

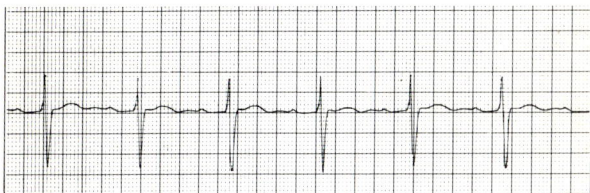

Fig. 19-19 First-degree AV block. *(From Jones KM, Ochs GM: Interpretation of the Electrocardiogram: A Review for Health Professionals. Long Beach, Ca, Capistrano Press Ltd, 1982. Used with permission.)*

Second-Degree Block

MOBITZ TYPE I (WENKEBACH): Progressive prolongation of the PR interval until the P wave is blocked and not followed by a QRS complex (Fig. 19-20).

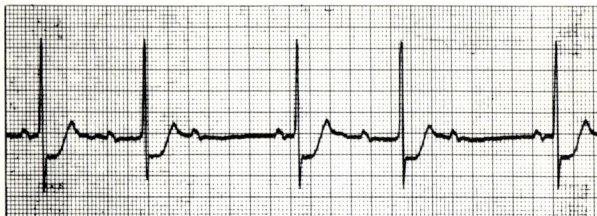

Fig. 19-20 Second-degree AV block (Wenkebach or Mobitz type I). *(From Jones KM, Ochs GM:* Interpretation of the Electrocardiogram: A Review for Health Professionals. *Long Beach, Ca, Capistrano Press Ltd, 1982. Used with permission.)*

Clinical Correlations: Seen with ischemic heart disease and digitalis toxicity. Can be transient. May progress to bradycardia (rare).

Treatment
- If bradycardia occurs: Atropine, isoproterenol, or a pacemaker

MOBITZ TYPE II: A series of P waves without QRS complexes (blocked) followed by a conducted P wave with a QRS complex (Fig. 19-21). May occur as a 2:1, 3:1, or 4:1 block. With a 4:1 block, every fourth P wave is followed by a QRS.

Clinical Correlations: Implies severe conduction system disease that can progress into complete heart block.

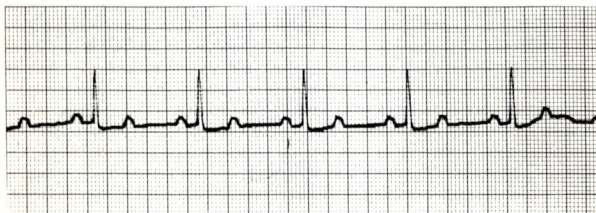

Fig. 19-21 Second-degree AV block (Mobitz type II). *(From Jones KM, Ochs GM:* Interpretation of the Electrocardiogram: A Review for Health Professionals. *Long Beach, Ca, Capistrano Press Ltd, 1982. Used with permission.)*

Treatment
- Usually with placement of a temporary cardiac pacemaker, particularly when associated with an acute anterior myocardial infarction

Third-Degree Block: Complete AV block with independent atrial and ventricular rates. Ventricular rate usually 20–40 BPM (Fig. 19-22).

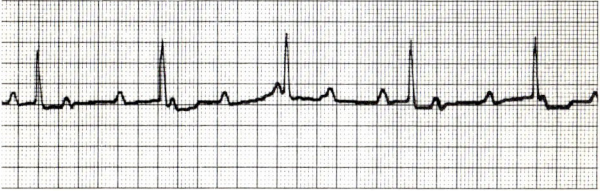

Fig. 19-22 Third-degree AV block (complete heart block). *(From Jones KM, Ochs GM:* Interpretation of the Electrocardiogram: A Review for Health Professionals. *Long Beach, Ca, Capistrano Press Ltd, 1982. Used with permission.)*

CLINICAL CORRELATIONS: May occur as the result of degenerative changes in the conduction system in the elderly, from digitalis toxicity, transiently after an acute inferior myocardial infarction (due to temporary ischemia of the AV junction). Can cause exacerbation of CHF or syncope.

TREATMENT
- With an acute myocardial infarction, usually requires placement of a temporary pacemaker

Bundle Branch Block (BBB): Complete BBB present when the QRS complex >0.12 seconds (or three small boxes on the ECG strip).

Right Bundle Branch Block (RBBB): RSR' pattern in V1 or V2 with secondary T wave inversion in V1 or V2 (Fig. 19-23). Also a wide S in V5 or V6.

CLINICAL CORRELATIONS: May be seen in normal person, but usually associated with diseases affecting the right side of the heart (pulmonary hypertension, atrial septal defect, ischemia); sudden onset associated with pulmonary embolism.

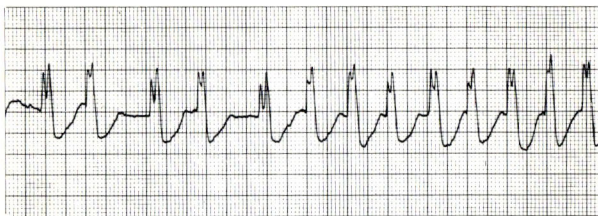

Fig. 19-23 Lead V2 showing RSR' pattern of right bundle branch block. *(From Jones KM, Ochs GM: Interpretation of the Electrocardiogram: A Review for Health Professionals. Long Beach, Ca, Capistrano Press Ltd, 1982. Used with permission.)*

Left Bundle Branch Block (LBBB): RR' in V5 or V6 with secondary T wave inversion in V5 or V6 with a wide S in V1 or V2 (Fig. 19-24).

CLINICAL CORRELATIONS: Associated with organic heart disease (hypertensive, valvular, and ischemic). Development of a new LBBB after an acute myocardial infarction may be an indication for inserting a temporary cardiac pacemaker.

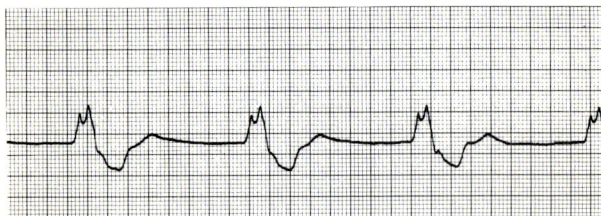

Fig. 19-24 Lead V6 showing RR' pattern of left bundle branch block. *(From Jones KM, Ochs GM: Interpretation of the Electrocardiogram: A Review for Health Professionals. Long Beach, Ca, Capistrano Press Ltd, 1982. Used with permission.)*

CARDIAC HYPERTROPHY

Atrial Hypertrophy

Atrial Hypertrophy: P wave >2.5 mm in height and >0.12 seconds wide (three small boxes on the ECG paper).

Right Atrial Enlargement (RAE): Tall, slender, peaked P waves in leads II, III, and AVF with a diphasic or inverted P wave in V1 ("P pulmonale pattern").

CLINICAL CORRELATIONS: Seen with chronic diffuse pulmonary disease, pulmonary hypertension, congenital heart disease (atrial septal defects).

Left Atrial Enlargement (LAE): Notched P wave ("P mitrale pattern") seen in leads I and II with a wide, slurred diphasic P in V1 with a wide terminal component (negative deflection).

CLINICAL CORRELATIONS: Seen with mitral stenosis or secondary to LVH with hypertensive cardiovascular disease.

Ventricular Hypertrophy

Right Ventricular Hypertrophy (RVH): Tall R wave in V1 (R wave > S wave in V1), persistent S waves in V5 and V6, progressively smaller R wave from V1 to V6, slightly enlarged QRS intervals, and a strain pattern with ST segment depression and T wave inversion in V1 to V3.

CLINICAL CORRELATIONS: Associated with mitral stenosis, chronic diffuse pulmonary disease, congenital heart disease (e.g., tetralogy of Fallot), LVH.

Left Ventricular Hypertrophy (LVH): Voltage criteria (in patients over age 35): R wave in AVL >13 mm or an R in V5 or V6 >27 mm or an S in V1 plus an R in V5 >35 mm. QRS complex may be >0.1 seconds wide in V5 or V6. ST segment depression and T wave inversion in V5 or V6.

CLINICAL CORRELATIONS: Hypertension, aortic stenosis or insufficiency, long-standing coronary artery disease, some forms of congenital heart disease.

MYOCARDIAL INFARCTION

Myocardial Ischemia: Inadequate oxygen supply to the myocardium due to blockage or spasm of the coronary arteries. The ECG can show ST segment depression (Fig. 19-25)

or symmetrically inverted T waves (Fig. 19-26) in the area of
ischemia (e.g., inferior ischemia in II, III, F; anterior ischemia
in V1 to V6; lateral ischemia in I, AVL).

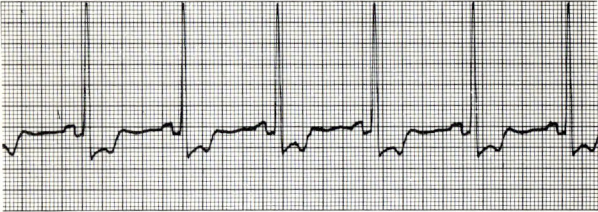

Fig. 19-25   ST segment depression. *(From Jones KM, Ochs GM:*
Interpretation of the Electrocardiogram: A Review for Health
Professionals. *Long Beach, Ca, Capistrano Press Ltd, 1982. Used
with permission.)*

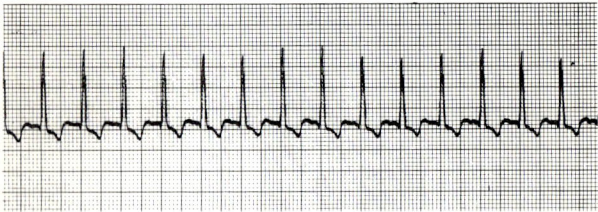

Fig. 19-26   Flipped T waves. *(From Jones KM, Ochs GM:* Interpretation of the Electrocardiogram: A Review for Health Professionals. *Long Beach, Ca, Capistrano Press Ltd, 1982. Used with
permission.)*

Myocardial Infarction (MI):   Refers to myocardial
necrosis due to severe ischemia. Can be transmural (Q waves
seen) or subendocardial (ischemia seen without evidence of Q
waves). The following table outlines the localization of
myocardial infarctions.

Acute Injury Phase: ST segment elevation (Fig. 19-27) and
tall positive hyperacute T waves (Fig. 19-28).

Evolving Phase: Occurs days to weeks after an MI. Deep T
wave inversion replaces ST segment elevation.

Myocardial Infarctions

Location of MI	Presence of Q Wave or ST Segment Elevation	Reciprocal ST Depression
Anterior	V1 to V4, I, AVL (also poor R wave progression in leads V1 to V6)*	II, III, AVF
Inferior	II, III, AVF	Anterior Leads
Posterior	Abnormally tall R and T waves in V1 to V3	V1 to V3
Subendocardial	No abnormal Q wave Have ST segment elevation in the anterior leads (I, AVL, V1 to V6) or the inferior leads (II, III, AVL)	None

*Normally in V1 to V6 the R wave amplitude gradually increases, and the S decreases with a "biphasic" QRS (R = S) in V3. With an anterior MI, there will be a loss of the R wave voltage, and the biphasic QRS will appear more laterally in V4 to V6. Hence the expression, "poor R wave progression."

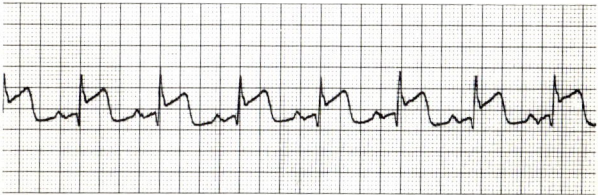

Fig. 19-27 ST segment elevation. *(From Jones KM, Ochs GM: Interpretation of the Electrocardiogram: A Review for Health Professionals. Long Beach, Ca, Capistrano Press Ltd, 1982. Used with permission.)*

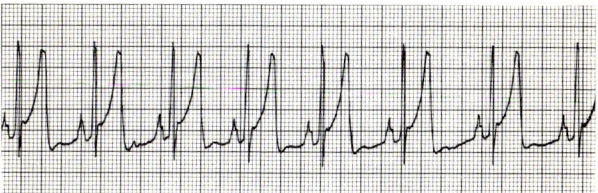

Fig. 19-28 ST segment elevation with hyperacute T waves. *(From Jones KM, Ochs GM: Interpretation of the Electrocardiogram: A Review for Health Professionals. Long Beach, Ca, Capistrano Press Ltd, 1982. Used with permission.)*

Q Waves: Occur 24 to 48 hours after a transmural MI. A Q wave is the initial negative deflection of the QRS complex. A "significant" Q wave is 0.04 seconds in duration and >25% the height of the R wave (Fig. 19-29).

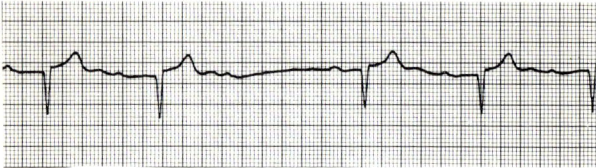

Fig. 19-29 Example of Q waves. *(From Jones KM, Ochs GM:* Interpretation of the Electrocardiogram: A Review for Health Professionals. *Long Beach, Ca, Capistrano Press Ltd, 1982. Used with permission.)*

ELECTROLYTE AND DRUG EFFECTS

Electrolytes

Hyperkalemia: Narrow, symmetrical, peaked T waves. With severe hyperkalemia, PR prolongation occurs, the P wave flattens and is lost, and the QRS widens and can progress to ventricular fibrillation.

Hypokalemia: ST segment depression with the appearance of U waves (a positive deflection after the T wave).

Hypercalcemia: Short QT interval.

Hypocalcemia: Long QT interval.

Drugs

Digitalis Effect: Down-sloping ST segment.

Digitalis Toxicity

  ARRHYTHMIAS: PVCs, bigeminy, trigeminy, ventricular tachycardia, ventricular fibrillation, PAT, nodal rhythms, sinus bradycardia.

  CONDUCTION ABNORMALITIES: First-degree, second-degree, third-degree heart blocks.

Quinidine and Procainamide: With toxic levels, see prolonged QT, flattened T wave, and QRS widening.

20
Critical Care

MANAGEMENT OF THE CRITICALLY ILL PATIENT

Patients with multiple system disease or injury are commonplace in the intensive care unit (ICU). The problems they present are complicated, often overwhelming, to the student or young house officer.

This chapter describes a system by system approach to the critically ill patient. This approach forces you, the clinician, to focus sequentially on each of the body's major organ systems and to evaluate each system's function over the previous 24 hours. You then integrate abnormalities within each given system to the problem of the patient as a whole. This approach lends itself well to the writing of a complete but concise daily progress note.

Attention is then turned towards understanding the cardio-vascular and respiratory parameters essential to the care of any ICU patient.

THE ICU PROGRESS NOTE

In the first part of the daily progress note, you should con-dense and organize the patient's course over the previous 24 hours. In the second part of the progress note—the plan—try to anticipate and avoid future complications.

Organization

A simple organizational approach to the organ system pro-gress note includes the following ten items:

1. General summary of major events
2. Assessment of neurological function
3. Assessment of respiratory function
4. Assessment of cardiovascular function
5. Assessment of gastrointestinal function
6. Assessment of genitourinary function
7. Evaluation of the extremities
8. Assessment of metabolic and nutritional status
9. Assessment of hematological and infectious status
10. Listing of the patient's medications

Each individual system should be approached in a uniform way. There are four basic categories to be scrutinized within each system:

1. Physical examination
2. X-ray examination
3. Laboratory results
4. Results of instrumentation

The evaluation of some systems may rely more heavily on one category or another, but it is always helpful to think of each system in light of each category.

The following table is an example of a progress note that uses the organ system approach.

Sample ICU Progress Note

Category	Comments
GENERAL	Motor vehicle accident Postoperative day #4 Splenectomy, pulmonary contusion Bronchoscopy yesterday
NEUROLOGICAL	Alert, moves all four extremities to command Glasgow Coma Scale 10 Repeat CT* scan wnl* Intracranial pressure 15–20 cm H_2O
RESPIRATORY	Decreased breath sounds right lung (L) chest tube in place—bubbling pO_2 80, pCO_2 50, pH 7.30, FIO_2 60% Rate 12, TV* 1000 PEEP* 12 CXR: White out (R) lung Compliance decreased Shunt fraction (Qs/Qt) increasing (now 28%)
CARDIOVASCULAR	BP 110/60 No rubs, murmurs, or gallops CPK MB <5% Wedge 10, PAP* 30/15, cardiac index 3 liters/min/m^2 Normal sinus rhythm
EXTREMITIES	Fx (fracture) left tibia and fibula Urine myoglobin negative Compartment pressure normal
GASTROINTESTINAL	Abdominal wound clean Penrose drainage 55 ml, serosanguineous Elevated (L) hemidiaphragm SGOT 155 (increased)
GENITOURINARY	Foley in place 2800 ml in/2500 out Creatinine 0.9, clearance 65 ml/min (decreased, 80 ml/min yesterday) 4 + bacteria—cultures pending
METABOLIC/ NUTRITIONAL	SMA-6 wnl Albumin 2.3, PO_4 2.2, Mg 2.0 TPN 4.25% amino acids, D25 at 125 ml/hr = >3000 cal/day Nitrogen balance: Positive by 4 gm/day

Sample ICU Progress Note (Continued)

Category	Comments
HEMATOLOGICAL/ INFECTIOUS	WBC 30,000 (increased), HCT 30 (decreased), PT 12/12, PTT 35/22 Temp to 103.6 F Blood cultures: Gram-negative rods sensitive to tobramycin Sputum: *Pseudomonas* sensitive to chloramphenicol Urine: No growth at 24 hours Skin tests: Anergic at 48 hours
MEDICATIONS	Tobramycin 80 mg IV q8h, peak 6.5, trough 1.2 Chloramphenicol 1 gm IV q6h Cleocin 300 mg IV q6h Digitalis 0.250 mg IV qd Cimetidine 300 mg IV q6h
PLAN	1. Watch pulmonary status • Decreased pO_2 will require increased PEEP • May need chest tube on (R) 2. Increased SGOT • Suspect liver failure secondary to hyperalimentation • Check NH_3, SGPT • Decrease INF to 75 ml/hr 3. Decreased creatinine clearance • Suspect tobramycin nephrotoxicity • Decrease tobramycin to 80 mg IV q12h • Repeat tobramycin levels 4. Increased WBC, increased temp with elevated (L) hemidiaphragm • Suspect (L) subphrenic abscess • May require surgical drainage 5. Medication changes in face of decreased renal function • Decrease cimetidine to 300 mg IV q12h • Decrease digitalis to 0.125 mg qd • Check digitalis level in A.M. • Check K in A.M.

*CT = computerized axial tomography; wnl = within normal limits; TV = tidal volume; PEEP = positive end expiratory pressure; PAP = pulmonary artery pressure.

CARDIOVASCULAR SYSTEM

Cardiovascular instability is one of the most common problems faced in the ICU. Understanding the approach to the evaluation of the cardiovascular system is essential to managing any critically ill patient.

Inspection

Inspection of the cardiovascular system is divided into three main areas:

- Inspection for jugular venous distension (JVD)
- Inspection for precordial contusion
- Inspection for extremity perfusion

Jugular Veins: Any daily examination of the patient in the ICU should include a brief glance at the neck veins to look for JVD. A patient sitting at a 45 degree angle who has distended neck veins has a CVP of 12 to 15 cm H_2O or higher.

Distended neck veins in the face of systemic hypotension in the acutely ill or injured patient suggest

- Tension pneumothorax
- Pericardial tamponade

Precordial Contusion: Bruising about the anterior chest wall is commonly associated with blunt trauma from a steering wheel. Such an injury pattern should alert the physician to the possibility of a myocardial contusion. The latter condition is worked up and treated in the same fashion as a myocardial infarction: Provide continuous ECG monitoring and vigorously treat arrhythmias.

Extremity Perfusion: Check all four extremities for distal perfusion. Pay special attention to the following areas:

- Sites distal to long bone fractures or dislocations
- Sites distal to indwelling arterial catheters

Blood Pressure

Blood pressure over the short term is considered adequate if renal perfusion is maintained. In a young previously healthy individual, an adequate blood pressure usually corresponds to a minimum systolic pressure of 90.

Systolic Hypertension: A systolic blood pressure >150 mm Hg with a normal diastolic pressure. In the acute care setting, thought to be secondary to increased cardiac output. Seen in the following situations:

- A generalized response to stress
- Thyrotoxicosis
- Anemia

Diastolic Hypertension: A diastolic pressure >90 mm Hg. Often associated with systolic hypertension. Isolated diastolic hypertension is ordinarily associated with three general disease categories:

- Renal disease
- Endocrine disorders
- Neurological disorders

TREATMENT FOR HYPERTENSION: Hypertension is of concern in the ICU in the face of a fresh myocardial infarction or a vascular anastomosis and especially following carotid artery surgery. Ideally the blood pressure in this instance is maintained above 130 and below 160. A systolic pressure >180 mm Hg usually requires immediate treatment. Drugs commonly used to treat acute hypertension are nitroprusside (Nipride) and hydralazine.

Pulse Pressure: The difference between systolic and diastolic blood pressure.

Pulse pressure = systolic pressure − diastolic pressure

WIDE PULSE PRESSURE: A pulse pressure >40 mm Hg. Associated with

- Thyrotoxicosis
- Arterial venous fistula
- Aortic insufficiency

NARROW PULSE PRESSURE: A pulse pressure <25 mm Hg. Associated with

- Significant tachycardia
- Pericarditis
- Pericardial effusion or tamponade
- Ascites

Mean Arterial Blood Pressure (MAP):   Calculated by taking the diastolic pressure plus one-third of the pulse pressure. Used to calculate the total peripheral resistance.

MAP = diastolic pressure + (pulse pressure ÷ 3)

Paradoxical Pulse: A function of the change in intrathoracic pressures during inspiration and expiration. Normally, systolic blood pressure will fall between 6 and 10 mm Hg with inspiration. This fall is reflected by a systolic blood pressure that varies with respiration. If this variation occurs over a range >10 mm Hg, the patient is said to have a paradoxical pulse (Fig. 20-1). One must always consider the diagnosis of pericardial tamponade if pulsus paradoxus is present. Other conditions associated with a paradoxical pulse are

- Asthma and COPD
- Pericardial effusion
- Ruptured diaphragm
- Pneumothorax

TECHNICAL TIP: The obese arm will give a systolic blood pressure reading 10 to 15 mm Hg higher if a normal blood pressure cuff is used rather than a thigh cuff.

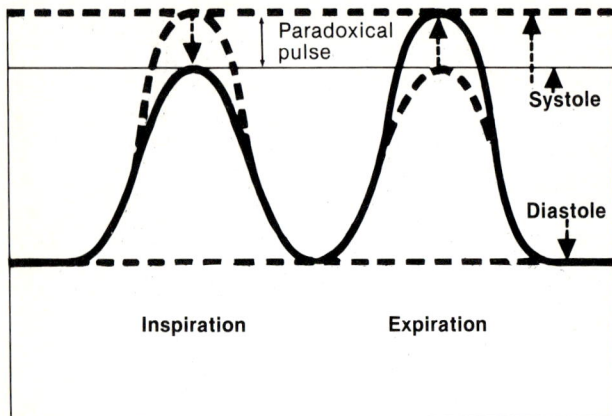

Fig. 20-1 The paradoxical pulse.

Heart Murmurs

It is important to listen for the development of a new murmur. Murmurs are classically described as systolic or diastolic. Diastolic murmurs are practically always pathological. All new murmurs should be characterized as to their intensity, location, and variation with position and respiration. Details on heart murmurs can be found in Chapter 2.

Systolic Murmurs: Abrupt onset caused by two conditions that have clinical significance for the acutely ill patient:

- Injury to the papillary muscle
- Rupture of an intraventricular septum

PAPILLARY MUSCLE INJURY: Papillary muscle dysfunction following acute myocardial infarction is characterized by an apical systolic murmur. The injury to the papillary muscle may cause a murmur of Grade I–II/VI. After rupture of the papillary muscle, a sudden pansystolic murmur of Grade II–IV/VI may appear. The diagnosis of papillary muscle rupture can be made either at cardiac catheterization or by echocardiography.

RUPTURE OF AN INTRAVENTRICULAR SEPTUM: May be indicated by the appearance of a loud systolic murmur of abrupt onset. A catastrophic event that may follow myocardial infarction. Usually accompanied by massive pulmonary edema. This situation is an indication for emergency cardiac catheterization.

Diastolic Murmurs and Bacterial Endocarditis: The major concern in the appearance of a diastolic murmur in the acutely injured patient is bacterial endocarditis, an entity that is becoming more common in acutely ill patients who are managed in ICUs for long periods of time. Foreign bodies such as central venous lines, hyperalimentation lines, and Swan-Ganz catheters all contribute to the increasing incidence of bacterial endocarditis.

Gallop: Defined as three sequential heart sounds in which the first two beats of the triplet are closer together than the third. The result is a sound that resembles the gallop of a horse. A newly occurring gallop may herald the onset of one or more of the following:

- Severe CHF
- Mitral regurgitation secondary to injury of the papillary muscle
- Anemia

Pericardial Friction Rub: Classically described as the sound of two pieces of leather rubbing together. Frequently high pitched and may be intermittent. Development of a pericardial friction rub should cause one to suspect one of the following:

- Pericarditis
- Pericardial effusion
- Myocardial infarction near the surface of the pericardium

Common following open heart surgery (in this setting does not necessarily indicate pathological changes).

CARDIOVASCULAR PHYSIOLOGY

Prior to a discussion of CVPs and Swan-Ganz catheters, a brief review of cardiovascular physiology may be helpful.

Definitions

Cardiac Output: Defined as the quantity of blood pumped by the heart each minute. Normal output in an adult is 3.5–5.5 liters/min.

Cardiac Index: Used to compensate for body size. Defined as the cardiac output divided by the patient's body surface area. The normal cardiac index is 2.8–3.2 liters/min/m^2.

Determinants of Cardiac Output

Cardiac output is determined by heart rate and stroke volume. Stroke volume depends on the following:

- Preload
- Afterload
- Contractility

Preload: The initial length of the myocardial muscle fiber is proportional to the left ventricular end diastolic volume. As the volume of blood remaining in the heart after each beat (end diastolic volume) increases, the stretch on individual myocardial muscle cells increases. As the stretch increases, the energy of contraction increases proportionally until an optimal tension is developed.

STARLING'S LAW: When the myocardial muscle cell is stretched, the developed tension increases to a maximum and then declines as the stretch becomes more extreme (Fig. 20-2).

Afterload: Defined as the resistance to ventricular ejection. Measured clinically by the calculation of total peripheral resistance (TPR).

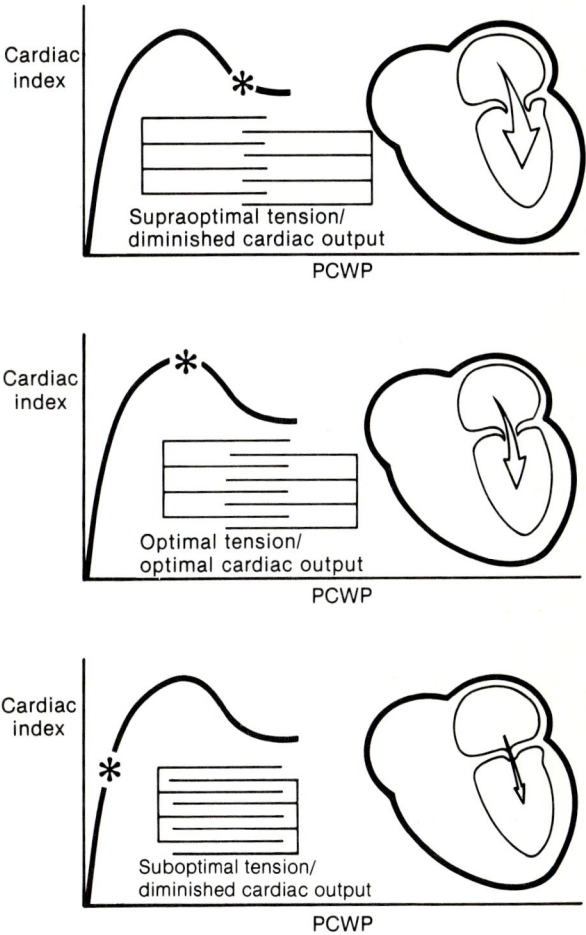

Fig. 20-2 Representation of Starling's Law.

Contractility: The ability of the heart to alter its contractile force and velocity INDEPENDENT of fiber length; in simple terms, it represents the intrinsic strength of the individual muscle fiber cells. A function of norepinephrine which is released by adrenergic nerve endings within the myocardial tissue in response to sympathetic stimulation.

BETA-1 RECEPTORS: Specific sites on the myocardial cell surface that stimulate the sinoatrial (SA) node to increase the heart rate and improve contractility. Activated by vasopressors.

BETA-2 RECEPTORS: Activated to varying degrees by vasopressors. Cause vasodilation of the peripheral vasculature and bronchodilation within the lung.

ALPHA RECEPTORS: Sympathetic receptors stimulated to varying degrees by vasopressors. Responsible for peripheral vasoconstriction and bronchoconstriction.

Vasopressors: A class of drugs that activates beta-1, beta-2, and alpha receptors (see the following table, "Receptor Actions"). Commonly used vasopressors include
- Dopamine
- Dobutamine
- Isoproterenol
- Norepinephrine

Receptor Actions

Receptor	Site	Action
Beta-1	Myocardium	Increased contractility
	SA Node	Increased heart rate
Beta-2	Arterioles	Vasodilation
Beta-2	Lungs	Bronchodilation
Alpha	Peripheral arterioles	Vasoconstriction

The following table describes the actions of these drugs on the three receptors.

Adrenergic Receptor Activity of Vasopressors

Drug	Effect on		
	Beta-1	Beta-2	Alpha
Dopamine	+ + + +	+ +	+ + + +
Dobutamine	+ + + +	+ +	+
Isoproterenol	+ + + +	+ + + +	0
Norepinephrine	+ + + +	0	+ + + +

CENTRAL VENOUS PRESSURES

The CVP catheter is one of two major devices used in cardiovascular instrumentation. The other major device, the Swan-Ganz catheter, is considered in the next section.

The CVP reading reflects the right ventricular filling pressure. This filling pressure defines the ability of the right heart to accept and pump blood.

Method

A 14 gauge intravenous catheter is inserted into the internal jugular or subclavian vein (see Chapter 4). A manometer that fluctuates with respiration provides the recordings. A chest x-ray is required to confirm the position of the catheter in the superior vena cava. The zero point for the manometer is usually 5 cm below the sternal notch, in the midaxillary line.

Implications

More important than the actual isolated measurements of pressure are the relative changes that take place as a patient's fluid or cardiac status changes. Therefore, serial readings are made. The implications of CVP readings are given in the following table.

Implications of CVP Readings

Reading (cm H_2O)	Description	Implications
<4	Low	Fluids may be pushed
4–10	Midrange	Not clinically useful
>10	High	Suspect CHF, cor pulmonale, or COPD

Limitations

- CVP does not reflect total blood volume or left ventricular function.
- CVP will be altered by changes in pulmonary artery resistance and compliance of the right ventricle.
- Use may be dramatically limited by changes in intrathoracic pressure such as those which occur during positive pressure ventilation, pneumothorax, or in the presence of tumors.
- CVP may be normal in the face of sepsis or hypovolemia accompanied by compromised myocardial function.
- Occult left ventricular failure may occur in the presence of normal CVP.
- Patients with COPD may require an elevated CVP to optimize their cardiac output.

Technical Tips

- If CVP readings do not fluctuate with respiration, the readings will be inaccurate.
- If possible, always remove the patient from the ventilator when taking a CVP reading.
- Have the head of the bed flat when taking readings so serial readings are comparable.
- Always use the same zero point (5 cm below the sternum in the midaxillary line) so that serial readings are comparable.
- Swan-Ganz catheter readings are far more accurate measurements of a patient's fluid and cardiac status than the CVP. CVPs are widely used because of the ease

of making these measurements as compared to using the Swan-Ganz catheter.

SWAN-GANZ CATHETER

The Swan-Ganz (SG) catheter is a device that allows the measurement of central circulatory parameters useful in the management of the acutely ill patient. Fluid balance, vascular tone (both pulmonary and peripheral), and the heart's pumping ability are all easily monitored with the SG catheter. The catheter actually passes through the heart; its distal end is in the pulmonary artery (Fig. 20-3). It allows the measurement of the pulmonary artery pressure (PAP), the pulmonary capillary wedge pressure (PCWP), the cardiac output, and the CVP.

Indications

- Acute heart failure
- Complex circulatory and fluid conditions (as in burn patients)
- Shock states
- Diagnosis of pericardial tamponade
- Intraoperative management (aneurysm repair, elderly patient undergoing major surgery)

Catheter Description

The most commonly used catheter has three lumens and a thermistor at the tip (Fig. 20-4).

Lumens

THE SQUARE WHITE PORT: For inflating the balloon.

THE DISTAL PORT (RED): Attached to a pressure transducer which provides continuous PAP tracings and allows intermittent PCWP monitoring. In addition, may be used to withdraw samples of mixed venous blood from the pulmonary artery.

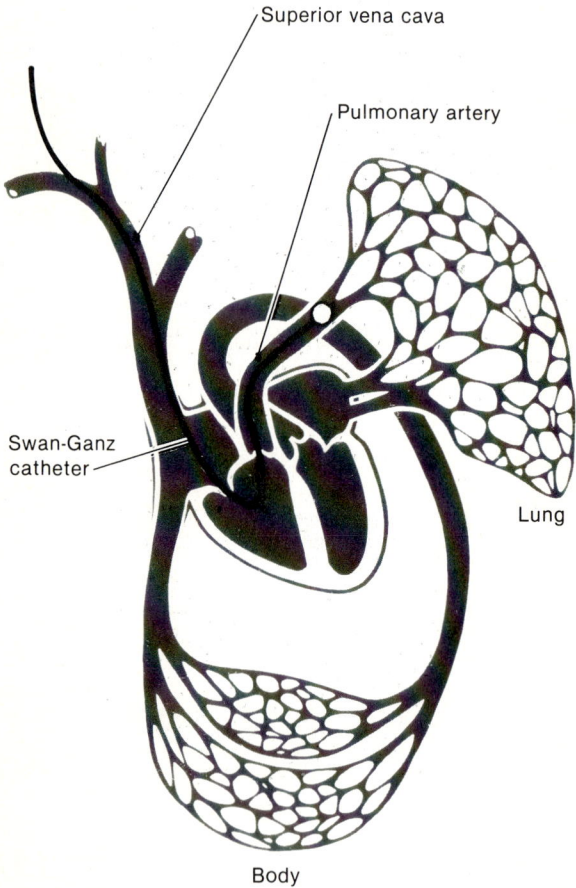

Fig. 20-3 Position of the Swan-Ganz catheter.

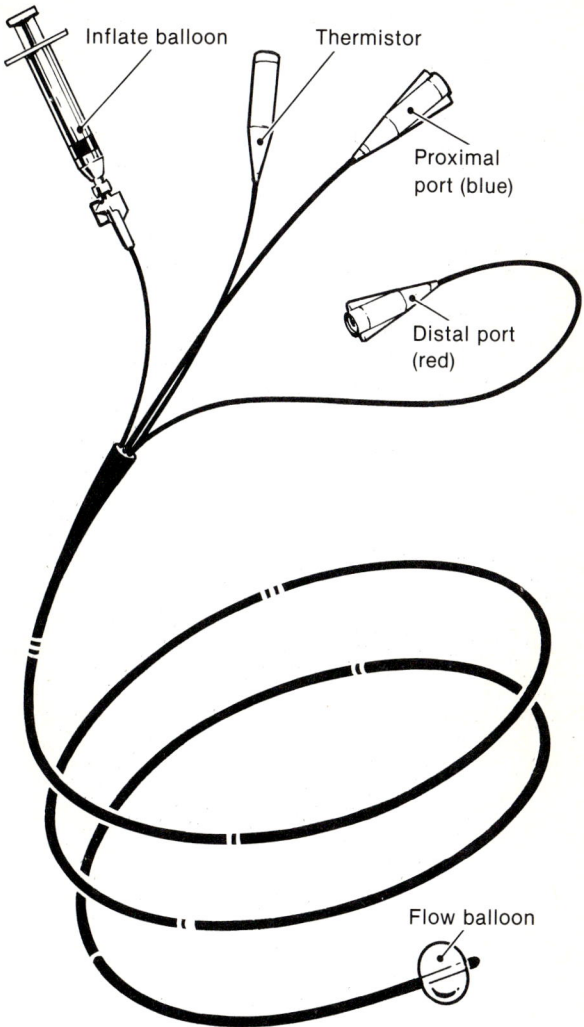

Fig. 20-4 The Swan-Ganz catheter.

THE PROXIMAL PORT (BLUE): Lies in the superior vena cava. May be used for the administration of routine IV fluids when not being employed in determinations of cardiac output.

THERMISTOR: A temperature sensor. Provides measurements used in the thermal dilution method for determination of the cardiac output. (This method is described later in this chapter.)

Procedure

The subclavian approach is the easiest, but any central venous access is acceptable.

1. Place a deep line as described in Chapter 4. Use a guide wire and a sheath and dilator to pass the catheter into the vein.

2. Advance the catheter under strict sterile technique into the right atrium.

3. At this point, the balloon at the tip (capacity 1.0 to 1.5 ml) may be partially inflated with air and allowed to flow with the blood through the right ventricle and out the pulmonary artery until it lodges in a secondary or tertiary branch. This is where it measures the PCWP.

4. Attach the catheter to a bedside monitor that displays the pressures at the tip of the catheter. See Fig. 20-5 for the normal pressures that can be seen as the catheter is advanced. In an adult, when the catheter is placed in the internal jugular or subclavian vein, the average distance to the pulmonary artery is 40 to 45 cm.

5. After insertion, take a chest x-ray to verify placement of the catheter and to check for a pneumothorax. A properly positioned SG catheter should lie just beyond the vertebral bodies.

Complications

- The patient must be constantly monitored via an ECG.

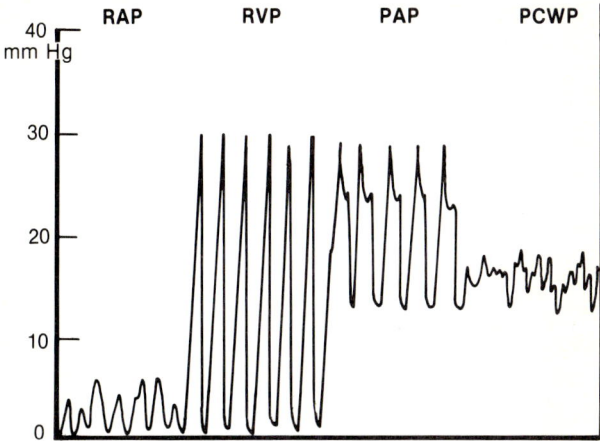

Fig. 20-5 Pressures seen as the Swan-Ganz catheter is advanced.

- Lidocaine and other resuscitation equipment must be readily available since arrhythmias frequently occur during insertion.
- Hazards of deep line placement including pneumothorax
- Chance of pulmonary infarction

Measurements

Pulmonary Artery Pressure (PAP): Measured when the Swan-Ganz catheter is in its resting position in the pulmonary artery (balloon deflated).

Pulmonary Capillary Wedge Pressure (PCWP): A reflection of the left atrial pressure (LAP). Measured when the balloon at the tip of the SG catheter is slowly inflated with air (maximum 1.5 ml) and carried out, by blood flow, into one of the smaller branches of the pulmonary artery. The balloon MUST be deflated after each PCWP measurement to avoid pulmonary infarction. In the absence of mitral valvular disease, correlates closely with the LAP and with the left ventricular end diastolic pressure (LVEDP).

Differential Diagnosis

The following two tables show normal Swan-Ganz measurements (see also Fig. 20-5) and the differential diagnosis based on these measurements.

Normal Swan-Ganz Measurements

Parameter	Range
Right atrial pressure (RAP)	1–7 mm Hg
Right ventricle pressure	
Systolic	15–25 mm Hg
Diastolic	0–8 mm Hg
PAP	
Systolic	15–25 mm Hg
Diastolic	8–15 mm Hg
Mean	10–20 mm Hg
PCWP ("wedge pressure")	6–12 mm Hg
Cardiac output	3.5–5.5 liters/min
Cardiac index	2.8–3.2 liters/min/m^2

Differential Diagnosis Based on Swan-Ganz Measurements

Measurement	Implications
PCWP	
6–12 mm Hg	Normal
Low	LVEDP is low and cardiac output can be increased by expanding circulating volume.
High	In the absence of severe underlying cardiac disease, signifies relative pulmonary congestion due to fluid overload or congestive failure.
PAP (DIASTOLIC) − PCWP	
5–10 mm Hg	Normal
>10 mm Hg	Suspect increased pulmonary vascular resistance (main cause, hypoxia), COPD, or adverse effects of ventilator PEEP.
RAP = PCWP	
	Biventricular compromise (cardiac tamponade, pericarditis)

Clinical Applications

The SG catheter allows the clinician to measure a patient's volume status and myocardial performance. As stated earlier, myocardial performance or cardiac output depends on stroke volume and heart rate. Stroke volume is, in turn, dependent on preload, afterload, and contractility.

Preload: Indicated by the PCWP, a reflection of left ventricular end diastolic volume. In simple terms, preload is the amount of blood in the heart prior to contraction. Consequently, preload represents the stretch placed on the individual myocardial cell. When the PCWP is optimized, myocardial performance is optimized according to the Starling curve.

CLINICAL IMPLICATIONS IN A HEALTHY HEART: A low PCWP means suboptimal myocardial muscle tension and, consequently, suboptimal myocardial performance. Cardiac output may be increased by the administration of fluids. The result is an increase in left ventricular end diastolic volume, an increase in myocardial muscle tension, and improved myocardial performance.

CLINICAL IMPLICATIONS IN A FAILING HEART: Long-standing myocardial disease may shift the Starling curve to the left. Consequently, a significantly elevated PCWP may be required to optimize myocardial performance. It is common for patients who have just undergone heart valve replacement to require a PCWP of 20 to 25 mm Hg to optimize cardiac output.

Afterload: Defined as the resistance to ventricular ejection. Measured clinically by the calculation of total peripheral resistance (TPR).

$$TPR = \frac{(MAP - CVP) \times 80}{Cardiac\ output\ (liters/min)}$$

Normal TPR = 900–1200 dynes/sec/cm^{-5}

INDICATIONS FOR AFTERLOAD REDUCTION
- Significant mitral regurgitation
- An increased PCWP in the face of an elevated TPR and a decreased cardiac index

Treatment: Nitroprusside (Nipride) is the drug of choice.

Contractility: The ability of the heart to alter its contractile force and velocity INDEPENDENT of fiber length. Difficult to measure clinically. Consequently, many critically ill patients receive digitalis empirically. Care should be maintained to insure normal levels of serum potassium prior to the administration of digitalis.

METABOLIC CAUSES FOR DEPRESSED CONTRACTILITY: Correctable causes include

- Hypoxia
- Acidosis (pH <7.3)
- Hypophosphatemia
- Adrenal insufficiency

The most common causes are hypoxia and acidosis. These must be corrected before inotropic therapy can be effective.

DETERMINATIONS OF CARDIAC OUTPUT

Arteriovenous Oxygen (A-VO$_2$) Difference

A reasonable estimate of cardiac index can be made on the basis of A-VO$_2$ difference. A-VO$_2$ difference is a measure of the difference between the oxygen content of arterial blood drawn from a peripheral artery and the oxygen content of mixed venous blood drawn from the distal lumen of the Swan-Ganz catheter.

A-VO$_2$ difference =

(Arterial O$_2$ content) − (Mixed venous O$_2$ content)

Concept: The A-VO$_2$ difference measures the extraction of oxygen by the tissues during a single transit time through the circulation.

IF CARDIAC OUTPUT IS LOW: Transit time is long and the tissues will extract large amounts of oxygen during a single circulation time. Thus, the oxygen content of mixed venous blood will be low and the A-VO$_2$ DIFFERENCE WILL BE LARGE.

IF CARDIAC OUTPUT IS HIGH: Circulation time is shorter and the amount of oxygen extracted will be low. Consequently, the A-VO$_2$ DIFFERENCE WILL BE LOW.

IN GENERAL: A-VO$_2$ difference is inversely proportional to cardiac output. Therefore, the approximations shown in the following table can be made.

Correlation Between A-VO$_2$ Difference and Cardiac Index

A-VO$_2$ Difference (vol %)	Cardiac Index* (liters/min/m^2)
>6	<2
4–5	3–4
<3	>5

*Cardiac Index = Cardiac output/Body surface area.

OXYGEN CARRYING CAPACITY: Hemoglobin carries 99% of the oxygen found in blood under standard conditions. If hemoglobin concentration is low, obviously less O$_2$ can be transported.

Saturation of hemoglobin reflects the percentage of hemoglobin molecules that are carrying oxygen molecules. Saturation is a function of peripheral arterial pO$_2$ as measured by routine blood gas determinations.

Conversion Factor: Each gram of hemoglobin can combine with 1.34 ml oxygen.

Calculation of A-VO$_2$ Difference

1. Place the patient on 100% O_2 for 15 minutes.

2. Draw a sample of heparinized peripheral arterial blood.

3. Draw a sample of heparinized mixed venous blood from the distal lumen of the Swan-Ganz catheter.

4. Obtain the hemoglobin concentration.

5. Calculate the oxygen content for both blood samples according to the following formula:

   O_2 content = Hgb × Saturation × Conversion factor

6. Calculate the A-VO$_2$ difference.

   Example

   Arterial O_2 content = 10.0 × 0.96 × 1.34 = 12.9

Mixed venous O_2 content = 10.0 × 0.40 × 1.34 = <u>5.4</u>

A-VO$_2$ difference = 12.9 − 5.4 = 7.5

From the previous table, an A-VO$_2$ difference of 7.5 corresponds to a cardiac index of <2 liter/min/m^2.

Thermal Dilution Technique

The thermal dilution technique is the most accurate way of calculating cardiac output. However, it is somewhat tedious and cannot be performed on an hour-to-hour basis. In addition, it requires that an expensive cardiac output computer be available.

Technique: A measured amount of iced saline (usually 10 ml) is injected into the proximal port of the Swan-Ganz catheter, and the temperature-sensitive thermistor located at the distal end of the pulmonary artery senses the temperature change in the surrounding blood. The cardiac output computer then integrates the magnitude and rate of change in temperature and calculates the cardiac output.

SHOCK

Shock is defined as tissue or organ blood flow that is inadequate to maintain normal cellular activities.

Types of Shock

Shock can be divided into four major classes:

- Oligemic (blood loss)
- Cardiogenic
- Septic
- Neurogenic

Oligemic: Characterized by a low cardiac output, a low PCWP, and an elevated TPR.

THERAPY: Should be directed towards volume replacement to improve myocardial performance.

Cardiogenic: Characterized by a low cardiac output, a high PCWP, and an elevated TPR. The basic defect is one of myocardial performance.

THERAPY: Should be aimed at increasing contractility while at the same time decreasing TPR.

Septic: Characterized by a high cardiac output, a low PCWP, and a low TPR.

THERAPY: Should be aimed at increasing PCWP and increasing TPR simultaneously.

Neurogenic: Characterized by a low cardiac output, a low PCWP, and a low TPR.

THERAPY: Should be aimed at increasing TPR.

CLINICAL PULMONARY PHYSIOLOGY

The goal of managing any critically ill patient is to optimize both oxygenation and tissue perfusion. Pulmonary and cardiovascular physiology are intimately interwoven to achieve this goal. It does little good to optimize cardiovascular function if, because of poor pulmonary function, there is no oxygen for the hemoglobin to transport. Ventilation refers to the mechanical movement of air in and out of the respiratory system. Oxygenation refers to the diffusion of oxygen from the alveoli to the blood in the pulmonary capillaries and from there to the tissues. Fig. 20-6 shows ventilation and oxygenation in typical alveoli.

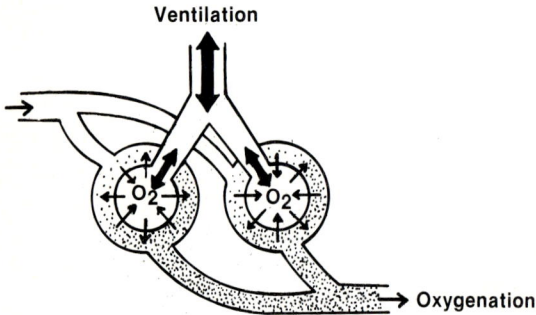

Fig. 20-6 Ventilation and oxygenation in typical alveoli.

Ventilation

The most important parameters of ventilation as depicted in Fig. 20-7 are

- Vital capacity

- Tidal volume

- Functional residual capacity

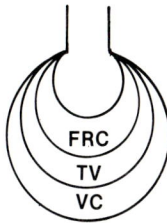

Fig. 20-7 Parameters of ventilation.

Vital Capacity (VC): The volume of gas moved in and out of the lungs during maximal inspiration followed by maximal expiration (Fig. 20-8). Frequently used in determining whether or not a patient can successfully be weaned from the ventilator. Normal vital capacity is 65–75 ml/kg. A vital capacity of <15 ml/kg is an indication for ventilator support.

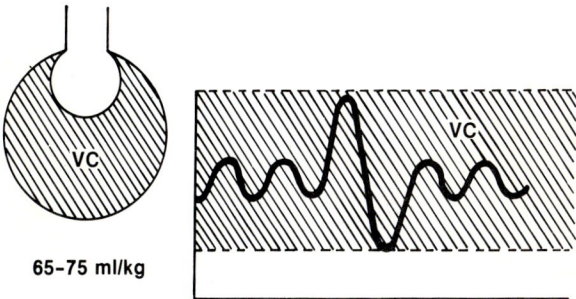

65–75 ml/kg

Fig. 20-8 Vital capacity.

Tidal Volume (TV): The total volume, both inspiration and expiration, of each breath (Fig. 20-9). Called tidal volume because, like the tide, the inspired gas moves back and forth over the same path. In normal individuals at rest, the tidal volume is 8–10 ml/kg. Postoperative patients who require ventilator support need larger tidal volumes of approximately 10–15 ml/kg.

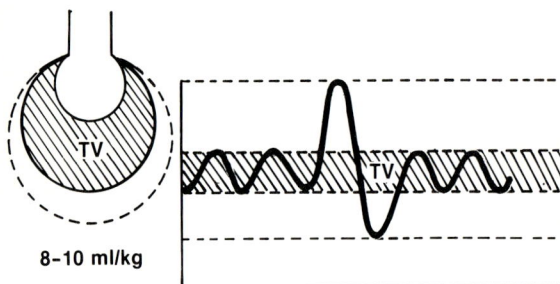

Fig. 20-9   Tidal volume.

Residual Volume (RV):   The volume of gas that remains in the lung even after maximal expiratory effort.

Functional Residual Capacity (FRC):   The gas remaining in the lung following normal expiration (tidal volume). Acts as a buffer against extreme changes in alveolar pO_2 and consequent dramatic changes in arterial pO_2 with each breath (Fig. 20-10).

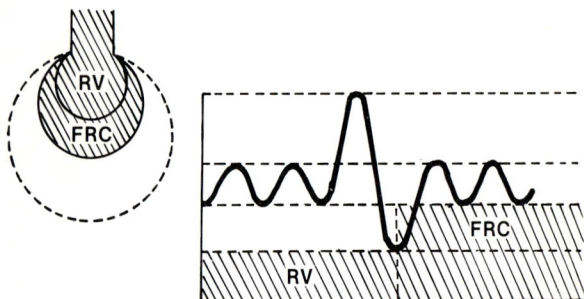

Fig. 20-10   Functional residual capacity.

Critical Closing Volume (CCV):   An expression of the tendency of alveoli to close at the end of expiration. As long as FRC is greater than the CCV, there is little tendency for alveolar collapse (Figure 20-11).

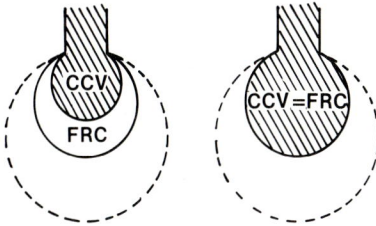

Fig. 20-11   FRC and critical closing volume.

However, when CCV exceeds FRC, alveolar collapse occurs, blood is shunted around the nonventilated alveolus, and hypoxia ensues (Fig. 20-12).

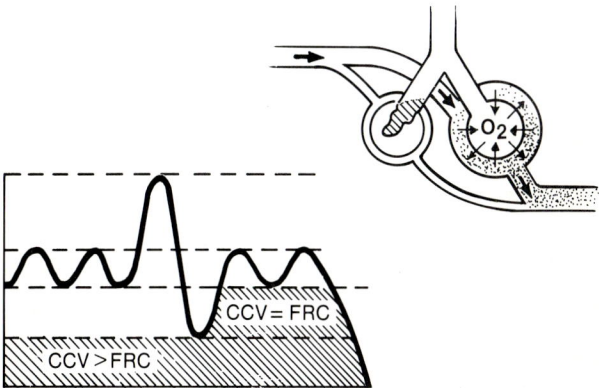

Fig. 20-12   Alveolar collapse when CCV exceeds FRC.

Positive End Expiratory Pressure (PEEP):   Commonplace in the management of critically ill patients. Improves alveolar ventilation, decreases the shunt fraction, and, consequently, improves hypoxia. The effect of PEEP is to increase FRC (Fig. 20-13). This increase is achieved by preventing alveolar collapse during expiration and by increasing the intra-alveolar pressure.

Note: Residual volume, FRC, and CCV are not bedside measurements. They are, however, essential concepts in understanding the use of PEEP.

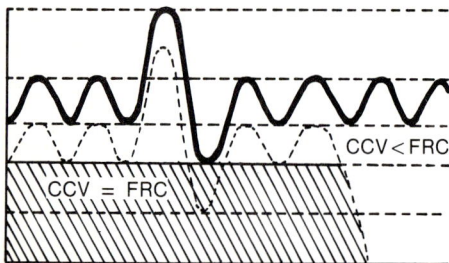

Fig. 20-13   The effect of PEEP is to increase the FRC.

Compliance: Measured at the bedside. A reflection of FRC and CCV. Relates the CHANGE in lung volume and the CHANGE in pressure required to produce the volume change.

$$\text{Compliance} = dV/dP$$

In concept, compliance reflects the ease with which ventilatory work may be performed (Fig. 20-14). It is a function of tissue elasticity and surface tension. As the lung becomes stiffer or less elastic, compliance decreases and ventilation is adversely affected.

MEASURING COMPLIANCE: Compliance is determined clinically by measuring tidal volume and dividing it by the peak inspiratory pressure read from the ventilator pressure gauge:

$$\text{Compliance} = \frac{\text{Tidal volume}}{(\text{Peak inspiratory pressure}) - (\text{PEEP})}$$

$$\text{Normal} = >100 \text{ ml/cm } H_2O$$

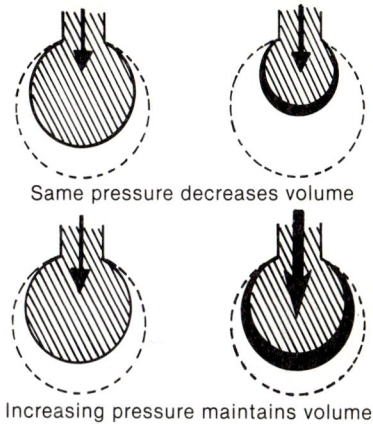

Same pressure decreases volume

Increasing pressure maintains volume

Fig. 20-14 Concept of compliance.

Note: PEEP may be increased up to 10 cm H_2O simply by following compliance. As long as the compliance remains stable, there is little chance of the unrecognized complications of PEEP occurring.

Oxygenation

Oxygenation is the process of transporting oxygen from the alveolus across the capillary membrane into the pulmonary circulation and subsequently distributing that oxygen to the body's tissues.

Common tests for the assessment of oxygenation include

- Calculation of alveolar to arterial gradient

- Calculation of arterial oxygen content

- Calculation of right to left shunt fraction (Qs/Qt)

Alveolar to Arterial Gradient: (A-a gradient or A-aDO$_2$) Provides an assessment of alveolar-capillary gas exchange.

CALCULATING THE A-a GRADIENT: To calculate the alveolar to arterial gradient one must determine

- Alveolar pO_2 (pAO_2)
- Arterial pO_2 (paO_2)

1. Place the patient on 100% oxygen (FIO_2) for 20 minutes.

2. Then obtain a peripheral arterial blood gas.

3. Calculate the alveolar pO_2. After breathing 100% oxygen for 20 minutes the only gases other than oxygen within the alveoli are H_2O and excreted CO_2 from tissue metabolism. Thus, the partial pressure of oxygen within the alveoli is easily calculated. The alveolar pO_2 equals

760	Barometric pressure (in torr)
-47	Partial pressure H_2O
-40	pCO_2 from peripheral sample
673	Alveolar pO_2 (pAO_2)

4. Subtract the peripheral arterial oxygen content (paO_2) from the alveolar pO_2 (pAO_2).

Example

Alveolar pO_2 =		673
Peripheral pO_2 =		-200
A-a gradient =		473

Rule: The larger the gradient, the more serious the degree of respiratory compromise. Any A-a gradient greater than 400 indicates severe respiratory distress. (Norm, 20–65)

Shunt Fraction: In clinical practice the A-a gradient is calculated primarily because it is a component of the shunt fraction equation. The shunt fraction (normal, <5%) is the ratio of ventilated alveoli to perfused pulmonary capillaries. In the normal state there is equality between the volume of lung ventilation and the volume of pulmonary capillary blood flow (Fig. 20-15). Alterations in these ventilation-perfusion relationships result from two sources:

- Relative obstruction of alveolar ventilation
- Relative obstruction of pulmonary blood flow

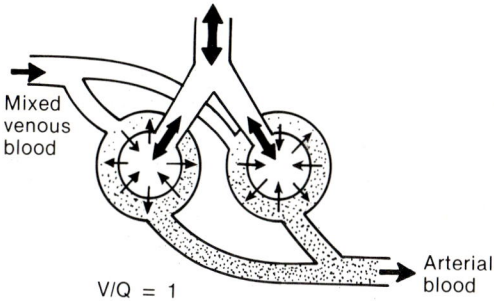

Fig. 20-15   Ventilation-perfusion ratio.

PERFUSION GREATER THAN VENTILATION: Fig. 20-16 depicts the extreme situation where alveolus A receives no ventilation but perfusion continues. Therefore, a complete pulmonary A-V shunt exists with respect to that alveolus.

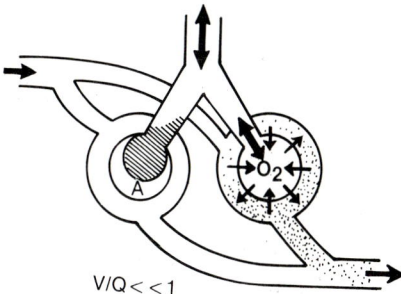

Fig. 20-16   Perfusion greater than ventilation.

VENTILATION GREATER THAN PERFUSION: Fig. 20-17 depicts uniform ventilation to A and B but no blood flow to alveolus A. This situation will cause an increase in physiological dead space.

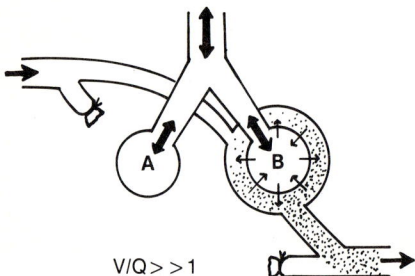

V/Q >> 1

Fig. 20-17 Ventilation greater than perfusion.

COMPENSATION MECHANISM: Fig. 20-18 represents the compensatory change that occurs when an alveolus is partially occluded. Blood flow is preferentially shunted to other, more efficiently ventilated alveolar units.

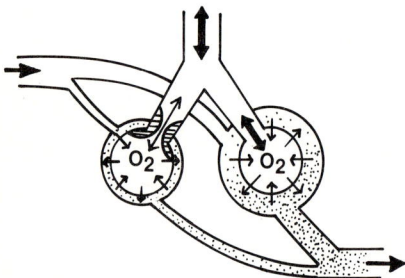

Fig. 20-18 Compensation for ventilation-perfusion mismatching.

PRINCIPLE: It is important to recognize that at any given time, even in the normal state, gradations of all these situations exist simultaneously within the lung. The normal shunt fraction is approximately 5%. Alterations in either ventilation or perfusion can seriously effect oxygenation.

Decreased Ventilation: Associated factors are

- Adult respiratory distress syndrome (ARDS)
- Pulmonary edema
- Atelectasis

Decreased Perfusion: Associated factors are

- Massive pulmonary embolus
- Continued micro pulmonary embolization

CALCULATION OF SHUNT FRACTION: Q is the mathematical symbol for flow. Therefore Qs is the symbol for the amount of flow through the shunt. Qs is defined as that portion of the cardiac output that does not participate in gas exchange, i.e., the volume of blood which is shunted past nonventilated alveoli. Qt is the symbol for total cardiac output. Therefore, the volume of blood shunted past nonventilated alveoli divided by the total cardiac output (shunted plus nonshunted blood) is Qs/Qt (Fig. 20-19).

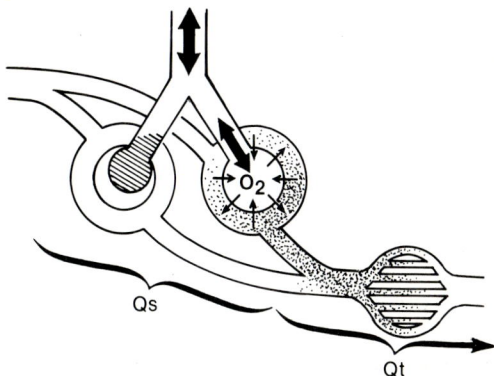

Fig. 20-19   Representation of shunt fraction.

Shunt fraction is defined as

$$\frac{Qs}{Qt} = \frac{(\text{A-a gradient}) \times (0.003)}{(\text{A-VO}_2 \text{ difference}) + (\text{A-a gradient} \times 0.003)}$$

where 0.003 is the solubility coefficient for oxygen dissolved in plasma.

Note: The shunt fraction is a difficult equation to master. However, if you break it into its component parts, alveolar capillary gas exchange as reflected by the A-a gradient and the cardiac output as reflected by A-VO$_2$ difference, the concept becomes easier to deal with.

Example: Employing the previous examples of an A-a gradient of 473 and an A-VO$_2$ difference of 7.5, the shunt fraction is

$$\frac{Qs}{Qt} = \frac{473 \times 0.003}{7.5 + (473 \times 0.003)}$$

This calculates out to a shunt fraction of approximately 16%.

Note: A rising shunt fraction is usually associated with progressive adult respiratory distress syndrome (ARDS). This is an indication for increasing PEEP.

Summary of Pulmonary and Hemodynamic Physiology

As the calculation of the shunt fraction implies, pulmonary and cardiovascular mechanics are intimately intertwined and must be considered as a complete unit. Advantageous changes in one parameter may result in disastrous changes in another parameter.

The absolute value of these numbers is not as important as the TREND of the numbers. If the trend is deteriorating, more aggressive intervention is indicated.

INDICATIONS FOR INTUBATION

The decision to intubate a patient for prolonged ventilator support is one of the most difficult decisions for clinicians to make. An endotracheal tube is extremely uncomfortable, and patients often beg the physician not to place them on the ventilator. In addition, it is easy for the physician to be lulled into a false sense of security by marginal blood gases. The following are some common indications for respirator support:

- Respiratory failure: (See the following table)

- Massive resuscitation in the face of multiple system trauma

- Suspected or impending ARDS

- Significant chest trauma (flail chest, crushed chest)

- Severe pulmonary edema

Indications for intubation are based primarily on clinical judgment. If the patient's respiratory work is increasing, the patient should be intubated electively and under controlled circumstances.

Indicators of Respiratory Failure

Condition	Normal Range (Adults)
Tachypnea >35 breaths/min	10–20
Vital capacity <15 ml/kg	40–70
Inspiratory force < −25 cm H_2O	> −50 to −100
paO_2 <70 mm Hg on 50% mask	80–100 on room air
$paCO_2$ >60 mm Hg	35–45
pH <7.25	7.38–7.42
A-a gradient >400 torr (on 100% oxygen)	20–65 torr

MECHANICAL VENTILATORS

Classes of Ventilators

Pressure Limited: Ventilator will deliver a volume of air until a preset pressure is reached. Used in IPPB and in some neonatal ventilators. Not generally used to ventilate patients because changes in airway pressure and in lung and chest wall compliance may result in an inadequate minute ventilation.

Volume Limited: A preset volume of air is delivered no matter what the opposing pressure is. The most commonly used type (Bennett MA-1, Bear, etc.).

Ventilator Modes

Intermittent Mandatory Ventilation (IMV): The respirator delivers a set number of breaths each minute and allows the patient to breathe in between. Allows the patient to use his own muscles to breathe and is excellent for weaning a patient. As the ventilator rate decreases progressively, the patient assumes more of the work of breathing.

Synchronous IMV (SIMV): Same as IMV, except the ventilator will sense when the patient is taking a breath and will not deliver the mandatory breath until after the patient's own breath is completed.

Controlled: Patient gets a breath only when it is delivered by the machine. He cannot initiate any of his own breaths. Used on patients who are intentionally paralyzed by drugs.

Assist Controlled: Patient sets his own breathing rate, but if he should become apneic, the machine will take over at a specified rate.

Assisted: Patient gets an assisted breath each time he initiates one.

Continuous Positive Airway Pressure (CPAP): Very similar to PEEP, except that the patient is doing all the breathing on his own. The ventilator is not cycling. The patient should be intubated. Often used as a last step before extubating a patient. Special CPAP face masks are available at some centers.

Sighs: Periodic large tidal volumes that help decrease atelectasis (usually 2X tidal volume).

VENTILATOR MANAGEMENT

For purposes of this discussion, ventilator management consists of

- Routine ventilator orders
- Ventilator setting changes
- Weaning from the respirator

The critical factor in monitoring the patient on the ventilator is the peripheral arterial pO_2. If the pO_2 is <60 or if the pO_2 is steadily deteriorating, something needs to be done.

Ventilator Orders

Once the decision has been made to place a patient on a ventilator, the patient must be intubated with an appropriate endotracheal tube (see Chapter 21) and the following orders written:

- FIO_2 40% to 100%
- Rate 8–12/min
- Tidal volume 10–15 ml/kg
- Mode (assist control, IMV)
- PEEP (0 to 10 or higher, if needed)

Note: The pO_2 tells you intervention is required. Swan-Ganz readings, compliance, and shunt calculations will help you decide what needs to be done.

Ventilator Setting Changes

There are three respiratory parameters that can be changed to improve ventilation and oxygenation:

- FIO_2
- Minute volume (tidal volume × rate)
- PEEP

FIO_2:   Because of the danger of oxygen toxicity, an FIO_2 >60% is to be avoided.

Minute Volume: Increased if the patient's peripheral arterial pO_2 continues to deteriorate or is <60. Usually done by increasing tidal volume to about 950 ml in the adult. Changes in rate are usually limited by a decrease in pCO_2 with a resultant respiratory alkalosis.

PEEP: Added if pO_2 still does not improve. Five cm of PEEP is considered physiological and often is enough to stabilize the pO_2. If the patient continues to deteriorate, PEEP is added in 2.5 cm increments until the 10 cm level is attained. Serial measurements of compliance are made to confirm improvement in pulmonary mechanics.

   HIGH DOSE PEEP: If additional PEEP is required, a Swan-Ganz catheter is essential to monitor cardiac output and shunt fraction. It should be noted that past a certain point increases in PEEP will increase intrathoracic pressure to the point where venous return is impaired. Consequently, cardiac output will fall. This point defines the maximum level of PEEP and may vary considerably from patient to patient or for the same patient over a period of time.

   PEEP SIDE EFFECTS

- Decreased cardiac output
- Barotrauma (pneumothorax, alveolar rupture, pneumomediastinum)

Principles

In summary, the application of respiratory and cardio-vascular physiology to critically ill patients includes the following principles:

- If the patient is deteriorating, intervene.
- Changes in FIO_2 are limited by oxygen toxicity.
- Changes in minute volume are limited by a decrease in pCO_2 with resultant alkalosis.
- Changes in PEEP are limited by decreases in cardiac output.

Ventilator Weaning

Prior to the successful weaning of a patient from the ventilator, one must assess the patient's pulmonary mechanics and oxygenation.

Pulmonary Mechanics: Provide useful information regarding a patient's ability to perform the work of respiration. Routine pulmonary mechanics consist of

- Vital capacity
- Tidal volume
- Lung compliance
- Inspiratory force

INSPIRATORY FORCE: The maximum subatmospheric pressure that can be exerted against a completely closed airway. A function of respiratory muscle strength. An inspiratory force between 0 and -25 would indicate that the patient is incapable of generating adequate inspiratory effort to allow extubation.

Criteria for Weaning: Based on the assessment of pulmonary mechanics and of oxygenation. Shown in the following table.

Criteria for Weaning

Parameter	Value
PULMONARY MECHANICS	
Vital capacity	>10–15 ml/kg
Resting minute ventilation (tidal volume × rate)	>10 liters/min
Inspiratory forces	> − 25 cm H_2O
OXYGENATION	
A-a gradient	<300–500 torr
Shunt fraction	<15%
pO_2 (on 40% FIO_2)	>70 mm Hg
pCO_2	<55 mm Hg

Checklist for Weaning

- Level of consciousness stable or improving
- Stable vital signs
- Respiratory rate <25
- Blood gases in the vicinity of
  paO_2 >70 mm Hg
  $paCO_2$ <55 mm Hg
  pH >7.35
- VC >15 ml/kg
- TV in adults (50 to 70 kg) >400 ml
- Inspiratory force >20 to 30 cm H_2O

IMV Weaning: Modern respirators are designed to facilitate weaning. Once the preceding criteria have been met, most employ the principle of intermittent mandatory ventilation (IMV).

IMV allows the patient to breathe spontaneously between preset ventilator cycles. The spontaneous breath maintains the same FIO_2 and PEEP as the mandatory cycles.

ORDER OF WEANING: The following steps are taken routinely:

1. Sequentially reduce FIO_2 by 10% until a FIO_2 of 40% is tolerated.

2. Sequentially reduce the IMV rate by 2 until a level of 4–6 breaths/min is achieved.

3. Sequentially reduce PEEP by 2.5 cm H_2O until level of 5 cm H_2O is achieved.

ESSENTIAL TIPS

- Check arterial blood gas (ABG) 30 minutes after each ventilator change.
- A pO_2 <60 requires return to previous levels of respiratory support.
- A pO_2 of 60 to 70 requires a hold at the current level of respiratory support.
- A pO_2 >70 allows for progression of weaning.
- Do NOT change more than one ventilator parameter at a time.

T PIECE: Patients without COPD are usually capable of going from IMV-4, FIO_2 40%, and PEEP of 5 cm H_2O to a "T" piece. The "T" piece provides humidified air (FIO_2 40%) but no other respiratory support. The "T" piece fits on the endotracheal tube. The ventilator remains at the bedside in case respiratory support needs to be restarted. Some employ CPAP of 5 cm for this procedure.

EXTUBATION: A patient who is able to maintain a pO_2 >70, a pCO_2 <45, and a respiratory rate <25 for one to two hours on a "T" piece is ready for extubation.

1. Remove the "T" piece.

2. Suction the patient's endotracheal tube and oral pharynx.

3. Deflate the endotracheal balloon.

4. Have the patient take a deep breath.

5. As the patient expires forcefully, remove the tube.

6. Apply 40% face mask.

7. Check postextubation blood gases.

ADULT RESPIRATORY DISTRESS SYNDROME

ARDS, also called "wet lung" or "shock lung," is respiratory failure associated with acute pulmonary injury manifested by marked respiratory distress and hypoxia.

There are two membrane systems within the lung:

- The pulmonary capillary membrane
- The alveolar membrane

Etiology

The etiology of ARDS is multifactorial. There are three primary mechanisms of injury:

- Substances that increase pulmonary vascular resistance
- Substances directly toxic to the pulmonary capillary membrane
- Substances directly toxic to the alveolar membrane

Increased Pulmonary Vascular Resistance: Neurogenic pulmonary edema is caused by a dramatic increase in pulmonary capillary hydrostatic pressure. This increase forces fluid across the capillary membrane and results in interstitial and then alveolar edema.

Permeability Edema: Circulating toxic substances within the bloodstream can cause the pulmonary capillary membrane to become leaky and allow extravasation of protein into the interstitial space. This extravasation increases the interstitial hydrostatic pressure and eventually results in injury to the alveolar membrane. At this point, fluid and protein migrate into the alveolar space and directly impede oxygen exchange. Sepsis is the primary etiology.

Injury to the Alveolar Membrane: Substances directly toxic to the alveolar membrane include

- Heat and smoke
- High doses of oxygen ($>60\%$ FIO_2)
- Aspiration

Treatment

The cardinal principle of treatment of ARDS is anticipation of the disease process. At that time, the patient should be intubated and PEEP should be started.

Clinical Correlations: ARDS should be anticipated in the following clinical situations:

- Severe head injury
- Severe trauma with prolonged hypotension
- Massive fluid resuscitation
- Sepsis
- Hemorrhagic pancreatitis
- Burn of the respiratory tract or aspiration
- Severe chest contusion

Steroids: MAY be helpful if given in massive doses very early in the following situations:

- Aspiration
- Septic ARDS

21
Emergencies

Basic Cardiopulmonary Resuscitation
Advanced Cardiac Life Support
Other Common Emergencies

BASIC CARDIOPULMONARY RESUSCITATION

In basic cardiopulmonary resuscitation (CPR), remember the ABCDs:

- Airway
- Breathing
- Circulation
- Drugs (See the next section, Advanced Cardiac Life Support.)

In Adults

1. Establish responsiveness (shake and shout); call out for help.

2. Open the airway (head tilt easiest).

The sections on basic CPR and ACLS are based on Standards and guidelines for cardiopulmonary resuscitation (CPR) and emergency cardiac care (ECC). *JAMA* **244**:511–512 (suppl), 1980.

3. Establish breathlessness (look, listen, and feel for air movement).

4. Remove airway obstruction, if present (back blows, abdominal thrusts).

5. Begin rescue breathing (four quick breaths, head tilted, nose pinched).

6. Check carotid pulse for 5 to 10 seconds to evaluate circulation.

7. If no pulse, begin cardiac compression (lower one-half of sternum, compress 1½ to 2 inches).

then

One-Man CPR

8. Continue with 15 compressions to two breaths (4 cycles/min).

9. Compress at a rate of 80/min ("1 and 2 and 3 and 4 and . . .").

or

Two-Man CPR

8. Continue with five compressions to one breath (12 cycles/min).

9. Compress at a rate of 60/min ("1 one thousand, 2 one thousand . . .").

10. Pause after one minute to evaluate pulse and respiration.

In Children

1.–6. Same as in adults, except use less force for breathing.

7. Compress lower one-half of sternum with heel of only one hand.

8. Compress 1 to 1½ inches at a rate of 80/min ("1 and 2 and 3 and . . .").

In Infants

Sequence (1 to 7) is the same as for adults except

1. Use only a "puff" of air from the cheeks to ventilate four times.

2. Palpate brachial pulse to evaluate circulation.

3. Use only two fingers to compress the middle of the sternum.

4. Compress ½ to 1 inch at a rate of 80–100/min.

5. Use a ratio of one breath to five compressions.

In Neonates

1. Ventilate at a rate of 30–40 puffs/min.

2. If a heart rate <80 is not restored with oxygen, begin CPR.

3. Use the two-handed chest-wrap-around method; compress with thumbs in the midsternum.

4. Compress ½ to ¾ inch at a rate of 100/min.

ADVANCED CARDIAC LIFE SUPPORT

Advanced cardiac life support (ACLS) includes the use of drugs, defibrillation, intubation, and military (medical) antishock trousers (MAST).

Basic Protocol

1. Begin basic CPR.

2. Determine circumstances, past history, current medications.

3. Begin IV and intubate.

4. Determine rhythms either on defibrillator paddles or on a monitor.

5. Begin appropriate drug therapy.

6. Determine blood gas as soon as possible.

Drugs

Atropine: Decreases vagal tone to increase heart rate (parasympatholytic)

   USES: Sinus bradycardia, high degree AV block

   DOSAGE: 0.5 mg IV q15min up to a total of 2.0 mg

Bretylium (Bretylol)

   USES: Ventricular fibrillation and ventricular tachycardia refractory to lidocaine, procainamide, and countershock

   DOSAGE
   - Ventricular tachycardia: 5–10 mg/kg IV over 10 minutes, then 1–2 mg/min drip
   - Ventricular fibrillaltion: 5–10 mg/kg bolus q15min, maximum 30 mg/kg

Calcium: Increases contractility, increases excitability

   USES: Asystole, electromechanical dissociation

   DOSAGE
   - Calcium chloride: 5–7 mg/kg q10min (500 mg approximate) or 5 ml of a 10% solution
   - Calcium gluconate: 10 ml of a 10% solution, about 1 gm

Dobutamine (Dobutrex): Direct beta agonist, increases cardiac output, little direct effect on blood pressure

USES: Pump failure

DOSAGE: 2.5–10.0 μg/kg/min (similar to dopamine), arrhythmias with doses >20 μg/kg/min

Dopamine (Intropin): Alpha, beta, and dopaminergic agonist, dose related

- 2–10 μg/kg/min (beta): Increases cardiac output, renal perfusion
- 10–20 μg/kg/min (alpha): Peripheral vasoconstriction, increases blood pressure
- >20 μg/kg/min: Peripheral and renal vasoconstriction

USES: Support cardiac output, blood pressure, and renal perfusion in shock states

DOSAGE: 1 amp (200 mg) in 250 ml to give 800 μg/ml; start at 2–5 μg/kg/min, about 20 microdrops/min average in adults; titrate to effect

Epinephrine: Alpha and beta agonist; increases heart rate, contractility, total peripheral resistance, automaticity

USES: Aystole, ventricular fibrillation (changes fine fibrillation to coarse fibrillation which is easier to defibrillate)

DOSAGE: 0.5 to 1.0 mg (5 to 10 ml of 1:10,000) IV q5min (can also be given via intracardiac or endobronchial routes)

Furosemide (Lasix): Loop diuretic and venodilator

USES: Acute pulmonary edema

DOSAGE: 0.5–1.9 mg/kg IV (onset 5 minutes, peak action in 30 minutes)

Isoproterenol (Isuprel): Pure beta agonist; increases heart rate, contractility, output

USES: Asystole, symptomatic heart block, bradycardia

DOSAGE: 1 mg in 250 ml to give 4 μg/ml, titrate to effect (2-20 μg/min)

Lidocaine (Xylocaine): Decreases automaticity, raises ventricular fibrillation threshold

USES: Suppress PVCs (>5/min or any PVCs after an acute myocardial infarction), ventricular tachycardia, ventricular fibrillation

DOSAGE: 1 mg/kg (50 to 100 mg) bolus, then 4 mg/min IV drip (to mix the drip, use 1 gm in 250 ml to give 4 mg/ml)

Procainamide (Pronestyl): Decreases cardiac excitability, slows conduction

USES: Suppress ventricular ectopics when lidocaine ineffective

DOSAGE: 100 mg IV at rate of 20 mg/min until dysrhythmia disappears or hypotension ensues (maximum dose 1 gm), then 1-4 mg/min drip (set up drip as for lidocaine)

Propranolol (Inderal): Beta blocker (caution in patients with COPD, wheezing, heart failure)

USES: Control of recurrent ventricular and atrial tachydysrhythmia

DOSAGE: 1 mg IV q5min up to 5 mg total

Sodium Bicarbonate

USES: Combat metabolic acidosis

DOSAGE: Based on blood gas values or empirically, 1 mEq/kg IV (50 to 100 mEq or 1 to 2 amps), then ½ the initial dose q10min

The following table gives the pediatric doses of ACLS drugs.

Pediatric Doses of ACLS Drugs

Drug	Dose
Atropine	0.01–0.02 mg/kg (minimum 0.1 mg)
Calcium Chloride	20 mg/kg/dose
Dopamine	As in adults
Epinephrine	0.1 ml/kg of a 1:10,000 solution
Furosemide	1 mg/kg/dose
Isoproterenol	Mix as in adults, start at 0.1 μg/kg/min, titrate to effect
Lidocaine	1 mg/kg/dose, IV drip at 30 μg/kg/min
Sodium Bicarbonate	1–2 mEq/kg/dose or 0.3 $\times$ kg $\times$ base deficit

Defibrillation

1. Use as soon as possible in ventricular fibrillation.

2. Occasionally, use if difficult to differentiate fine ventricular fibrillation from asystole.

3. If myocardium is anoxic or acidotic, use basic CPR and bicarbonate first, then defibrillate.

Energy Levels: (watt-second = joule)

1. Initially use 200 to 300 joules; if unsuccessful, repeat at same level.

2. If still no response, continue CPR, give epinephrine and bicarbonate, and repeat at full output (400 joules).

3. If the patient weighs <50 kg, begin at 2 joules/kg and advance to a maximum of 6 joules/kg.

Cardioversion: Used for ventricular tachycardia, atrial fibrillation with rapid ventricular response; an attempt to slow the heart or convert rhythm; procedure like defibrillation EXCEPT

1. USE LOW ENERGY LEVELS (20 to 50 joules).

2. KEEP THE SYNCHRONIZER SWITCH ON (prevents shocking during vulnerable part of QRS complex when shock may cause ventricular fibrillation, so-called "R on T phenomenon").

Defibrillation Procedure

1. Use paste or pads on skin.

2. Charge defibrillator as for cardioversion, SYNCHRONIZATION SWITCH OFF (if ON, the defibrillator may not fire).

3. Place paddles as directed on the handles: one at the right upper sternum and one at the left anterior axillary line (apex).

4. Apply paddles with firm pressure.

5. Shout, "clear area!" and make sure no one is touching the patient or bed.

6. Press both paddle buttons simultaneously to fire the unit, and observe for any change in the dysrhythmia.

Intubation

1. Fill the cuff with 5 to 10 ml of air or until the cuff no longer leaks air around it.

2. Choose the size (approximate) of the endotracheal tubes according to the following table.

Approximate Sizes for Endotracheal Tubes

Patient	Internal Diameter (mm) of Tube
Newborn	3.0 uncuffed
Children up to 8 yr old	3.5–6.0 uncuffed (measure little finger)
Children 8–16 yr old	6.0–7.0 cuffed
Adult female	8.0–8.5 cuffed
Adult male	8.5–9.0 cuffed

Military (Medical) Anti-Shock Trousers

MAST, also called PASG (pneumatic anti-shock garment), are inflated to keep blood pressure >100 mm Hg.

Indications

- Hypovolemic shock
- Can also be used to stabilize fractures of the lower extremities

Contraindication

- Cardiogenic shock

Procedure

1. Inflate one leg, then the other leg, and finally the abdominal section.

2. While blood volume is being replaced, deflate the trousers SLOWLY in the opposite order in which they were inflated. Maintain a blood pressure >100 mm Hg.

Patient Management Protocols

Uncomplicated Myocardial Infarction

1. Monitor ECG, begin IV with D5W at keep-open rate.

2. Give oxygen (nasal cannula, 4–6 liters/min).

3. Sublingual nitroglycerin is helpful.

4. Relieve pain with morphine sulfate 2 to 5 mg IV prn (as needed).

5. Consider the use of prophylactic lidocaine.

Acute Myocardial Infarction with Dysrhythmias

PVCs

1. Suppress with lidocaine.

BRADYCARDIA

1. Give atropine if rate <60 associated with PVCs or hypotension or if rate <50 without any PVCs.

SUPRAVENTRICULAR TACHYCARDIA

1. If hypovolemic, give fluids.

2. If cardiac output high, consider propranolol.

3. If cardiac output low, consider dopamine.

4. If due to atrial fibrillation or flutter, countershock (50 joules, synchronized) or give digitalis or verapamil IV.

Asystole

1. Use basic CPR, begin IV, intubate.

2. Give epinephrine 5 to 10 ml of 1:10,000 solution q5min AND bicarbonate 1 mEq/kg, then ½ initial dose q10min.

3. If ineffective, give 500 mg calcium chloride.

4. If ineffective, give 0.5 to 1.0 mg atropine.

5. If ineffective, use isoproterenol 1 mg in 250 ml; titrate to effect.

6. Repeat steps 2 to 5. If ineffective, as a last resort, consider giving epinephrine intracardially or using a transvenous pacemaker.

Ventricular Fibrillation

1. Use basic CPR, begin IV, intubate.

2. Use precordial thump ONLY IF A MONITORED, WITNESSED ARREST.

3. Defibrillate with 200 to 300 joules; repeat once if needed.

4. If no response, give epinephrine, bicarbonate as described for asystole.

5. Defibrillate with full output (400 joules).

6. Use lidocaine or procainamide.

7. If still no response, use bretylium.

8. After successful conversion, ALWAYS use a lidocaine drip.

Electromechanical Dissociation

1. Use basic CPR, begin IV, intubate.

2. Give epinephrine and bicarbonate as described for asystole.

3. If no response, use calcium chloride 500 mg IV.

4. Continue epinephrine and bicarbonate.

5. Consider isoproterenol drip.

6. Other modalities include MAST trousers, pericardiocentesis, or intra-aortic balloon pump.

Ventricular Tachycardia

1. Begin lidocaine.

2. Use CPR if no effective circulation.

3. Use precordial thump ONLY IF A MONITORED, WIT-NESSED ARREST.

4. Consider cardioversion and procainamide or bretylium if lidocaine is ineffective.

5. Determine contributing factors (high K, hypoxia, low HCT, myocardial infarction).

OTHER COMMON EMERGENCIES

The following material gives the treatment for other common emergencies. Dosages are for adults unless stated otherwise.

Anaphylaxis

Mild

- Epinephrine: 1:1000 solution SQ

  ADULT: 0.3 to 0.5 ml

  CHILDREN: 0.01 mg/kg

Severe

- Epinephrine, then diphenydramine (Benadryl) 50 to 100 mg IM

Asthmatic Attack

Mild to Moderate

- Epinephrine: 1:1000 SQ

ADULT: 0.3 to 0.5 ml q20min up to three doses

CHILDREN: 0.01 ml/kg, up to 0.30 ml/kg q20min up to three doses

then, if no relief

- Aminophylline: Load both children and adults with 6 mg/kg IV, then

ADULT: 0.9 mg/kg/hr IV

CHILDREN: 1.0 mg/kg/hr IV

Severe Attack

- Aminophylline: As for mild to moderate cases

ADULT MAXIMUM: 1.35 mg/kg/hr IV

CHILDREN MAXIMUM: 1.65 mg/kg/hr IV

then consider

- Hydrocortisone sodium: 4 mg/kg IV q2–4h OR
- Methylprednisolone: 2–4 mg/kg IV q4h

Anticholinergic Crisis: Usually related to drug overdose

- Physostigmine: 0.5 to 2.0 mg IV S-L-O-W-L-Y (may cause seizures if given rapidly)

Coma

1. Draw STAT SMA-6, calcium.

2. Give 1 amp (50 ml) of D50 IV and 100 mg thiamine IV.

3. Give naloxone (Narcan) as for a narcotics overdose.

Hypercalcemia: Usually emergency treatment if Ca >15 mEq/liter

1. Use saline diuresis: D5NS at 300–400 ml/hr.

2. Give furosemide (Lasix) 80 to 100 mg IV (Saline and Lasix will treat most cases).

3. Give phosphate 50 mg IV over six to eight hours (last resort).

4. Give mithramycin 25 μg/kg IV over two to three hours (last resort).

Hyperkalemia: (See Chapter 11.)

Hypertensive Crisis

- Diazoxide (Hyperstat): 200 to 300 mg bolus IV OR
- Hydralazine: 10 to 50 mg IM OR
- Nitroprusside (Nipride) drip: 50 mg in 500 ml, titrate to effect

Hypoglycemia

1. Draw a STAT serum glucose.

2. Give orange juice with sugar if the patient is awake and alert; if not, give 1 amp of D50 IV.

Narcotics Overdose

- Naloxone (Narcan)

ADULT: 0.4 to 0.8 mg IV or IM, repeat as needed

CHILD: 0.01 mg/kg IV or IM, repeat as needed

Poisoning

1. Support airway, respiration, and circulation, if needed.

2. Determine ingested substance; give specific antidote, if available.

3. Prevent further absorption.

   Unconscious patient

   - Protect airway with an endotracheal tube.
   - Lavage with 28 French or larger NG tube or Ewald tube.
   - Use 300 ml normal saline for adults and 20 ml/kg in children at a time.
   - Activated charcoal can be added.

   Conscious patient

   - Use SYRUP OF IPECAC to induce vomiting (Do not use with acid, alkali, or petroleum products): children up to 1 year old, 10 ml; children 1 to 12 years old, 15 ml; adults, 30 ml.
   - Ambulate the patient and give large quantities of water.
   - May repeat the dose of ipecac in 15 minutes if no result.
   - ACTIVATED CHARCOAL can be given after vomiting. Use 50 gm in children, 120 gm in adults, with 100 to 200 ml of water.

4. Promote excretion (alkalinize or acidfy urine, use hemodialysis).

Shock

Hypovolemic

1. Initially, use fluids such as NS, D5LR, blood, albumin, Plasmanate, or hetastarch.

2. If poor response and no Swan-Ganz catheter, use dopamine: Add 1 amp (200 mg) to 250 ml D5W to give 800 µg/ml; begin at 2–5 µg/kg/min (see the section on ACLS).

Status Epilepticus:

The drugs of choice are given in the following table. Use diazepam first, then move down the list as needed.

Drugs for Treatment of Status Epilepticus

Drug	Dose (mg/kg) in Children	Dose in Adults	Maximum Rate (mg/min)
Diazepam (Valium)	0.10–0.20 IV	5–10 mg IV (up to 30 mg)	3–5
Phenytoin (Dilantin)*	15 IV	same as child	50
Phenobarbital	10 IV or IM	120–140 mg IV	25
Paraldehyde	0.15 deep IM	3–5 ml deep IM	n.a.†

*When given IV, use a maximum dose of 50 mg/min and monitor ECG and vital signs closely. Can cause severe hypotension and bradycardia.
†n.a. = not applicable

22
Commonly Used Drugs

List of Generic Drugs
Generic Drugs:
  Indications, Actions,
  and Dosage

Chemotherapeutic Agents
Drug Levels
Aminoglycoside Dosing

This chapter is designed to serve as a general reference to some of the more commonly prescribed medications. Only a few fixed-dosage combination drugs are included. Selected information on indications, actions, and adult and pediatric dosages is presented. In addition, the way each drug is supplied is included. The latter information is particularly useful when writing prescriptions for patients being discharged. When prescribing any drug, you should be fully aware of all potential contraindications and side effects associated with that medication. This information can be found in detail in the *Hospital Formulary Service*, package insert, or the *Physicians Desk Reference* (PDR).

Drugs in this section are listed in alphabetical order by generic names. The more common trade names are listed for each medication. Where no pediatric dosage is provided, the implication is that the use of the agent is not well established in this age group.

LIST OF GENERIC DRUGS

Analgesic/Anti-Inflammatory/Antipyretic

Acetaminophen
Acetaminophen with
   Codeine
Aspirin
Codeine
Hydromorphone
Ibuprofen
Indomethacin
Meperidine

Methadone
Morphine Sulfate
Naproxen
Oxycodone
Pentazocine
Phenazopyridine
Phenylbutazone
Propoxyphene
Zomepirac

Antacids/Anti-gas

Aluminum Hydroxide
Aluminum Hydroxide with
   Magnesium Hydroxide
Aluminum Hydroxide with
   Magnesium Hydroxide
   and Simethicone

Magnesium Hydroxide
Milk of Magnesia
Simethicone

Antianxiety

Chlordiazepoxide
Diazepam

Antiasthmatic

Aminophylline
Beclomethazone
Epinephrine
Metaproterenol

Oxtriphylline
Terbutaline
Theophylline

Antibiotic

Amikacin
Amoxicillin
Amphotericin B
Ampicillin
Carbenicillin
Cefaclor
Cefamandole

Cefazolin
Cefoxitin
Cephalexin
Cephalothin
Cephapirin
Cephradine
Chloramphenicol

Clindamycin
Cloxacillin
Dicloxacillin
Doxycycline
Erythromycin
Gentamicin
Isoniazid
Methicillin
Metronidazole
Moxalactam
Nafcillin
Neomycin Sulfate
Nitrofurantoin
Nystatin
Penicillin G (Aqueous)
Penicillin G (Benzathine)
Penicillin G (Procaine)
Penicillin V
Rifampin
Silver Sulfadiazine
Streptomycin
Sulfasalazine
Sulfisoxazole
Tetracycline
Ticarcillin
Tobramycin
Trimethoprim
Trimethoprim-
  Sulfamethoxazole
Vancomycin

Anticoagulant

Heparin
Warfarin

Anticonvulsant

Carbamazepine
Diazepam
Phenobarbital
Phenytoin
Valproic Acid

Antidepressant/Antipsychotic

Amitriptyline
Chlorpromazine
Doxepin
Haloperidol
Imipramine
Lithium Carbonate
Prochlorperazine
Thioridazine

Antidiabetic

Chlorpropamide
Insulins
Tolbutamide

Antidiarrheal

Diphenoxylate with
  Atropine
Kaolin-Pectin
Lactobacillus
Loperamide

Antigout

Allopurinol
Colchicine

Probenecid
Sulfinpyrazone

Antihistaminic

Diphenhydramine
Hydroxyzine
Promethazine

Antihypertensive

Captopril
Clonidine
Diazoxide
Hydralazine
Methyldopa

Metoprolol
Nitroprusside
Prazosin
Propranolol
Timolol

Cardiac Drugs

Atenolol
Atropine
Bretylium
Calcium Chloride
Calcium Gluconate
Digoxin
Disopyramide
Dobutamine
Dopamine
Edrophonium
Epinephrine
Isoproterenol

Isosorbide Dinitrate
Lidocaine
Metoprolol
Nifedipine
Nitroglycerin
Procainamide
Propranolol
Quinidine
Sodium Bicarbonate
Timolol
Verapamil

Cathartics/Laxatives

Bisacodyl
Dioctyl Calcium
  Sulfosuccinate
Dioctyl Sodium
  Sulfosuccinate

Magnesium Citrate
Milk of Magnesia
Mineral Oil
Psyllium

Cough and Cold Preparations

Guaifenesin
Pseudoephedrine
Triprolidine-Pseudoephedrine

Diuretic

Acetazolamide
Ethacrynic Acid
Furosemide

Hydrochlorothiazide
Mannitol
Spironolactone

Emetics/Antiemetics

Benzquinamide
Chlorpromazine
Ipecac Syrup

Prochlorperazine
Trimethobenzamide

Gastrointestinal Agents

Cimetidine
Metoclopramide
Pancreatin

Pancrelipase
Simethicone
Sucralfate

Hormones/Synthetic Substitutes

Corticosteroids
Cortisone
Dexamethasone
Dienestrol
Hydrocortisone
Methylprednisolone

Oxytocin
Prednisone
Prednisolone
Steroids
Vasopressin

Local Anesthetic Agents

Anusol
Dibucaine

Lidocaine
Phenazopyridine

Plasma Volume Expanders

Albumin
Hetastarch
Plasma Protein Fraction

Sedatives/Hypnotics

Chloral Hydrate
Chlordiazepoxide
Diazepam
Flurazepam

Pentobarbital
Phenobarbital
Promethazine
Secobarbital

Supplements

Calcium Salts
Ferrous Sulfate and
    Gluconate
Folic Acid
Iron Dextran

Magnesium Sulfate
Phytonadione (Vitamin K)
Potassium Supplements
Pyridoxine
Thiamine

Thyroid/Antithyroid

Levothyroxine
Methimazole
Propylthiouracil

Toxoids/Vaccines/Serums

Hepatitis B Immune
    Globulin
Pneumococcal Vaccine,
    Polyvalent

Rh_O D Immune Globulin
Tetanus Toxoid

Urinary Tract Agents

Bethanechol
Methenamine Mandelate

Oxybutynin
Propantheline

Miscellaneous

Benztropine
Bromocriptine
Carbidopa/Levodopa
Gamma Benzene
    Hexachloride
Lactulose
Naloxone

Pancuronium
Physostigmine
Protamine Sulfate
Sodium Polystyrene Sulfonate
Streptokinase
Trihexaphenidyl

GENERIC DRUGS: INDICATIONS, ACTIONS, AND DOSAGE

Acetaminophen (Tylenol, Others)

Indications: Mild pain, headache, fever

Actions: Non-narcotic analgesic, antipyretic

Dosage

ADULT: 325–650 mg po or pr (given rectally) q4–6h

PEDS

<3 Months: 30 mg

3 Months to 1 Year: 60 mg

1 to 3 Years: 60 to 120 mg

6 to 12 Years: 240 mg

Supplied: Tablets, 80, 120 mg; chewable, 300, 325, 500, 650 mg; suppositories 120, 125, 130, 300, 325, 600, 650 mg; capsules; wafers; elixirs; syrup; drops

Notes: Overdose causes hepatotoxicity; treated with N-acetylcysteine; unlike aspirin has no anti-inflammatory, platelet-inhibiting action.

Acetaminophen with Codeine (Tylenol #1, #2, #3, #4)

Indications: #1, #2, #3 for relief of mild to moderate pain; #4 for relief of moderate to severe pain

Actions: Combined effects of acetaminophen and narcotic analgesic

Dosage: 1–2 tablets q3–4h prn

Supplied: Tablets, 300 mg acetaminophen plus codeine; elixir

Notes: Codeine in #1 = 7.5 mg, #2 = 15 mg, #3 = 30 mg, #4 = 60 mg.

Acetazolamide (Diamox)

Indications: Diuresis, glaucoma, epilepsy, alkalinization of urine

Actions: Carbonic anhydrase inhibitor

Dosage

ADULT: 250 mg IV or po q24h in divided doses

PEDS
- Epilepsy: 8–30 mg/kg/24 hr in 4 divided doses
- Diuretic: 5 mg/kg/24 hr

Supplied: Tablets, 125, 250, 500 mg; IV solution

Notes: Contraindicated in renal failure, sulfa hypersensitivity; follow Na and K; watch for metabolic acidosis.

Albumin (Albumisol, Albuspan, Albutein, Others)

Indications: Plasma volume expansion for shock resulting from burns, surgery, hemorrhage, or other trauma; temporary protein source for hypoalbuminemia

Actions: Expands plasma volume by contribution of colloids (oncotic pressure of plasma)

Dosage

ADULT: 25 gm IV initially; subsequent infusions should depend upon clinical situation and response

PEDS: 25% to 50% of adult dose initially; subsequent infusions same as adults

Supplied: Injectable forms (12.5 gm/50 ml of 25% solution)

Note: Contains 130–160 mEq Na/liter; see also Chapter 11.

Allopurinol (Zyloprim)

Indications: Gout, treatment of hyperuricemia of malignant disease

Actions: Xanthine oxidase inhibitor

Dosage

ADULT: Initial 100 mg po qd; usual 300 mg po qd

PEDS

<6 Years: 150 mg po qd

6 to 10 Years: 300 mg po qd (use ONLY for treating malignancy in children)

Supplied: Tablets, 100, 300 mg

Notes: Not useful in acute gout attack.

Aluminum Hydroxide (Amphojel)

Indications: Hyperacidity (peptic ulcer, hiatal hernia, etc.)

Actions: Antacid

Dosage: 10 ml po or 1 tablet (0.6 gm) five to six times daily

Supplied: Tablets, suspension

Notes: Can be used in renal insufficiency; can cause constipation.

Aluminum Hydroxide with Magnesium Hydroxide (Maalox)

Indications: Hyperacidity (peptic ulcer, hiatal hernia, etc.)

Actions: Antacid

Dosage: 10–20 ml po qid or prn or 2–4 tablets po qid or prn

Supplied: Chewable tablets, suspension

Notes: Doses qid best given after meals and at bedtime; caution in renal failure (can cause hypermagnesemia).

Aluminum Hydroxide with Magnesium Hydroxide and Simethicone (Mylanta, Mylanta II)

Indications: Hyperacidity with bloating (peptic ulcer, etc.)

Actions: Antacid with antiflatulent combination

Dosage: 5–10 ml po or 1–2 tablets q2–4h prn and at bedtime (hs)

Supplied: Chewable tablets, suspension

Notes: Caution in renal insufficiency (can cause hypermagnesemia); Mylanta II contains twice the amount of aluminum and magnesium hydroxide as Mylanta.

Amikacin (Amikin)

Indications: Short-term therapy of serious infections due to gram-negatives and penicillinase-producing staphylococci

Actions: Aminoglycoside, bactericidal, inhibits protein synthesis

Dosage

ADULT: Based on renal function; refer to Aminoglycoside Dosing Chart in this chapter

PEDS: Same as adult dosage

Supplied: Injectable forms

Notes: Not a first-line drug; monitor renal function carefully for dosage adjustments.

Aminophylline

Indications: Asthma, bronchospasm

Actions: Xanthine derivative with beta-like effects (smooth muscle relaxation, bronchodilation)

Dosage

ADULT
- Acute asthmatic attack: See Chapter 21
- Chronic asthma: 3 mg/kg po q6h, advance as needed

PEDS
- Acute asthmatic attack: See Chapter 21
- Chronic asthma: 16 mg/kg/24 hr in 3 to 4 divided doses, advance as needed to 24 mg/kg/24 hr

Supplied: Multiple po, pr, and IV forms

Notes: Each dosage must be individualized; signs of toxicity include nausea, vomiting, irritability, tachycardia; following serum levels is helpful, especially with CHF or hepatic disease (see the section on Drug Levels in this chapter); aminophylline is about 85% theophylline; erratic absorption of rectal doses.

Amitriptyline (Elavil, Others)

Indications: Endogenous depression

Actions: Tricyclic antidepressant

Dosage: Initially, 50–100 mg po qhs; can increase to 300 mg qhs

Supplied: Tablets, 10, 25, 50, 75, 100, 150 mg; injectable forms

Notes: When symptoms are controlled, can decrease dose to lowest amount effective.

Amoxicillin (Amoxil, Robamox, Trimox, Others)

Indications: Treatment of susceptible gram-negatives (*H. influenzae, E. coli, P. mirabilis, N. gonorrhoeae*) and gram-positives (streptococci, nonpenicillinase-producing staphylococci)

Actions: Semisynthetic penicillin, bactericidal, inhibits cell wall synthesis

Dosage

ADULT: 250–500 mg po tid

PEDS: 20–40 mg/kg/24 hr po tid

Supplied: Capsules, 250, 500 mg; suspension, 125 or 250 mg/5 ml

Notes: Cross-hypersensitivity with penicillin.

Ampicillin (Amcil, Omnipen, Others)

Indications: Treatment of susceptible gram-negatives (*Shigella, Salmonella, E. coli, H. influenzae, P. mirabilis, N. gonorrhoeae*) and gram-positives (streptococci, nonpenicillinase-producing staphylococci)

Actions: Semisynthetic penicillin, bactericidal, inhibits cell wall synthesis

Dosage

ADULT: 500 mg–1 gm po, IM, or IV qid

PEDS

Weight <40 kg: 50–100 mg/kg/24 hr po, IM, or IV in 4 doses

Weight >40 kg: As in adults

Supplied: Capsules, 250, 500 mg; suspension, 125 or 250 mg/5 ml; injectable forms

Notes: Cross-hypersensitivity with penicillin.

Amphotericin B (Fungizone)

Indications: Severe, systemic fungal infections

Actions: Antifungal, alters cell membrane

Dosage: 0.25 mg/kg IV over six hours initially; gradually increase dose as tolerated up to 1.0–1.5 mg/kg/24 hr IV over six hours; total dose varies with indication

Supplied: Injectable forms

Notes: Severe side effects; monitor liver, blood, and renal function.

Anusol

Indications: Symptomatic relief of pain from external and internal hemorrhoids and anorectal surgery

Actions: Surface analgesic and lubricant

Dosage: 1 suppository qAM (every morning), hs, and following each bowel movement; apply cream freely to anal area q6–12h

Supplied: Suppositories, cream (Anusol-HC also contains hydrocortisone for anti-inflammatory effect)

Aspirin

Indications: Mild pain, headache, fever, inflammation, prevention of emboli

Actions: Prostaglandin inhibitor, anti-inflammatory, analgesic, antipyretic, platelet inhibitory action

Dosage

ADULT
- Pain, fever: 325–650 mg q4h po or pr
- Rheumatoid arthritis: 3–6 gm/day
- Platelet inhibitory action: 650 mg bid

PEDS: 60 mg/kg/24 hr po or pr in divided doses (CAUTION: Use linked to Reye's syndrome)

Supplied: Multiple po and pr forms including enteric-coated tablets; "standard" adult tablet contains 325 mg

Notes: GI upset, erosion common adverse reactions; can be prevented by ingestion with food.

Atenolol (Tenormin)

Indications: Hypertension

Actions: Cardioselective beta-adrenergic antagonist

Dosage: 50 mg po qd

Supplied: Tablets, 50, 100 mg

Notes: Can increase dose to 100 mg after two weeks; doses >100 mg unlikely to produce further benefit; extend to qod dosing with creatinine clearance <15 ml/min.

Atropine

Indications: Pre-anesthetic, symptomatic bradycardia

Actions: Parasympatholytic, vagolytic (dries mucous membranes, speeds heart)

Dosage

- Emergency cardiac care: See Chapter 21

ADULT

- Pre-anesthetic: 0.3 to 0.6 mg IM

PEDS

- Pre-anesthetic: 0.01 mg/kg/dose IM (maximum 0.4 mg)

Supplied: Multiple IM, IV forms

Notes: Can cause blurred vision, urinary retention, dried mucous membranes.

Beclomethasone (Beclovent, Vanceril)

Indications: Chronic asthma

Actions: Topical steroid, anti-inflammatory

Dosage

ADULT: 2 inhalations tid–qid (maximum 20/day)

PEDS: 1–2 inhalations tid–qid (maximum 10/day)

Supplied: Metered dose inhaler

Notes: Not effective for acute asthmatic attacks.

Benzquinamide (Emete-Con)

Indications: Nausea and vomiting

Actions: Antiemetic unrelated to the phenothiazines or antihistamines

Dosage: 50 mg IM q3–4h prn

Supplied: Injectable form

Notes: Alternative antiemetic when phenothiazine or antihistamine contraindicated.

Benztropine (Cogentin):   See trihexyphenidyl

Dosage: 1 to 6 mg po, IM, or IV in divided doses

Supplied: Tablets, injectable forms

Notes: Anticholinergic side effects.

Bethanechol (Urecholine)

Indications: Neurogenic atony of the bladder with retention, acute postoperative and postpartum functional (nonobstructive) urinary retention

Actions: Parasympathetic nervous system stimulant

Dosage

ADULT: 10–50 mg po tid–qid or 5 mg SQ tid–qid and prn

PEDS: 0.3–0.6 mg/kg po tid–qid or ⅓ the oral dose SQ

Supplied: Tablets, 5, 10, 25, 50 mg; injectable form

Notes: Contraindicated in bladder neck obstruction, asthma.

Bisacodyl (Dulcolax)

Indications: Constipation, bowel prep

Actions: Contact laxative

Dosage

ADULT: Usual 10 mg po or pr prn, can increase as needed

PEDS

<2 Years: 5 mg po or pr

>2 Years: 10 mg po or pr

Supplied: Tablets, 5 mg; suppositories, 10 mg

Notes: Do not use with an acute abdomen or bowel obstruction.

Bretylium (Bretylol):   (See Chapter 21.)

Indications: Acute treatment of ventricular fibrillation or tachycardia unresponsive to conventional therapy

Actions: Adrenergic blocking agent, prevents norepinephrine reuptake at adrenergic nerve terminals

Dosage: 5 mg/kg IV rapid injection (one minute); may repeat q15–30min with 10 mg/kg (maximum of 30 mg/kg); maintenance, 1–2 mg/min IV infusion

Supplied: Injectable form

Note: Nausea and vomiting associated with rapid IV push; should gradually reduce dose and discontinue in three to five days; effects seen within first 10 to 15 minutes; transient rise in BP seen initially.

Bromocriptine (Parlodel)

Indications: Short-term treatment of galactorrhea (especially postpartum where nursing is not desired)

Actions: Nonhormonal prolactin inhibitor

Dosage: 2.5 mg po bid–tid

Supplied: Tablets, 2.5 mg

Notes: Nausea, vertigo common side effects.

Calcium Salts (Chloride, Gluconate [Chloripe, Glucanate, Others])

Indications: Calcium replacement, ventricular fibrillation, asystole

Actions: Dietary supplement, increases myocardial contractility and automaticity

Dosage: (See also Chapter 21)

ADULT
- Replacement: 1–2 gm po qd
- Cardiac emergencies: 0.5–1.0 gm IV q10min (calcium chloride) OR 1.0–2.0 gm IV q10min (calcium gluconate)

PEDS
- Replacement: Gluconate 500 mg/kg/day po q4–8h
- Cardiac emergencies: 20 mg/kg/dose q10min

Supplied: Tablets, suspension, injectable forms

Notes: Calcium chloride contains 270 mg (13.6 mEq) elemental calcium per gram; calcium gluconate contains 90 mg (14.7 mEq) elemental calcium per gram; calcium carbonate used 650 mg po tid–qid effective in slowing diarrhea induced by tube feeding.

Captopril (Capoten)

Indications: Hypertension refractory to usual therapy

Actions: Inhibits angiotensin-1-converting enzyme which causes decreased aldosterone secretion

Dosage: Initially, 25 mg po tid; titrate maintenance every one to two weeks by 25 mg increments per dose (maximum 450 mg/day)

Supplied: Tablets, 25, 50, 100 mg

Notes: Caution with renal failure; give one hour before meals; can cause rash and proteinuria; not a first-line drug.

Carbamazepine (Tegretol)

Indications: Seizure disorders that do not respond to other medications (psychomotor, temporal lobe, grand mal, but NOT petit mal)

Actions: Anticonvulsant, actions unknown

Dosage

ADULT: 200 mg bid, initially; increase by 200 mg/day; usual 800–1200 mg/day

PEDS: 10 mg/kg/day po bid–tid, increase every two weeks until controlled (maximum 1.6 gm/day)

Supplied: Tablets, 200 mg

Notes: Can cause severe hematological side effects; monitor blood.

Carbenicillin (Geocillin, Geopen)

Indications: Active against most strains of *Pseudomonas, Proteus,* some *E. coli*; particularly good for urinary tract infections

Actions: Extended spectrum penicillin

Dosage

ADULT: 1–2 tablets po qid or 1–2 gm or 200 mg/kg/day IV or IM q6h

PEDS: Usual range 100–200 mg/kg/24 hr IV in 4 divided doses

Supplied: Injectable forms; tablets, 382 mg

Notes: Usually used with another antibiotic; resistance develops rapidly; synergistic with aminoglycosides for *Pseudomonas;* coagulation abnormalities and bleeding have been reported with intravenous use; high sodium content of IV form (4.7 mEq/gm) can cause hypernatremia.

Carbidopa/Levodopa (Sinemet)

Indications: Parkinson's disease

Actions: Raises central nervous system levels of dopamine

Dosage

ADULT: Start at 10/100 bid–tid, titrate as needed

Supplied: Tablets, (mg carbidopa/mg levodopa) 10/100, 25/100, 25/250

Notes: Psychic disturbances, orthostatic hypotension, dyskinesias, cardiac arrhythmias associated with this combination.

Cefaclor (Ceclor)

Indications: Active against gram-positive bacteria (staphylococci and streptococci), gram-negative bacteria (*H. influenzae, E. coli, K. pneumoniae, P. mirabilis*), anaerobic gram-positive cocci, and *Bacteroides* species except *B. fragilis*

Dosage

    ADULT: 250–500 mg po q6–8h

    PEDS: 20–40 mg/kg/24 hr in 3 doses (maximum 1.5 gm/day)

Supplied: Capsules, 250, 500 mg

Notes: May prove more effective than cephalexin for some gram-negative bacterial infections; reduce dose in renal failure: severe— ¼ dose, moderate— ½ dose.

Cefamandole (Mandol)

Indications: Active against gram-positive bacteria, gram-negative cocci, gram-negative aerobic bacilli (*E. coli, P. mirabilis, Klebsiella* species, and *H. influenzae*), gram-negative anaerobic bacilli except *B. fragilis*

Actions: Inhibits cell wall synthesis, bactericidal or bacteriostatic depending on many factors

Dosage

    ADULT: 1–2 gm IM or IV q4–8h

    PEDS: 50–100 mg/kg/24 hr IM or IV in 3 to 6 divided doses

Supplied: Injectable forms

Notes: Third-generation cephalosporin.

Cefazolin (Ancef, Kefzol):   See cephalothin

Dosage

    ADULT: 250 mg–2 gm IM or IV tid–qid

    PEDS: 25–50 mg/kg/24 hr IM or IV in 3 to 4 divided doses

Notes: Decrease dose with renal insufficiency; more activity against *E. coli*; biliary concentrations high; IM route less painful than with other cephalosporins.

Cefoxitin (Mefoxin) See cefamandole

Dosage

ADULT: 1–2 gm IM or IV q4–8h

Supplied: Injectable forms

Notes: Third-generation cephalosporin; poor for methicillin-resistant staphylococci; active against most anaerobes (*B. fragilis*).

Cephalexin (Keflex): See cephalothin

Dosage

ADULT: 250–500 mg po q6h

PEDS: 25–50 mg/kg/24 hr po in 4 divided doses

Supplied: Capsules, 250, 500 mg; oral suspension; drops

Notes: Excellent absorption of doses given orally; double dosage for moderate to severe infections.

Cephalothin (Keflin)

Indications: Active against most aerobic and anaerobic gram-positive penicillinase-producing cocci, gram-positive bacilli, gram-negative aerobic bacteria

Actions: Bactericidal or bacteriostatic depending on many factors, inhibits cell wall synthesis

Dosage

ADULT: 500 mg–2 gm IM or IV q4–6h

PEDS: 80–160 mg/kg/24 hr IM or IV in divided doses q4–6h

Supplied: Injectable forms

Notes: Best studied of cephalosporins; reliable drug against staphylococci; usually effective against methicillin-resistant staphylococci; IM route is painful.

Cephapirin (Cefadyl, Cefatrexil):   See cephalothin

Dosage

   ADULT: 500 mg–2 gm IM or IV q4–6h

   PEDS: 40–80 mg/kg/24 hr IM or IV in 4 divided doses

Supplied: Injectable forms

Notes: May cause less phlebitis than other cephalosporins but has not been confirmed.

Cephradine (Velosef, Anspor):   See cephalothin

Dosage

   ADULT: 250–500 mg po, IM, or IV q6h

   PEDS: 25–50 mg/kg/24 hr po, IM, or IV in 2 to 4 divided doses

Supplied: Capsules, 250, 500 mg; tablets, 1 gm; oral, injectable forms

Notes: Oral form similar to cephalexin.

Chloral Hydrate (Noctec, Somnos)

Indications: Insomnia

Actions: Sedative-hypnotic (nonbarbiturate)

Dosage

ADULT: 500 mg–1 gm po qhs prn (maximum 2 gm/day)

PEDS
- Sedative: 25 mg/kg/dose
- Hypnotic: 50 mg/kg/dose
- Maximum dose: 1 gm

Supplied: Capsules, 250, 500 mg; suppositories; elixir; syrup

Notes: May be habit forming; causes gastric and mucosal irritation.

Chloramphenicol (Chloromycetin)

Indications: Serious infections caused by gram-positive cocci and bacilli, gram-negative aerobic and anaerobic bacteria; *Pseudomonas aeruginosa* almost always resistant

Actions: Bacteriostatic, interferes with protein synthesis

Dosage

ADULT: 25–100 mg/kg/day po or IV in 4 divided doses

PEDS

<1 Week: 25 mg/kg/24 hr IV (continuous infusion) or po in 1 to 4 divided doses

>2 Weeks: 50 mg/kg/24 hr IV (continuous infusion) or po in 4 divided doses

Supplied: Capsules, 50, 100, 250 mg; suspension; injectable, topical forms

Notes: Aplastic anemia common; monitor blood studies (reticulocyte and platelet counts) carefully; reduce dose with hepatic impairment.

Chlordiazepoxide (Librium)

Indications: Anxiety, tension, alcohol withdrawal

Actions: Benzodiazepine, sedative and antianxiety effect, cross tolerance with alcohol

Dosage

ADULT
- Mild anxiety, tension: 5–10 mg po tid–qid or prn
- Severe anxiety, tension: 25–50 mg IM or IV tid–qid or prn
- Alcohol withdrawal: 50 to 100 mg IM or IV; repeat in 2 to 4 hours if needed, up to 300 mg in 24 hours; gradually taper daily dosage

PEDS

>6 Years ONLY: 0.5 mg/kg/24 hr in divided doses

Supplied: Capsules and tablets, 5, 10, 25 mg; injectable form

Notes: Reduce dosage in elderly; absorption of IM doses can be erratic; can be habit forming.

Chlorpromazine (Thorazine)

Indications: Psychotic disorders, apprehension, intractable hiccups

Actions: Phenothiazine, antipsychotic, antiemetic, sedative-tranquilizer

Dosage

- Acute anxiety, agitation: 10–25 mg po or pr bid–tid
- Severe symptoms: 25 mg IM; can repeat in one hour, then 25–50 mg po or pr tid

- Outpatient antipsychotic: 10–25 mg po bid–tid
- Hiccups: 25–50 mg po bid–tid

PEDS: 2 mg/kg/24 hr in 4 to 6 divided doses

Notes: Beware of extrapyramidal side effects; sedation; has alpha adrenergic blocking properties.

Chlorpropamide (Diabinese)

Indications: Adult onset diabetes that cannot be controlled by diet

Actions: Hypoglycemic agent, stimulation of endogenous insulin release and synthesis

Dosage: 250 mg po qd usual; do not exceed 750 mg/day

Supplied: Tablets, 100 to 250 mg

Notes: Contraindicated in juvenile onset diabetes mellitus (JODM), brittle diabetes, diabetes complicated by other factors (ketosis, infection, etc.)

Cimetidine (Tagamet)

Indications: Duodenal ulcer; ulcer prophylaxis in hyper-secretory states such as severe trauma, burns, Zollinger-Ellison syndrome, etc.

Actions: Histamine H2 receptor antagonist

Dosage

ADULT: 300 mg po or IV tid–qid

PEDS: 25–40 mg/kg/24 hr po or IV in 4 divided doses

Supplied: Tablets, 200, 300 mg; liquid; injectable form

Notes: No absolute contraindications; increased effectiveness when used with antacids, however absorption of cimetidine may be decreased; extend dosing interval to q12h with creatinine clearance <30 ml/min.

Clindamycin (Cleocin)

Indications: Serious infections caused by gram-negative anaerobes (*B. fragilis*) or for serious staphylococcal or streptococcal infections in patients allergic to penicillin, not effective against gram-negative aerobes

Actions: Bacteriostatic antibiotic, inhibits protein synthesis

Dosage

ADULT: 150–450 mg po qid or 600 mg–2.7 gm/day IM or IV in 2 to 4 divided doses

PEDS: 8–25 mg/kg/24 hr po, IM, or IV in 3 to 4 divided doses

Supplied: Capsules, 75, 150 mg; solution; injectable forms

Notes: Beware of severe diarrhea that may represent pseudomembranous colitis caused by *Clostridium difficile*; treat by stopping drug and giving vancomycin.

Clonidine (Catapres)

Indications: Hypertension

Actions: Centrally acting sympatholytic agent

Dosage: 0.05–0.10 mg po bid–qid adjusted daily by 0.10 to 0.20 mg increments (maximum 2.4 mg/day)

Supplied: Tablets, 0.1, 0.2, 0.3 mg

Notes: Dry mouth, drowsiness, sedation occur frequently; more effective when combined with a diuretic.

Cloxacillin (Cloxapen, Tegopen)

Indications: Treatment of susceptible gram-positive cocci, especially penicillinase-producing *Staphylococcus*

Actions: Semisynthetic penicillin, penicillinase resistant, inhibits cell wall synthesis

Dosage

ADULT: 250–500 mg po qid

PEDS

Weight <20 kg: 50–100 mg/kg/24 hr po in 4 divided doses

Weight >20 kg: Adult dosage

Supplied: Capsules, 250 mg; oral solution

Notes: Beware of possible penicillin cross-hypersensitivity.

Codeine

Indications: Mild to moderate pain, symptomatic relief of cough

Actions: Mild narcotic analgesic, antitussive

Dosage

ADULT
- Analgesic: 15–60 mg po, SQ, or IM qid prn
- Antitussive: 5–15 mg po or SQ q4h prn

PEDS
- Analgesic: 0.5–3.0 mg/kg/dose po or SQ q4h prn
- Antitussive: ⅓ analgesic dose po q4h prn

Supplied: Tablets, 15, 30, 60 mg; powder; elixir; injectable forms

Notes: Can be habit forming; 120 mg equivalent to 10 mg morphine.

Colchicine

Indications: Acute gouty attack

Actions: Antigout agent, not a uricosuric agent

Dosage: Initially 1 to 2 tablets po, then 1 tab q1–2h until GI side effects develop (maximum 16 tablets/day); or 1 to 2 mg IV, then 0.5 mg q6–12h up to 4 mg/day

Supplied: Tablets, 0.6 mg; injectable form

Notes: Caution in elderly and renal impairment.

Corticosteroids: See steroids

Cortisone: See steroids

Dexamethasone (Decadron): See steroids

Diazepam (Valium)

Indications: Anxiety, muscle spasm, status epilepticus, pre-operative sedation

Actions: Benzodiazepine, antianxiety, sedative, anti-spasmotic

Dosage
- Status epilepticus: See Chapter 21

  ADULT
  - Anxiety, muscle spasm: 2–10 mg po, IM, or IV tid–qid prn
  - Preoperative: 5 to 10 mg po or IM 20 to 30 minutes before procedure

  PEDS: 0.12–0.80 mg/kg/24 hr in 3 to 4 divided doses

Supplied: Tablets, 2, 5, 10 mg; injectable forms

Notes: Caution with glaucoma; respiratory depression with IV use; absorption of IM dose can be erratic.

Diazoxide (Hyperstat)

Indications: Hypertensive emergencies

Actions: Rapid arterial dilation

Dosage

ADULT: 150 to 300 mg IV bolus over 10 to 30 seconds; may repeat 30 minutes later, then at 4 to 24 hour intervals

PEDS: 3–5 mg/kg rapidly IV

Supplied: Injectable form

Notes: Sodium retention and hyperglycemia frequently occur; possible thiazide diuretic cross-hypersensitivity; decrease in blood pressure from drug; cannot be titrated.

Dibucaine (Nupercaine)

Indications: Anesthetic action in abrasions, sunburn, hemorrhoids, etc.

Actions: Local anesthetic

Dosage: Apply lotion or ointment or insert suppository prn

Supplied: 0.5% to 1.0% cream, ointment, suppositories

Notes: Ointment supplied with rectal applicator.

Dicloxacillin (Dynapen, Dycill)

Indications: Infections caused by penicillinase-producing staphylococci

Actions: Semisynthetic penicillin, penicillinase resistant, inhibits cell wall synthesis

Dosage

ADULT: 125–500 mg po qid

PEDS

Weight <40 kg: 12.5–25.0 mg/kg/24 hr in 4 divided doses

Weight >40 mg: Adult dosage

Supplied: Capsules, 125, 250, 500 mg; oral suspension

Notes: Beware of possible penicillin cross-hypersensitivity; more active than cloxacillin against streptococci and pneumococci; give one to two hours before meals.

Dienestrol (AVC Cream)

Indications: Atrophic vaginitis, related disorders

Actions: Topical estrogen replacement

Dosage: 35 ml (500 mg) of 0.01% cream intravaginally qd for one to two weeks; reduce to ½ initial dose for one-half week; after restoration of vaginal mucosa, reduce to 5 ml one to three times every week

Supplied: Vaginal cream, 0.01%, with 5 ml applicators

Digoxin (Lanoxin)

Indications: CHF, atrial fibrillation and flutter, paroxysmal atrial tachycardia

Actions: Increases force of myocardial contraction, increases refractory period of AV node to slow AV conduction

Dosage

ADULT

- po digitalization: 0.50 to 0.75 mg po; then 0.25 mg po q6–8h until a total dose between 1.0 to 1.5 mg
- IV or IM digitalization: 0.25 to 0.50 mg IM or IV; then 0.25 mg q4–6h to a total dose of about 1 mg
- Daily maintenance: 0.125–0.500 mg po, IM, or IV qd (average daily dose 0.125 to 0.250 mg)

PEDS

Infant

- Digitalization: 0.03–0.05 mg/kg IM or IV divided in 3 q6h doses, then
- Maintenance 1/10–1/5 original dose qd

2 Weeks to 2 Years

- Digitalization: 0.06–0.08 mg/kg po divided in 3 q6h doses, then
- Maintenance: 1/5–1/3 original dose qd

>2 Years

- Digitalization: 0.04–0.06 mg/kg po divided in 3 q6h doses, then
- Maintenance: 1/5–1/3 original dose qd

Supplied: Tablets, 0.125, 0.25, 0.50 mg; elixir; injectable form

Notes: Can cause heart block; low potassium can potentiate toxicity; reduce dose in renal failure; symptoms of toxicity include nausea, vomiting, headache, fatigue, visual disturbances (yellow-green halos around lights), cardiac arrhythmias (see the section on drug levels in this chapter for therapeutic levels); absorption of IM dose can be erratic; IM route may be painful.

Dioctyl Calcium Sulfate (Surfak, Others)

Indications: Constipation-prone patient (bedrest, medication, etc.)

Actions: Stool softener, surfactant cathartic

Dosage

ADULT: 240 mg po qd

PEDS: 50–150 mg po qd

Supplied: Capsules, 50, 240 mg

Notes: No significant side effects, no laxative action.

Dioctyl Sodium Sulfosuccinate (DOSS) (Colace, Others)

Indications: Constipation-prone patient, adjunct to painful anorectal conditions

Actions: Stool softener, surfactant cathartic

Dosage

ADULT: 50–200 mg po qd

PEDS: 5 mg/kg/24 hr in 3 to 4 divided doses

Supplied: Tablets, 50, 60, 100, 240, 300 mg; capsules, 50, 60, 100, 120, 240, 250, 300 mg; solutions; syrup; 100 mg suppositories

Notes: No significant side effects, no laxative action.

Diphenhydramine (Benadryl, Others)

Indications: Allergic reactions, motion sickness, potentiate narcotics, sedation, extrapyramidal reactions

Actions: Antihistamine

Dosage

ADULT: 25–50 mg po or IM bid–tid

PEDS: 5 mg/kg/24 hr po or IM in 4 divided doses

Supplied: Tablets and capsules, 25, 50 mg; elixir; syrup; injectable form

Notes: Many anticholinergic side effects including dry mouth, urinary retention; increase dosing interval in moderate to severe renal failure.

Diphenoxylate with Atropine (Lomotil)

Indications: Diarrhea

Actions: Mild narcotic to slow bowel motility

Dosage

ADULT: Initially 2 tabs or 10 ml po tid or qid until under control; then 1 tab or 5 ml po bid

PEDS

2 to 5 Years: 6 mg/24 hr po divided tid

5 to 8 Years: 8 mg/24 hr po divided qid

8 to 12 Years: 10 mg/24 hr po divided in 5 doses

Supplied: Tablet, 2.5 mg; liquid (5 ml = 1 tablet)

Notes: Can be habit forming, atropine-type side effects.

Disopyramide (Norpace)

Indications: Adjunct to therapy for atrial fibrillation or flutter; suppression of premature ventricular contractions, other ventricular arrhythmias

Actions: Antiarrhythmic agent similar to procainamide and quinidine

Dosage
- Load: 200 to 300 mg po
- Maintenance: 100 mg q6h

Supplied: Capsules, 100, 150 mg

Notes: Has anticholinergic side effects (urinary retention); can induce or aggravate heart failure; decrease dose in impaired hepatic function.

Dobutamine (Dobutrex): See Chapter 21

Dopamine (Intropin): See Chapter 21

Doxepin (Sinequan)

Indications: Depression or anxiety

Actions: Tricyclic antidepressant

Dosage: 50–150 mg po qd usually qhs but can be divided dose

Supplied: Capsules, 10, 25, 50, 75, 100, 150 mg; oral concentrate

Notes: Anticholinergic, central nervous system (CNS), cardiovascular side effects.

Doxycycline (Vibramycin)

Indications: Broad spectrum antibotic against rickettsiae, *Mycoplasma pneumoniae*, bacteroides, many others

Actions: See tetracycline

Dosage

ADULT: 100 mg po q12h first day, then 100 mg po daily in single or bid dose q12h or 100–200 mg IV qd

PEDS

Weight <45 kg: 4.4 mg/kg/24 hr po or IV in 2 divided doses, then ½ that dose bid

Weight >45 kg: Adult dosage

Supplied: Capsules, 50, 100, 300 mg; suspension; syrup; injectable forms

Notes: Useful for chronic bronchitis and prostatitis; tetracycline of choice for patients with renal impairment; caution with use in pregnancy and children <8 years old.

Edrophonium (Tensilon)

Indications: Diagnosis of myasthenia gravis, acute myasthenic crisis, curare antagonist, paroxysmal atrial tachycardia

Actions: Anticholinesterase, raises acetylcholine levels

Dosage
- Tensilon test for myasthenia gravis in adults and children: 0.2 mg/kg; give 1/5 dose IV in one minute; if tolerated, give the remainder of the dose; a positive test is a brief increase in strength
- Curare antagonist and PAT: 10 mg IV to a maximum of 40 mg

Supplied: Injectable form

Notes: Can cause severe cholinergic effects; keep atropine available.

Epinephrine (Adrenalin, Sus-Phrine, Others)

Indications: Cardiac arrest, anaphylactic reactions

Actions: Primarily beta adrenergic agonist although does exhibit some alpha adrenergic properties

Dosage

- Cardiac arrest: See Chapter 21

ADULT
- Anaphylaxis: 0.3 to 0.5 ml of 1:1000 dilution SQ; may repeat q10–15min to maximum of 1 mg/dose and 5 mg/day
- Asthma: 0.3 to 0.5 ml of 1:1000 dilution SQ repeated at 20 minute to four hour intervals OR 1 inhalation (metered dose); may repeat in one to two minutes; see Chapter 21 also

PEDS
- Anaphylaxis: 0.01 ml/kg of 1:1000 dilution SQ, repeat q15min twice, then q4h prn
- Asthma: See Chapter 21

Supplied: Injectable forms, metered inhaler, ophthalmic solutions

Notes: Contraindicated in closed angle glaucoma; do not use if solution has brown color or has precipitated.

Erythromycin (E-Mycin, Ilosone, Erythrocin, Others)

Indications: Group A streptococci (*S. pyogenes*), alpha-hemolytic streptococci and *N. gonorrhoeae* infections in penicillin-sensitive patients, *S. pneumoniae, Mycoplasma pneumoniae,* Legionnaire's disease, and soft tissue infection caused by *S. aureus*

Dosage

ADULT: 250–500 mg po qid or 500 mg–1 gm IV qid

PEDS: 30–100 mg/kg/24 hr in 4 divided doses

Supplied: Tablets, capsules, suspension (200 or 400 mg/5 ml), solutions, injectable form

Notes: Frequent mild GI disturbances; Ilosone has been associated with cholestatic jaundice. Erythromycin base not well absorbed from the GI tract and often used as part of a bowel prep for colonic surgery known as the "Condon Prep." This procedure involves a two to three day prep that includes oral laxatives and cleansing enemas. Then, for an 8 A.M. operation 1 gm of erythromycin base and 1 gm of neomycin are given at about 1 P.M., 3 P.M., and 11 P.M. to help "sterilize" the bowel.

Ethacrynic Acid (Edecrin)

Indications: Edema, CHF, ascites, anytime rapid diuresis is desired

Actions: Loop diuretic, inhibits Na and Cl reabsorption at loop of Henle

Dosage

   ADULT: 50–100 mg po qd up to usual dose of 50 to 200 mg or 0.5–1.0 mg/kg IV; change injection site after first dose

   PEDS: (Contraindicated in infants) 25 mg po qd; increase by 25 mg to obtain effect

Supplied: Tablets, 25, 50 mg; injectable form

Notes: Contraindicated in anuria; many severe side effects.

Ferrous Sulfate and Gluconate

Indications: Iron deficiency anemia

Actions: Iron supplement

Dosage

   ADULT: 300 mg po qd–tid with meals

PEDS
- Prophylaxis: 1 mg/kg/24 hr in single or divided dose
- Treatment: 6 mg/kg/24 hr in 3 divided doses

Supplied: Capsules, tablets, elixir, syrup, drops (standard is 300 to 325 mg tablets)

Notes: Will turn stools and urine dark; can cause GI upset, constipation; the sulfate salt contains more elemental iron per dosage unit.

Flurazepam (Dalmane)

Indications: Insomnia

Actions: Benzodiazepine, sedative-hypnotic

Dosage: 15–30 mg po qhs prn

Supplied: Capsules, 15, 30 mg

Notes: Reduce dose in elderly.

Folic Acid

Indications: Macrocytic (folate deficiency) anemia, pregnancy

Actions: B-complex vitamin needed for nucleoprotein synthesis

Dosage
- Supplement: 0.10 mg po qd
- Folate deficiency: 0.25–1.00 mg po qd

Supplied: Tablets, 0.25, 1.0 mg; many other combination forms

Furosemide (Lasix)

Indications: Edema, hypertension, CHF

Actions: Loop diuretic, inhibits Na and Cl reabsorption at loop of Henle

Dosage

ADULT: Usual from 20–80 mg po or IV qd or bid

PEDS: 1–2 mg/kg po or IV qd or bid; maximum 6 mg/kg/dose

Supplied: Tablets, 20, 40, 80 mg; solution; injectable forms

Notes: Need to monitor for hypokalemia; use with caution in hepatic disease, may precipitate hepatic encephalopathy.

Gamma Benzene Hexachloride (Kwell, Gamene)

Indications: Head lice, crab lice, scabies

Actions: Parasiticide

Dosage
- Cream or lotion: Apply thin layer after bathing and leave in place for 24 hours; pour on laundry
- Shampoo: Apply 30 ml and develop lather with warm water for four minutes; comb out nits

Supplied: Cream, lotion, shampoo

Notes: Caution with overuse, may be absorbed into blood.

Gentamicin (Garamycin)

Indications: Serious infections caused by susceptible *Pseudomonas, Proteus, E. coli, Klebsiella, Enterobacter, Serratia,* and for initial treatment of gram-negative sepsis

Actions: Aminoglycoside, bactericidal, inhibits protein synthesis

Dosage: Based on renal function; refer to aminoglycoside dosing at the end of this chapter

Supplied: Injectable forms, ophthalmic solutions

Notes: Nephrotoxic and ototoxic; decrease dose with renal insufficiency; monitor creatinine clearance and serum levels for dosage adjustments; see later in this chapter for drug levels.

Guaifenesin (Robitussin, Others)

Indications: Symptomatic relief of cough, expectorant

Actions: Decreases viscosity of respiratory secretions

Dosage

ADULT: 100 mg (usually 5 ml) po q4h

PEDS: 12 mg/kg/24 hr po q4h

Supplied: Many single and combination oral dosage forms

Haloperidol (Haldol)

Indications: Management of psychotic disorders (schizophrenia, psychoses), agitation ("sundowning" in elderly)

Actions: Butyrophenone, antipsychotic, neuroleptic

Dosage
- Moderate symptoms: 0.5–2.0 mg po bid–tid
- Severe symptoms or agitation: 3–5 mg po bid–bid OR 1–5 mg IM q4h prn (maximum 100 mg/day)

Supplied: Tablets, 0.5, 1, 2, 5, 10 mg; solution; injectable form

Notes: Can cause extrapyramidal symptoms, hypotension; reduce dose in elderly patient.

Heparin Sodium

Indications: Venous thrombosis, prevention of venous thrombosis and pulmonary emboli, atrial fibrillation with emboli formation, acute arterial occlusion

Actions: Acts with antithrombin III to inactivate thrombin and to inhibit thromboplastin formation

Dosage

- Prophylaxis: "Mini dose" 3,000–5,000 units SQ q8–12h
- Treatment of thrombosis: Loading dose 50–75 units/kg IV, then about 25 units/kg IV qh (adjust based on PTT)

Supplied: Many injectable forms

Notes: Follow PTT, thrombin time, or activated clotting time to assess effectiveness; heparin has little effect on the prothrombin time; with proper dose PTT is about 2 to 2½ times the control.

Hepatitis B Immune Globulin (HyperHep, Others)

Indications: Exposure to HB_sAg-positive materials such as blood, plasma, or serum (accidental needle-stick, mucous membrane contact, oral ingestion)

Actions: Passive immunization

Dosage: 0.06 ml/kg IM preferably within seven days after exposure; repeat 28 to 30 days after exposure

Note: Administered in gluteal or deltoid muscle, preferably gluteal.

Hetastarch (Hespan): See also Chapter 11

Indications: Plasma volume expansion as an adjunct in treatment of shock due to hemorrhage, surgery, burns, other trauma

Actions: Synthetic colloid with properties similar to albumin

Dosage: Usually 500 to 1000 ml (do not usually exceed 1500 ml/day) IV at a rate not to exceed 20 ml/kg/hr

Supplied: 500 ml injectable 6% solution

Notes: Not a substitute for blood or plasma; contraindicated in patients with severe bleeding disorders, severe CHF, or renal failure with oliguria or anuria.

Hydralazine (Apresoline)

Indications: Severe hypertension

Actions: Direct relaxation of vascular smooth muscle

Dosage

ADULT: Begin at 10 mg po qid, then increase to 25 mg qid to a maximum of 300 mg/day; for rapid control of pressure, 20 to 40 mg IM prn

PEDS: 0.75 mg/kg/24 hr po in 4 divided doses or 1.7–3.5 mg/kg/24 hr IM or IV up to q4h

Supplied: Tablets, 10, 25, 50, 100 mg; injectable forms

Notes: Caution with impaired renal function, coronary artery disease; compensatory sinus tachycardia can be eliminated with addition of propranolol.

Hydrochlorothiazide (Hydrodiuril, Esidrix, Others)

Indications: Edema, hypertension, CHF

Actions: Thiazide diuretic, causes sodium and chloride excretion

Dosage

ADULT: 50–100 mg po qd–bid

PEDS

<6 Months: Up to 3 mg/kg/24 hr in 2 doses

>6 Months: 2–3 mg/kg/24 hr in 2 doses

Supplied: Tablets, 25, 50, 100 mg

Notes: Hypokalemia frequent; hyperglycemia, hyperuricemia common.

Hydromorphone (Dilaudid)

Indications: Moderate to severe pain (surgery, cancer, etc.)

Actions: Potent narcotic analgesic

Dosage: 2–4 mg po, IM, IV, SQ, or pr q4–6h prn

Supplied: Tablets, 1, 2, 3, 4 mg; powder; injectable forms; suppositories

Notes: Can be habit forming; 1.5 mg IM equivalent to 10 mg morphine.

Hydroxyzine (Atarax, Vistaril)

Indications: Anxiety, tension, sedation, itching

Actions: Antihistamine, sedative effects, potentiates narcotics

Dosage

ADULT

- Anxiety or preop: 50–100 mg po or IM qid or prn (maximum 600 mg/day)
- Itching: 25 mg po or IM tid–qid

PEDS: 0.5–1.0 mg/kg/dose IM q4h prn or 2 mg/kg/24 hr in 4 divided doses

Supplied: Tablets, 10, 25, 50, 100 mg; capsules, 25, 50, 100 mg; suspension; liquid; injectable forms

Notes: Useful in potentiating the effect of narcotics; not for IV use.

Ibuprofen (Motrin)

Indications: Rheumatoid arthritis, osteoarthritis, mild pain, dysmenorrhea

Actions: Nonsteroidal anti-inflammatory, antipyretic

Dosage: 300, 400, or 600 mg po tid–qid; titrate as needed (maximum 2.4 gm/24 hr)

Supplied: Tablets, 300, 400, 600 mg

Notes: Can cause GI upset.

Imipramine (Tofranil)

Indications: Depression, childhood enuresis

Actions: Tricyclic antidepressant

Dosage

ADULT

Hospitalized: Start at 100 mg/24 hr in divided doses; can increase over several weeks to 250–300 mg/24 hr

Outpatient: Maintenance 50–150 mg/24 hr in divided doses not to exceed 200 mg/24 hr

PEDS
- Enuresis: >6 years old, 25–50 mg po qhs
- Sedation: 1.5 mg/kg/24 hr po or IM in 3 divided doses (maximum 100 mg/24 hr)

Supplied: Tablets, 10, 25, 50 mg; capsules, 75, 100, 125, 150 mg; injectable forms

Notes: Do not use with MAO inhibitors; less sedation than amitriptyline.

Indomethacin (Indocin)

Indications: Severe rheumatoid arthritis, osteoarthritis, severe ankylosing spondylitis, acute gouty attack

Actions: Nonsteroidal anti-inflammatory

Dosage
- Acute gouty attack: 50 mg tid
- Other: 25 mg po bid–tid; titrate up to 200 mg/day maximum

Supplied: Capsules 25, 50 mg

Notes: Large number of severe side effects; discolors feces and urine; use with care in elderly.

Insulin (Iletin)

Indications: Diabetes mellitus that cannot be controlled by diet

Actions: Like endogenous insulin, hypoglycemic agent

Dosage: Based on serum glucose levels; usually given SQ, can also be given IV or IM

Supplied: See the following comparison charts

Notes: The highly purified insulins provide an increase in free insulin; monitor patients closely for several weeks when changing from standard to highly purified insulin; may need to decrease dose to get same effect; highly purified insulins more expensive, therefore, only indicated at present for patients with insulin allergies, lipodystrophies, or intermittent therapy.

Comparison of Standard Insulins

Type of Insulin	Onset (hr)	Peak (hr)	Duration (hr)
RAPID			
Regular	0.5–1.0	2–4	5–7
Semilente	1.0–2.0	2–4	12–16
INTERMEDIATE			
NPH	2.0–4.0	6–12	24–48
Lente	2.0–4.0	6–12	24–48
PROLONGED			
Protamine zinc (PZI)	2.0–6.0	14–24	36 +
Ultralente	2.0–6.0	18–24	36 +

Comparison of New Highly Purified Insulins

Type of Insulin	Onset (hr)	Peak (hr)	Duration (hr)
RAPID			
Actrapid	0.5	2.5–5.0	8
Semitard	0.5	5.0–10.0	16
Regular Iletin II	0.5–1.0	2.0–4.0	5–7
INTERMEDIATE			
Monotard	2.5	7–15	22
Lentard	2.5	7–15	24
NPH Iletin II	3.0–4.0	6–12	24–28
Lente Iletin II	1.0–3.0	6–12	24–28
PROLONGED			
Ultratard	4.0	10–30	36
Protamine zinc Iletin II	4.0–6.0	14–24	36 +

Ipecac Syrup

Indications: Emetic for use in drug overdose and certain cases of poisoning

Actions: Emetic agent

Dosage: See Chapter 21 for the treatment of poisoning

Supplied: Syrup

Notes: Do not use for ingestion of petroleum, strong acid, base, or other corrosive or caustic agents; not for use in comatose, unconscious, CNS depression, depressant overdose; may turn patient around in circles or ambulate for better results.

Iron Dextran (Imferon)

Indications: Iron deficiency

Actions: Replenishes iron stores when oral intake is not possible

Dosage: Based on estimate of iron deficiency (See package insert)

   ADULT: Average dose 4 ml IM qd for one week

Supplied: Injectable form

Notes: Must give a test dose since anaphylaxis common; may be given deep IM using "Z-track" technique although IV route most preferred.

Isoniazid (INH)

Indications: Active tuberculosis and the prevention of tuberculosis

Actions: Antituberculous antibiotic

Dosage

   ADULT
- Active TB: 5 mg/kg/24 hr po single dose (maximum 300 mg/day)
- Prevention: 300 mg/24 hr po

   PEDS
- Active TB: 10–20 mg/kg/24 hr po or IM in 2 divided doses

- Prevention: 10 mg/kg/24 hr po or IM single or divided dose

Supplied: Tablets, 50, 100, 300 mg; syrup; powder; injectable forms

Notes: Can cause severe hepatitis; usually used with other antituberculous drugs; treatment usually lasts 18 to 24 months; IM and IV routes rarely used; to prevent peripheral neuropathy can give pyridoxine 50–100 mg/day.

Isoproterenol (Isuprel)

Indications: Shock, cardiac arrest, AV nodal block, antiasthmatic

Actions: Pure beta adrenergic agonist

Dosage
- Cardiac arrest: See Chapter 21
- Shock: Titrate to desired effect (usually 1–4 μg/min IV)
- AV nodal block: 0.02 to 0.06 mg IV push (may repeat q3–5 min); 1–5 μg/min IV infusion for maintenance
- Antiasthmatic: 1–2 inhalations q1–5h (metered doses, maximum 6 repetitions qd)

Supplied: Injectable forms, metered inhaler

Notes: Contraindications include tachycardia due to digitalis intoxication; pulse >130 BPM may induce ventricular arrhythmias.

Isosorbide Dinitrate (Isordil)

Indications: Angina pectoris

Actions: Nitrate, smooth muscle relaxant

Dosage
- Acute angina: 2.5–10.0 mg po (chewable tablet) or SL q2–3h or prn q5–10min (>3 doses should not be given in 15 to 30 minute period)
- Angina prophylaxis: 5–30 mg po qid

Supplied: Chewable tablets, 5, 10 mg; tablets, 2.5, 5, 10, 20, 40 mg; sublingual (SL) 2.5, 5 mg

Notes: Can cause headaches; usually need to give a higher oral dose to achieve same results as with sublingual forms.

Kaolin-Pectin (Kaopectate, Others)

Indications: Treatment of diarrhea

Actions: Adsorbent demulcent

Dosage: 15 to 30 ml po prn

Supplied: Suspension

Lactobacillus (Lactinex Granules)

Indications: Control of diarrhea, especially after antibiotic therapy

Actions: Replaces normal intestinal flora

Dosage: 1 gm or 4 tablets with meals or liquids tid

Supplied: Tablets, granules

Lactulose

Indications: Hepatic (portal-systemic) encephalopathy

Actions: Acidification of colonic contents causes diffusion of ammonium iron into the colon from the blood; results in decreased serum ammonia.

Dosage: 20–30 gm po tid–qid; adjust dosage every one to two days to produce 2 to 3 soft stools qd

Supplied: Liquid forms

Notes: Can cause severe diarrhea.

Levothyroxine (Synthroid)

Indications: Hypothyroidism

Actions: Like L-thyroxine

Dosage: 25–50 μg/day initially; increase by 25–50 μg/day every month, usually 100–200 μg/day

Supplied: Tablets, 0.025, 0.05, 0.10, 0.15, 0.20, 0.30 mg; injectable forms

Notes: Titrate dosage based on clinical response and thyroid function tests; drug of choice for thyroid hormone replacement; dosage can be increased more rapidly in young to middle-aged patients.

Lidocaine (Xylocaine)

Indications: Local anesthetic, treatment of cardiac arrhythmias

Actions
- Anesthetic: Stabilizes neuronal membrane
- Antiarrhythmic: Increases myocardial stimulation threshold

Dosage
- Emergency cardiac care: See Chapter 21
- Local anesthesia: Maximum 4.5 mg/kg or 300 mg total in adults

Supplied: Injectable forms for cardiac use, injectable forms with and without epinephrine, topical solutions, jelly, ointment, suppositories

Notes: Epinephrine added to injectable forms for anesthesia to prolong effect and help decrease bleeding; for IV forms, dosage reduction is required with liver disease, CHF; dizziness, paresthesias, convulsions associated with toxicity.

Lithium Carbonate (Eskalith, Others)

Indications: Manic episodes of manic-depressive illness, maintenance therapy in recurrent disease

Actions: Uncertain

Dosage
- Acute mania: 600 mg po tid
- Maintenance: 300 mg po tid–qid

Supplied: Tablets, 300 mg; capsules, 300 mg

Notes: Dosage must be titrated; follow serum levels (see the section on drug levels in this chapter); common side effects are polyuria, tremor; contraindicated in patients with severe renal impairment; sodium retention on diuresis may potentiate toxicity.

Loperamide (Imodium)

Indications: Diarrhea

Actions: Slows intestinal transit time, non-narcotic

Dosage: 4 mg po initially, with 2 mg for each loose stool, up to 16 mg/day

Supplied: Tablets, 2 mg

Notes: Do not use in acute diarrhea caused by *Salmonella, Shigella,* or pseudomembranous colitis.

Magnesium Hydroxide (Milk of Magnesia)

Indications: Constipation, hyperacidity

Actions: Mild cathartic, antacid

Dosage

ADULT
- Antacid: 5 to 10 ml po prn
- Laxative: 15 to 30 ml po prn

PEDS: 0.5 ml/kg dose

Supplied: Liquid forms, tablets

Notes: Do not use in renal insufficiency or intestinal obstruction.

Magnesium Citrate

Indications: Vigorous bowel prep (barium enema), constipation

Actions: Saline cathartic

Dosage: 120 to 240 ml po prn

Supplied: Liquid forms

Notes: Do not use in renal insufficiency, intestinal obstruction.

Magnesium Sulfate

Indications: Anticonvulsant (especially for toxemia of pregnancy), replacement for low plasma levels (alcoholism, hyperalimentation)

Actions: Magnesium replacement, CNS depressant

Dosage: 1 to 2 gm IM or IV until desired response

Supplied: Injectable forms

Notes: Do not use in renal insufficiency.

Mannitol

Indications: When osmotic diuresis indicated (cerebral edema, oliguria, anuria, myoglobinuria, etc.)

Actions: Osmotic diuretic, rapid volume expansion, osmotic cathartic

Dosage

ADULT: Test dose, 12.5 gm IV over 10 minutes; then 50–200 gm/24 hr IV in divided doses

PEDS: Same test dose; 2 gm/kg over two to six hours of a 15% to 20% solution

Supplied: Injectable forms

Notes: Caution with CHF or volume overload.

Meperidine (Demerol)

Indications: Relief of moderate to severe pain, pre op medication

Actions: Synthetic narcotic analgesic similar to morphine

Dosage

ADULT: 50–100 mg po or IM q3–4h prn

PEDS: 6 mg/kg/24 hr po, IM, or SQ in 6 divided doses

Supplied: Tablets, 50, 100 mg; syrup; injectable forms

Notes: 75 mg IM equivalent to 10 mg morphine IM; beware of respiratory depression, addiction; a useful pre-procedure powerful sedative, particularly in children, is a so-called "cardiac cocktail" consisting of (per 30 lb or 66 kg) 30 mg Demerol, 6.25 mg Thorazine, and 6.25 mg Phenergan given IM.

Metaproterenol (Alupent, Metaprel)

Indications: Bronchodilator for asthma and reversible bronchospasm

Actions: Beta adrenergic agonist

Dosage: 1-3 inhalations q3-4h, maximum 12/day (allow at least two minutes between inhalations) or 20 mg po q6-8h

Supplied: Metered inhalers; tablets, 20 mg

Notes: Fewer beta-1 effects than isoproterenol and longer acting.

Methadone (Dolophine)

Indications: Severe pain, detoxification and maintenance of narcotics addiction

Actions: Narcotic analgesic, synthetic

Dosage: 2.5-10.0 mg q4h IM OR 5-15 mg po q4h (titrate dosage as needed)

Supplied: Liquid, injectable form

Notes: Equianalgesic with parenteral morphine.

Methenamine Mandelate (Mandelamine, Others)

Indications: Suppression of chronic urinary tract infection

Actions: In acid urine converted to formaldehyde (bactericidal)

Dosage

ADULT: 1 gm po qid

PEDS

<6 Years: 50 mg/kg/24 hr in 3 divided doses

>6 Years: 125 mg po qid

Supplied: Tablets, 0.25, 0.5, 1 gm; oral suspension

Notes: For maximum effect, urinary pH should be <5.5; use oral vitamin C or ammonium chloride to acidify urine; GI distress, urinary tract irritation common.

Methicillin (Staphcillin, Others)

Indications: Infections due to penicillinase-producing staphylococci

Actions: Synthetic penicillin, penicillinase resistant

Dosage

ADULT: 1 gm IM or IV q4–6h (may double in severe case)

PEDS: 100 mg/kg/24 hr IM in 4 to 6 divided doses

Supplied: Injectable forms

Notes: Can cause interstitial nephritis; caution with penicillin hypersensitivity; excreted primarily unchanged in urine.

Methimazole (Tapazole)

Indications: Hyperthyroidism, prep for thyroid surgery or radiation

Actions: Blocks organification and formation of T_3 and T_4

Dosage: Start at 15–60 mg/24 hr in 3 divided doses; maintenance, 5–15 mg po qd

Supplied: Tablets, 5, 10 mg

Notes: Follow patient clinically; follow thyroid function tests.

Methyldopa (Aldomet)

Indications: Hypertension

Actions: Central acting antihypertensive, possibly blocks formation of dopamine

Dosage

ADULT: Usual, 250 mg po bid–tid (maximum 2–3 gm/day) or 250 mg–1 gm IV q4–8h

PEDS: 10 mg/kg/24 hr po in 2 to 3 divided doses (maximum 65 mg/kg/24 hr)

Supplied: Tablets, 125, 250, 500 mg; injectable forms

Notes: Do not use in presence of liver disease; can discolor urine; initial transient sedation or drowsiness occurs frequently.

Metoclopramide (Reglan)

Indications: Treatment of delayed gastric emptying

Actions: Stimulates motility of upper GI tract without stimulation of gastric, biliary, or pancreatic secretions

Dosage: 10 mg po 30 minutes ac (before meals) and hs

Supplied: Tablets, 10 mg

Notes: Contraindicated with GI tract mechanical obstruction, perforation, or hemorrhage.

Methylprednisolone: See steroids

Metoprolol (Lopressor)

Indications: Hypertension

Actions: Selective beta-1 blocker

Dosage: Usual, 50–100 mg po bid

Supplied: Tablets, 50, 100 mg

Notes: Slowly increase dose for desired effect; can acquire beta-2 antagonist effect with high doses; good choice for patients with COPD; relatively contraindicated in CHF, AV block.

Metronidazole (Flagyl)

Indications: Amebiasis, trichomoniasis, *B. fragilis*; IV form indicated for serious anaerobic infections

Actions: Antiprotozoan antibiotic

Dosage: For IV use, see PDR or package insert

ADULT
- Amebic dysentery: 750 mg po qd (5 to 10 days)
- Trichomoniasis: 250 mg po tid (seven days) or 2 gm po in one day

PEDS
- Amebic dysentery: 40 mg/kg/24 hr in 3 divided doses for 5 to 10 days

Supplied: Tablets, 250 mg; injectable form

Notes: For *Trichomonas* infections, treat partner also; reduce dose in hepatic failure; effective in *B. fragilis* infections resistant to clindamycin, chloramphenicol, and penicillin.

Milk of Magnesia: See magnesium hydroxide

Mineral Oil

Indications: Constipation

Actions: Emollient laxative, lubricates stool

Dosage: 15 to 45 ml po prn

Supplied: Liquid forms

Morphine Sulfate

Indications: Relief of severe pain

Actions: Potent narcotic analgesic, cerebral and respiratory depression, pupillary constriction

Dosage

ADULT: 8–10 mg po or 5–15 mg SQ or IM or 4–10 mg IV slowly q4h prn

PEDS: 0.1–0.2 mg/kg/dose SQ (maximum 15 mg)

Supplied: Tablets, 10, 15, 30 mg; injectable forms; elixir

Notes: Large number of narcotic side effects; may require scheduled dosing to relieve severe chronic pain.

Moxalactam (Moxam)

Indications: Chronic upper respiratory tract infection (URI), septicemia, bone and joint infections due to gram-positive and gram-negative aerobes and some anaerobes

Actions: Semisynthetic beta-lactam, broad spectrum antibiotic

Dosage: 0.5–2.0 gm IV q12h

Supplied: Injectable forms

Notes: Stable against beta-lactamases from many gram-negative bacteria.

Nafcillin (Nafcil, Unipen)

Indications: Infections caused by penicillinase-producing staphylococci

Actions: See methicillin

Dosage

ADULT: 250 mg–1.5 gm po, IM, or IV q4–6h

PEDS

Newborn: 40–60 mg/kg/24 hr IM in 2 to 3 doses

Others: 50–100 mg/kg/24 hr IM in 4 doses

Supplied: Injectable forms, tablets, capsules, oral solutions

Notes: Penicillin-like side effects possible; change to po anti-staphylococcal agent when able; less incidence of interstitial nephritis than methicillin; caution with penicillin hypersensitivity.

Naloxone (Narcan)

Indications: Reversal of narcotic effect or suspected narcotic overdose

Actions: Competitive narcotic antagonist

Dosage

ADULT: 0.4–0.8 mg IV q5min for 3 doses

PEDS: 0.01 mg/kg IM, IV, or SQ; may repeat IV q3min for 3 doses

Supplied: Injectable forms

Notes: May precipitate acute withdrawal in addicts; if no response after 3 doses, suspect a non-narcotic cause.

Naproxen (Naprosyn)

Indications: Symptomatic treatment of acute and chronic rheumatoid arthritis

Actions: Nonsteroidal anti-inflammatory agent

Dosage: 250 mg po bid, adjust dosage according to clinical response or tolerance

Supplied: Tablets, 250 mg

Notes: Doses >750 mg/day not recommended; GI disturbances.

Neomycin Sulfate

Indications: Infectious diarrhea with pathogenic *E. coli*, hepatic coma, pre op bowel prep, topical antibiotic

Actions: Antibiotic

Dosage

   ADULT: 3–12 gm/24 hr po in 3 to 4 divided doses

   PEDS: 50–100 mg/kg/24 hr in 3 to 4 divided doses

Supplied: Many oral, topical, injectable forms

Notes: Part of Condon bowel prep (see erythromycin).

Nifedipine (Procardia)

Indications: Vasospastic, chronic stable angina

Actions: Inhibits cellular uptake of calcium, potent inhibitor of coronary artery spasm, dilates coronary and peripheral resistance vessels

Dosage: Initially, 10 mg po q8h; titrate to effect (maximum 180 mg/day)

Supplied: Capsules, 10 mg

Notes: Combine with nitrates for intractable angina.

Nitrofurantoin (Macrodantin, Furadantin)

Indications: Specific for urinary tract infections

Actions: Blocks enzyme systems, usually bactericidal

Dosage

ADULT
- Suppression: 50–100 mg po qd
- Usual dose: 50–100 mg po qid

PEDS

>1 Month: 5–7 mg/kg/day in 4 divided doses

Supplied: Tablets, 50, 100 mg; capsules, 25, 50, 100 mg; liquid; injectable form

Notes: GI side effects common; should be taken with food, milk, or antacid.

Nitroglycerine (Nitrostat, Nitro-Bid Ointment, Nitrobid IV, Others)

Indications: Angina pectoris, acute and prophylactic

Actions: Nitrate; smooth muscle relaxant, especially systemic venous beds

Dosage: 1 tablet SL q5min prn or topical 1–2 inches q3–4h prn (maximum 4 to 5 inches); refer to package insert or PDR for IV dosing instructions

Supplied: Tablets, 0.15 mg (1/400 grain [gr]), 0.30 mg (1/200 gr), 0.4 mg (1/150 gr), 0.6 mg (1/100 gr); 2% ointment; injectable forms; capsules, 2.5, 6.5 mg

Notes: Potent tablets should give burning under tongue and headache; larger doses of oral capsules often required for equivalent effect.

Nitroprusside (Nipride)

Indications: Hypertensive emergency, aortic dissection, acute myocardial infarction, CHF

Actions: Relaxation of arterial and venous smooth muscle

Dosage

ADULT: 0.5–8.0 µg/kg/min IV infusion (may be titrated for desired effect)

PEDS: Average, 1–3 µg/kg/min IV infusion

Supplied: Injectable form

Notes: Thiocyanate, the metabolite, is excreted by the kidney; thiocyanate toxicity occurs at plasma levels of 5–10 mg/dl.

Nystatin (Mycostatin, Nilstat)

Indications: Treatment of *Candida* infections (thrush, vaginitis)

Actions: Antifungal, polyene antibiotic; affects cell membrane

Dosage

ADULT
- Thrush: 400,000–600,000 units po "swish and swallow" qid
- Vaginitis: 1 tab per vagina qd or bid for two weeks

PEDS

Infants: 400,000 units po divided into 4 doses

Children: Adult dosage

Supplied: Tablets, oral suspension, topical ointment

Notes: Negligible oral absorption.

Oxtriphyilline (Choledyl)

Indications: Asthma, bronchospasm

Actions: Methyl xanthine, smooth muscle relaxant, equivalent to theophylline

Dosage

ADULT: 200 mg po qid

PEDS

>6 Years: Start at 6 mg/kg/24 hr in 4 divided doses (maximum 11 mg/kg/24 hr)

Supplied: Tablets, 100, 200 mg; elixir

Notes: Contains 64% theophylline.

Oxybutynin (Ditropan)

Indications: Symptomatic relief of urgency, nocturia, incontinence associated with neurogenic or reflex neurogenic bladder

Actions: Spasmolytic agent, anticholinergic

Dosage:

ADULT: 5 mg po bid–qid

PEDS

>5 Years: 5 mg po bid–tid

Supplied: Tablets, 5 mg; liquid, 5 mg/5 ml

Notes: Typical anticholinergic side effects.

Oxycodone (Percocet, Percodan, Tylox)

Indications: Moderate to moderately severe pain

Actions: Synthetic narcotic analgesic plus actions of additives

Dosage: 1 tablet po q4–6h

Supplied: Combination dosage tablets only

PERCOCET: 5 mg oxycodone, 325 mg acetaminophen

PERCODAN: 4.5 mg oxycodone, aspirin

TYLOX: 4.5 mg oxycodone, 500 mg acetaminophen

Notes: Cautions as with other narcotics.

Oxytocin (Pitocin)

Indications: Induction of labor, control of postpartum hemorrhage, stimulate flow of breast milk

Actions: Stimulates muscular contractions of uterus and breast

Dosage
- Induction of labor: 0.001–0.002 units/min IV, titrate effect; or buccal tablets, 1500–2000 units in 200 unit doses q30min
- Postpartum hemorrhage: 10 to 40 units in 1 liter of fluid, titrate rate to effect

Supplied: Injectable forms, buccal tablets

Notes: Can cause uterine rupture and fetal death; monitor vital signs closely.

Pancreatin (Viokase, Others)

Indications: Poor food digestion due to pancreatic hypofunction

Actions: Contains digestive enzymes, primarily amylase, from fresh pancreas

Dosage: 500 mg po with meals (may sprinkle granules over food)

Supplied: Capsules, granules, powder, tablets

Pancrelipase (Cotazym, Others)

Indications: Conditions in which pancreatic insufficiency impairs fat digestion

Actions: Contains pancreatic enzymes including lipase, trypsin, and amylase

Dosage: Determined by fat content of diet (300 mg/17 gm dietary fat)

Supplied: Capsules, tablets

Notes: Capsules may be opened and contents sprinkled on food.

Pancuronium (Pavulon)

Indications: Muscle relaxant for anesthesia, aid in management of patient on mechanical ventilator (THE PATIENT MUST BE INTUBATED OR MUST BE IMMEDIATELY INTUBATED)

Actions: Nondepolarizing neuromuscular blocker (curariform)

Dosage

ADULT: 2-4 mg IV q2-4h prn (0.04-0.10 mg/kg); additional doses of 0.010-0.015 mg/kg q30-60min prn

PEDS

Neonates: 0.02 mg/kg/dose

Older Children: Adult dosage

Supplied: Injectable forms

Notes: Use with extreme caution; patient should be intubated; use adequate amount of sedation or analgesia (morphine, etc.).

Penicillin G (Potassium or Sodium Aqueous)

Indications: Most gram-positive infections (except penicillin-resistant staphylococci) including streptococci (*S. viridans, S. pneumoniae*, group A), *N. gonorrhoeae, N. meningitidis*, syphilis, clostridia, corynebacteria, prophylaxis of bacterial endocarditis, some coliforms and others

Actions: Bacteriostatic, inhibits cell wall synthesis

Dosage

ADULT: 250-500 mg (400,000-800,000 units) po qid; IV doses vary greatly depending on indication, range from 1.2 to 24 million units/day; IM route very painful and not recommended; use benzathine or procaine form if IM route needed

PEDS

<12 Years: 25,000-300,000 units/kg/24 hr po, IM, IV, or SQ in 4 to 6 divided doses

Supplied: Multiple tablets, suspension, injectable forms

Notes: Beware of hypersensitivity reactions; drug of choice for group A streptococcal and pneumococcal infections.

Penicillin G Benzathine (Bicillin)

Indications: Useful as a single dose treatment regimen for streptococcal pharyngitis, rheumatic fever and glomerulo-nephritis prophylaxis, syphilis and SBE prophylaxis

Actions: See penicillin G; sustained action

Dosage

ADULT: 1.2–2.4 million units deep IM every 2–4 weeks and prn

PEDS: 300,000–1.2 million units IM monthly or prn

Supplied: Injectable form

Notes: Considered drug of choice for treatment of noncongenital syphilis; Bicillin L-A contains the benzathine salt only; Bicillin C-R contains a combination of the benzathine and procaine salts.

Penicillin G Procaine (Wycillin, Others)

Indications: Moderately severe penicillin G-sensitive organisms that respond to low persistent serum levels (gonorrhea, syphilis, uncomplicated pneumococcal pneumonia)

Actions: A long acting parenteral penicillin

Dosage

ADULT
- Gonorrhea: 4.8 million units IM in 2 divided doses in different sites with 1 gm of probenecid po
- Pneumonia: 600,000–1.2 million units/day IM

PEDS: 50,000–100,000 units/kg/day in divided doses

Supplied: Injectable form

Notes: Give probenecid at least 30 minutes prior to administration of penicillin.

Penicillin V (Pen-Vee K, Others)

Indications: See penicillin G

Actions: See penicillin G

Dosage

ADULT: 250–500 mg po q6h

PEDS: 25,000–50,000 units/kg/24 hr po in 4 divided doses

Supplied: Tablets, 125, 250, 500 mg; oral suspensions

Notes: A well-tolerated oral penicillin; 1 mg = 1695 units.

Pentazocine (Talwin)

Indications: Moderate to severe pain, pre op medication

Actions: Non-narcotic analgesic, mild narcotic antagonism

Dosage: 30 mg IM or IV or 50–100 mg po q3–4h prn

Supplied: Tablets, 50 mg; injectable form

Notes: 30 to 60 mg IM equianalgesic to 10 mg morphine IM.

Pentobarbital (Nembutal, Others)

Indications: Insomnia, anxiety, convulsions

Actions: CNS depressant, sedative-hypnotic, barbiturate

Dosage

ADULT
- Sedative: 20–40 mg po q6–12h
- Hypnotic: 100–200 mg po qhs

- Antianxiety-anticonvulsant: 0.25 mg/kg IV; additional small increments can be administered to total of 200 to 500 mg

PEDS
- Sedative: 2–3 mg/kg/day po or pr in 3 divided doses

Supplied: Capsules, 30, 50, 100 mg; tablets, 100 mg; elixir; suppositories; injectable forms

Notes: Can be habit forming; can cause respiratory depression; fairly short acting agent of barbiturate class; tolerance to sedative-hypnotic effect acquired within one to two weeks.

Phenazopyridine (Pyridium, Others)

Indications: Symptomatic relief of discomfort from lower urinary tract irritation (surgery, endoscopic procedures, catheters, infection)

Actions: Analgesic, local anesthetic

Dosage

ADULT: 200 mg po tid

PEDS: 12 mg/kg/24 hr in 3 divided doses

Supplied: Tablets, 100, 200 mg

Notes: GI disturbances; causes red-orange urine color.

Phenobarbital

Indications: Seizure disorders, insomnia, anxiety

Actions: Barbiturate, anticonvulsant, sedative-hypnotic

Dosage
- Status epilepticus: See Chapter 21

ADULT
- Sedative-hypnotic: 30–120 mg po or IM qd prn
- Anticonvulsant: 1–5 mg/kg/day po initially; usually 100–200 mg qd

PEDS
- Sedative: 1–2 mg/kg/24 hr po or pr in 3 divided doses
- Hypnotic: 2–4 mg/kg po or pr qhs prn
- Anticonvulsant: 4–6 mg/kg/24 hr po divided in 2 to 3 doses

Supplied: Tablets, capsules, elixirs, suppositories, injectable form

Notes: Tolerance develops to sedation; paradoxical hyperactivity seen in pediatric patients; long half-life allows single daily dosing; see the section on Drug Levels at the end of this chapter.

Phenylbutazone (Butazolidin, Azolid, Others)

Indications: Symptomatic treatment of acute gouty arthritis, rheumatoid spondylitis, musculoskeletal disorders (peritendinitis, bursitis, etc.), acute perivascular inflammation

Actions: Nonsteroidal anti-inflammatory agent

Dosage: 300–600 mg/day in 3 to 4 divided doses; should reduce maintenance dose to minimum effective dose (maximum 400 mg/day)

Supplied: Tablets, 100 mg

Notes: Discontinue after one week if favorable response is absent; should limit length of therapy because of serious side effects (especially hematological).

Phenytoin (Dilantin)

Indications: Grand mal and psychomotor seizures

Actions: Inhibits spread of seizure in motor cortex

Dosage
- Status epilepticus: See Chapter 21

ADULT
- Actively seizing: 15–18 mg/kg IV (50 mg/min maximum infusion rate)
- Prophylaxis of seizures: 11 mg/kg IV (50 mg/min) or 30 mg/kg po (3 divided doses)
- Maintenance: 4–8 mg/kg/day IV, IM, or po in 2 divided doses

PEDS: Same as adults

Supplied: Capsules, 30, 100 mg; chewable tablets, 50 mg; suspension; injectable forms

Notes: May use a loading dose; caution with cardiac side effects, especially with IV forms; follow levels as needed (see the end of this chapter for levels); nystagmus and ataxia early signs of toxicity; gum hyperplasia occurs often.

Physostigmine (Antilirium)

Indications: Antidote for tricyclic antidepressant, atropine, scopolamine overdose (see Chapter 21); stimulation of peristalsis from postoperative intestinal atony

Actions: Anticholinesterase, acetylcholinesterase inhibitor

Dosage

ADULT
- Antidote: 1 to 4 mg IV slowly prn, 1 mg SQ q15min
- Peristalsis: 0.5 to 2.0 mg IV or IM

PEDS
- Antidote: 0.5 mg IV q5min until cholinergic effects seen (maximum 2 mg)

Supplied: Injectable forms

Notes: Rapid IV administration associated with convulsions; cholinergic side effects.

Phytonadione (Vitamin K) (AquaMEPHYTON, Others)

Indications: Correction of a prolonged prothrombin time (caused by Coumadin or a decrease in absorption or synthesis of vitamin K from the gut), hyperalimentation, hemorrhagic disease of the newborn

Actions: Like natural vitamin K, needed for the production of Factors II, VII, IX, and X

Dosage

ADULT
- Anticoagulant-induced prothrombin deficiency: 2.5 to 10.0 mg po or 10 to 50 mg IV SLOWLY
- Hyperalimentation: 10 mg IM every week

PEDS
- Hemorrhagic disease
  - Prophylaxis: 1 mg IM or SQ, single dose
  - Treatment: 5 to 10 mg IM, IV, or SQ, single dose
- Other deficiencies: 5–10 mg po qd

Supplied: Tablets, 5 mg; injectable forms

Notes: With parenteral treatment, prothrombin deficit usually controlled in four to eight hours; anaphylaxis can result from IV dosage.

Plasma Protein Fraction (Plasmanate, Others)

Indications: Plasma volume expansion for shock from burns, surgery, hemorrhage, other trauma, or other conditions

Actions: Causes osmotic shift of interstitial fluids into the circulation

Dosage

ADULT: 250 to 500 ml IV initially (not >10 ml/min); subsequent infusions should depend upon clinical situation and response

PEDS: 4.5–6.8 ml/kg IV initially (not >10 ml/min); subsequent infusions same as adults

Supplied: Injectable forms, 5%

Notes: Hypotension associated with rapid infusion; see Chapters 11 and 21 for additional information.

Pneumococcal Vaccine, Polyvalent (Pneumovax)

Indications: Immunization against pneumococcal infections in patients predisposed or at high risk of acquiring these infections (elderly, pediatric, sickle cell disease, anatomic or functional asplenia)

Actions: Immunization against pneumococcal infections

Dosage

ADULT: 0.5 ml IM or SQ

PEDS

>2 Years: Same as adults

Supplied: Injectable form

Notes: Not to be performed at intervals ©three years; covers approximately 80% of pneumococcal disease isolates.

Potassium Supplements (Kay Ciel, K-Lor, Slow-K, Others)

Indications: Prevention or treatment of hypokalemia (most commonly diuretic-related)

Actions: Oral potassium replacement, KCl

Dosage: See Chapter 11 for treatment of hypokalemia

ADULT
- Diuretic therapy: 8–40 mEq po qd

PEDS
- Diuretic therapy: 1–2 mEq/kg/day, increase as needed.

Supplied: Tablets, liquids, powders

Notes: Can cause GI irritation and bleeding; powder and liquids must be mixed with a beverage (unsalted tomato juice very palatable); Slo-K tablets contain 8 mEq KCl/tablet.

Prazosin (Minipres)

Indications: Hypertension

Actions: Peripheral vasodilation by peripheral alpha-l adrenergic blockade

Dosage: 1 mg po test dose, then 1 mg po tid; can increase to a total daily dose of 20 mg

Supplied: Capsules, 1, 2, 5 mg

Notes: Can cause orthostatic hypotension, therefore, patient should take first dose at bedtime; tolerance develops to this effect; not a first-line drug.

Prednisone: See steroids

Prednisolone: See steroids

Probenecid (Benemid, Others)

Indications: Gout, maintenance of serum levels of penicillin

Actions: Uricosuric agent, inhibits tubular secretion of penicillins and cephalosporins

Dosage
- Gout: 0.25 gm bid for one week; then 0.5 gm po bid
- Penicillin effect: 1 to 2 gm po 30 minutes prior to dose of penicillin

Supplied: Tablets, 0.5 gm

Procainamide (Pronestyl)

Indications: Treatment of supraventricular and ventricular arrhythmias

Actions: Antiarrhythmic; depresses cardiac excitability and slows conduction; effect similar to quinidine

Dosage
- Emergency cardiac care: See Chapter 21

ADULT: 50 mg/kg/day po in divided doses q4–6h

PEDS: Same as adults

Supplied: Tablets and capsules, 250, 375, 500 mg; injectable forms

Notes: Can cause hypotension and a lupus-like syndrome; dosage adjustment required with renal impairment.

Prochlorperizine (Compazine)

Indications: Nausea, vomiting, agitation, psychotic disorders

Actions: A phenothiazine, antiemetic, antipsychotic

Dosage

ADULT
- Antiemetic: 5–10 mg po tid–qid or 25 mg pr bid or 5–10 mg deep IM q4–6h
- Antipsychotic: 10 to 20 mg IM acutely or 5–10 mg po tid–qid for maintenance

PEDS
>2 Years: 0.4 mg/kg/24 hr po in 3 to 4 divided doses or deep IM using ½ the po dose

Supplied: Tablets, 5, 10 mg; syrup; suppositories; injectable forms

Notes: Much larger doses required for antipsychotic effect; extrapyramidal side effects common; treat acute extrapyramidal reactions with diphenhydramine.

Promethazine (Phenergan)

Indications: Nausea, vomiting, motion sickness, potentiate narcotics

Actions: A phenothiazine, antiemetic, some antihistamine effects

Dosage

ADULT: 25–50 mg po, pr, or IM bid–qid prn

PEDS: 0.25–0.50 mg/kg/dose po, pr, or IM bid–qid prn

Supplied: Tablets, 12.5, 25, 50 mg; syrup; suppositories; injectable form

Notes: High incidence of drowsiness.

Propantheline (Pro-Banthine)

Indications: Symptomatic treatment of small intestine hypermotility, spastic colon, ureteral spasm, bladder spasm, pylorospasm

Actions: Parasympatholytic, inhibits GI and urinary tract motility

Dosage: 15–30 mg po, IV, or IM q6h

Supplied: Tablets, 7.5, 15 mg; injectable forms

Notes: Up to 60 mg q6h may be required, especially with urogenital spasm.

Propoxyphene (Darvon, Darvocet, Dolene, SK-65)

Indications: Mild to moderate pain

Actions: Mild narcotic analgesic related to methadone

Dosage: 1 tablet (32–65 mg) po q4h prn

Supplied
- Darvon: 32, 65 mg
- Darvon-N: 100 mg required to supply 65 mg of propoxyphene
- Darvocet-N: Propoxyphene with acetaminophen
- Darvon Compound: Propoxyphene, aspirin, phenacetin, caffeine

Notes: Caution as with all narcotics.

Propranolol (Inderal)

Indications: Angina, hypertension, arrhythmias, pheochromocytoma, thyroid storm, migraine prophylaxis

Actions: Mixed beta-1 and beta-2 adrenergic antagonist

Dosage
- Emergency cardiac care: See Chapter 21

ADULT
- Angina pectoris: 10–40 mg po tid–qid (maximum 320 mg/day)
- Hypertension: 160–480 mg/day po in divided doses
- Arrhythmias: 10–30 mg po tid–qid
- Migraine prophylaxis: 80 mg initially, up to 160–240 mg qd in divided doses

PEDS: 0.5–1.0 mg/kg/24 hr in 3 to 4 divided doses

Supplied: Tablets, 10, 40, 80 mg; injectable forms

Notes: Relatively contraindicated in COPD, CHF, AV block.

Propylthiouracil (PTU) (Propacil, Others)

Indications: Hyperthyroidism

Actions: Inhibits production and conversion of T_3 and T_4

Dosage

ADULT: Begin at 100 mg po q8h (may need up to 1200 mg/day for control); after patient euthyroid (six to eight weeks), taper dose by ⅓ every four to six weeks to a maintenance dose of 50–150 mg/day; treatment usually complete in two to three years

PEDS

6 to 10 Years: 50–150 mg/day po in 3 divided doses; then 50 mg po bid when euthyroid

>10 Years: 150–300 mg/day in 3 divided doses; then 50–100 mg po bid when euthyroid

Supplied: Tablets, 50, 250 mg

Notes: Follow patient clinically; monitor thyroid function tests.

Protamine Sulfate

Indications: Reversal of heparin effect

Actions: Heparin antagonist, binds heparin

Dosage: Based on amount of heparin reversal desired; given slow IV, 1 mg will reverse approximately 100 units of heparin

Supplied: Injectable forms

Notes: Follow coagulation studies; may have anticoagulant effect if given without heparin.

Pseudoephedrine (Sudafed, Novafed, Afrinol, Others)

Indications: Symptomatic relief of nasal or eustachian tube congestion

Actions: Sympathomimetic, alpha and beta effects; decongestant

Dosage

ADULT: 60 mg po q4h (time-release capsules, q8–12h)

PEDS: 4–8 mg/kg/24 hr in 4 divided doses

Supplied: Tablets, 30, 60 mg; capsules (time release), 60, 120 mg; liquid

Notes: Contraindicated with hypertensive patient, coronary artery disease, patients taking MAO inhibitors.

Psyllium (Metamucil, Serutan, Effersyllium)

Indications: Constipation, diverticular disease of the colon

Actions: Bulk laxative, holds water in stool

Dosage: 1 teaspoon (7 gm) in a glass of water qd–tid

Supplied: Powders, flakes, granules

Notes: Do not use in suspected bowel obstruction; one of the safest laxatives.

Pyridoxine (Various)

Indications: Treatment and prevention of vitamin B_6 deficiency

Actions: Vitamin B$_6$ supplement

Dosage
- Treatment: 2.5–10.0 mg po qd
- Drug-induced deficiency: 50–100 mg po qd

Supplied: Capsules, tablets, injectable forms

Notes: Given with isoniazid to prevent peripheral neuropathy during TB therapy.

Quinidine (Quinidex, Quinaglute)

Indications: Prevention of tachydysrhythmias (PAT, atrial fibrillation, ventricular tachycardia, PVCs, etc.)

Actions: Depresses automaticity and conduction of the myocardium, prolongs the refractory period

Dosage

ADULT
- PAC, PVCs: 200–300 mg po tid–qid
- PAT: 400–600 mg po q2–3h until terminated
- Conversion of atrial fibrillation or flutter: Use after digitalization, 200 mg q2–3h for 8 doses; then increase daily dose to maximum of 3 to 4 gm or until normal rhythm

PEDS
- Sulfate: 3–6 mg/kg/dose q2–3h or
- Gluconate: 2–10 mg/kg/dose q3–6h

Supplied: As two salts

SULFATE SALT: Contains 83% quinidine; capsules, 200, 300 mg; tablets 100, 130, 200, 325 mg; injectable forms

GLUCONATE SALT: Contains 62% quinidine; tablets (extended release), 324 mg; injectable forms

Notes: Contraindicated in digitalis toxicity, AV block; follow serum levels if available (see table on drug levels at the end of this chapter); extreme hypotension seen with IV administration.

Rh$_O$ (D) Immune Globulin (Rh$_O$GAM)

Indications: Prevention of maternal sensitization to the Rh$_O$ (D) factor and help in prevention of erythroblastosis fetalis in future pregnancies

Actions: Suppresses the immune response of Rh-negative mothers who receive Rh-positive blood as a result of feto-maternal hemorrhage at delivery

Dosage: Administer 1 vial IM within 72 hours following Rh-incompatible delivery; need to crossmatch sample to recipient

Supplied: Injectable form

Rifampin (Ritadin)

Indications: Tuberculosis, treatment of *N. meningitidis* carrier

Actions: Antibiotic, blocks DNA-dependent RNA polymerase

Dosage

ADULT: 600 mg po qd (treat meningitis carriers for two days)

PEDS: 20 mg/kg/day 1 dose (treat carriers for two days)

Supplied: Capsules, 300 mg

Notes: Multiple side effects; not a first-line TB drug.

Secobarbital (Seconal)

Indications: Insomnia, preoperative sedation

Actions: A barbiturate, rapidly acting sedative-hypnotic

Dosage

ADULTS: 100 mg po or pr OR 1–2 mg/kg IM qhs

PEDS: 2–6 mg/kg/day in 3 divided doses

Supplied: Capsules, tablets, elixir, suppositories, injectable form

Notes: Beware of respiratory depression; can be habit forming; tolerance acquired within one to two weeks.

Silver Sulfadiazine (Silvadene)

Indications: Prevention of sepsis in second-degree and third-degree burns

Actions: A sulfonamide, broad spectrum topical antibiotic

Dosage: Aseptically cover affected area with 1/16 inch coating bid

Supplied: Topical cream

Notes: Can be systemic absorption with extensive application.

Simethicone (Mylicon)

Indications: Symptomatic treatment of flatulence

Actions: Defoaming action to disperse gas

Dosage: 40–80 mg po pc (after meals) and hs prn

Supplied: Chewable tablets, 40, 80 mg; drops; suspension

Sodium Bicarbonate: See Chapter 21

Sodium Polystyrene Sulfonate (Kayexalate)

Indications: Treatment of hyperkalemia

Actions: Sodium and potassium ion exchange resin, lowers serum potassium

Dosage: See Chapters 11 and 21

Supplied: Powder for oral and rectal use

Notes: Can cause hypernatremia and increased intravascular volume.

Spironolactone (Aldactone)

Indications: Treatment of hyperaldosteronism, essential hypertension, edematous states (CHF, cirrhosis)

Actions: Aldosterone antagonist, causes increased sodium and water excretion, spares potassium loss

Dosage

ADULT: 100 mg/day po in divided doses; adjust after two weeks (up to 400 mg/day for primary aldosteronism)

PEDS: 1.7–3.3 mg/kg/24 hr in divided doses

Supplied: Tablets, 25 mg

Notes: Can cause hyperkalemia and gynecomastia; avoid prolonged use; diuretic of choice for cirrhotic edema and ascites.

Steroids: The following relates only to the commonly used systemic glucocorticoids

Indications: Endocrine disorders (adrenal insufficiency), rheumatoid disorders, collagen diseases, dermatological diseases, allergic states, edematous states (cerebral, nephrotic syndrome), others

Actions: Potent anti-inflammatory effects, some mineralo-corticoid effects

Dosage: Varies with indications

Supplied: See the following table, "Comparison of Gluco-corticoids."

Notes: All can cause hyperglycemia, adrenal suppression; never acutely stop steroids, especially if chronic treatment; need to gradually taper dose to allow adrenals to respond.

Comparison of Glucocorticoids

Drug	Equivalent Dose (mg)	Moderate Daily Dose (mg)	Route*
CORTISONE (Deltasone)	25.00	100–150	PO, IM
HYDROCORTISONE (Solu-Cortef)	20.00	80–120	PO, IM, IV
PREDNISONE (Deltasone)	5.00	20–40	PO
PREDNISOLONE (Delta-Cortef)	5.00	20–40	PO, IM, IV
METHYLPREDNISOLONE (Depo-Medrol, Solu-Medrol)	4.00	16–24	PO, IM, IV
DEXAMETHASONE (Decadron)	0.75	3–6	PO, IV

*Given orally (PO), intramuscularly (IM), intravenously (IV)

Streptokinase (Streptase, Others)

Indications: Acute massive pulmonary embolism, deep vein thrombosis, some occluded vascular grafts

Actions: Thrombolytic agent

Dosage

LOAD: 250,000 IU IV over 30 minutes

MAINTENANCE
- Pulmonary embolus: 100,000 IU/hr IV for 24 to 72 hours
- Deep venous thrombosis: 100,000 IU/hr IV for 72 hours

Supplied: Injectable form

Notes: If maintenance infusion not adequate to maintain thrombin clotting time two to five times control, refer to package insert, PDR, or *Hospital Formulary Service* for adjustments.

Streptomycin (Various)

Indications: Tuberculosis, bacterial endocarditis, other serious bacterial infections

Actions: An aminoglycoside, bactericidal, inhibits protein synthesis

Dosage

ADULT: 1–4 gm/day IM in 2 to 4 divided doses

PEDS: 20–40 mg/kg/24 hr IM in 3 divided doses (up to 10 days total)

Supplied: Injectable forms

Notes: Nephrotoxic, ototoxic; decrease dose in renal impairment.

Sucralfate (Carafate)

Indications: Short-term treatment of duodenal ulcers

Actions: Local formation of acid-resistant barrier, inhibits pepsin activity, absorbs bile salts

Dosage: 1 gm po qid

Supplied: Tablets, 1 gm

Notes: Administer one hour prior to meals and hs; antacids may also be used if taken ½ hour prior to sucralfate; treatment should be continued for four to eight weeks unless healing demonstrated by x-ray or endoscopy; constipation most frequent side effect.

Sulfasalazine (Azulfidine)

Indications: Ulcerative colitis

Actions: A sulfonamide and immunosuppressant, actions not clear

Dosage

  ADULTS: 1 to 2 gm initially, increasing to maximum of 8 gm/day in 3 to 4 divided doses; maintenance, 500 mg qid

  PEDS: 40–60 mg/kg/day in 3 to 6 divided doses initially; maintenance, 30 mg/kg/day in 4 divided doses

Supplied: Tablets, 500 mg

Notes: Can cause severe GI upset; discolors urine; enteric-coated tablet available.

Sulfinpyrazone (Anturane)

Indications: Maintenance of chronic gout

Actions: Uricosuric agent, decreases serum uric acid levels

Dosage: 200–400 mg po bid

Supplied: Tablets, 100 mg; capsules, 200 mg

Notes: Because of GI upset, should be given with meals.

Sulfisoxazole (Gantrisin, Various)

Indications: Acute uncomplicated urinary tract infections (sensitive organisms such as *E. coli* and staphylococci)

Actions: Inhibits synthesis of dihydrofolic acid

Dosage

ADULT: 2 to 4 gm po initially; then 4–8 gm/day in 4 to 6 divided doses

PEDS

>2 Months: 75 mg/kg po initially; then 150 mg/kg/day in 4 to 6 divided doses

Supplied: Suspension, 500 mg/5 ml; tablets; syrup; ointments; creams; injectable forms

Notes: Avoid use in last half of pregnancy (causes fetal hyperbilirubinemia).

Terbutaline (Brethine, Bricanyl)

Indications: Reversible bronchospasm (asthma, COPD)

Actions: Primarily adrenergic beta-2 agonist, bronchodilator

Dosage

ADULT: 2.5–5.0 mg po qid (maximum 15 mg/day); or 0.25 mg SQ, can repeat in 15 minutes (maximum 0.5 mg in four hours)

PEDS

12 to 15 Years: 7.5 mg/24 hr po in 3 divided doses

Supplied: Tablets, 2.5, 5 mg; injectable forms

Notes: Caution with diabetes, hypertension, hyperthyroidism; high doses may precipitate beta-1 adrenergic effects.

Tetanus Toxoid

Indications: Protection against tetanus

Actions: Active immunization against tetanus

Dosage: See Chapter 17 and Appendix

Supplied: Injectable forms

Tetracyclines

Indications: Broad spectrum antibiotic treatment against *Staphylococcus, Streptococcus*, acne, and others and when penicillin contraindicated

Actions: Bacteriostatic, inhibits protein synthesis

Dosage

ADULT: 250–500 mg po bid–qid

PEDS: 25–50 mg/kg/24 hr po in 2 to 4 divided doses; DO NOT USE IN CHILDREN LESS THAN 8 YEARS OLD

Supplied: Many oral, topical, injectable forms

Notes: IM and IV routes not recommended; can stain enamel and depress bone formation in children; caution with use in pregnancy; do not use in presence of impaired renal function (see doxycycline).

Theophylline (Theolair, Somophyllin, Others)

Indications: See aminophylline

Actions: See aminophylline

Dosage

ADULT: 200–250 mg po q6h or 250–500 mg pr bid–tid

PEDS: 16–25 mg/kg/day po in 4 divided doses or 5–7 mg/kg/day pr in 2 to 3 divided doses

Supplied: Capsules, tablets, elixirs, suppositories, time-release forms

Notes: Can only be given po or pr; aminophylline (85% theophylline) can be used IV if needed; see aminophylline for side effects; suppositories are erratically absorbed.

Thiamine (Vitamin B$_1$)

Indications: Thiamine deficiency (alcoholism, beriberi)

Actions: Needed for decarboxylation reactions (carbohydrate metabolism)

Dosage: 5–10 mg po tid for one month; 5–100 mg IM or IV q8h

Supplied: Tablets, elixir, injectable forms

Thioridazine (Mellaril)

Indications: Psychotic disorders, short-term treatment of depression, agitation, organic brain syndrome

Actions: A phenothiazine, antipsychotic, sedative

Dosage: Initially 50–100 mg po tid; maintenance, 200 to 800 mg po in 2 to 4 divided doses

Supplied: Multiple oral forms

Notes: Low incidence of extrapyramidal effects.

Ticarcillin (Ticar)

Indications: See carbenicillin

Actions: See carbenicillin

Dosage

ADULT: 200–300 mg/kg/24 hr IV in 4 to 6 divided doses

PEDS: Same as adults

Supplied: Injectable forms

Notes: Reduce dose in renal impairment; more active in vitro against *Pseudomonas aeruginosa* than carbenicillin; because of lower dose, less sodium load each day than with carbenicillin.

Timolol (Timoptic, Blocadren)

Indications: Glaucoma, hypertension, reduction in risk of reinfarction or cardiovascular mortality immediately following an acute myocardial infarction

Actions: Beta-1 and beta-2 adrenergic antagonist, decreases intraocular pressure

Dosage:

- Glaucoma: 1 drop (gtt) of 0.25% to 0.50% solution in each eye bid
- Hypertension: 20–40 mg/day po in 2 divided doses (maximum 60 mg/day)
- Reinfarction: 20 mg/day po in 2 divided doses after a myocardial infarction

Supplied: Optic solutions, 0.25%, 0.50%; tablets

Notes: Titrate dose every seven days for hypertension.

Tobramycin (Nebcin)

Indications: Serious gram-negative infections, especially *Pseudomonas*

Actions: See gentamicin

Dosage: Based on renal function; refer to Aminoglycoside Dosing at the end of this chapter.

Supplied: Injectable forms

Notes: See gentamicin.

Tolbutamide (Orinase)

Indications: Adult onset diabetes mellitus

Actions: Stimulates production and release of endogenous insulin

Dosage: Initially, 1 to 2 gm po single or divided dose; then maintenance, 250 mg to 3 gm po in single or divided dose

Supplied: Tablets, 250, 500 mg

Notes: Do not use in complicated diabetes (JODM, brittle, ketosis); usually first oral hypoglycemic of choice.

Trihexyphenidyl (Artane)

Indications: Parkinsonism, drug-induced extrapyramidal disorders

Actions: Anticholinergic

Dosage: 1–15 mg/day po in divided doses

Supplied: Tablets, capsules, elixir

Notes: Contraindicated in narrow angle glaucoma.

Trimethobenzamide (Tigan)

Indications: Nausea and vomiting

Actions: Antiemetic, antihistamine

Dosage

ADULT: 250 mg po or 200 mg pr or IM tid–qid prn

PEDS: 20 mg/kg/24 hr po OR 15 mg/kg/24 hr pr or IM in 3 to 4 divided doses (not recommended for infants)

Supplied: Capsules, 100, 250 mg; suppositories; injectable form

Trimethoprim (Trimpex, Proloprim)

Indications: Urinary tract infections due to susceptible gram-positive and gram-negative organisms

Actions: Inhibits dihydrofolate reductase

Dosage: 100 mg po bid

Supplied: Tablets, 100 mg

Notes: Good for initial, uncomplicated UTI.

Trimethoprim-Sulfamethoxazole (Co-trimoxazole) (Bactrim, Septra)

Indications: Urinary tract infections, otitis media, *Shigella*, *Pneumocystis carinii*

Actions: Sulfamethoxazole inhibits synthesis of dihydrofolic acid; trimethoprim inhibits dihydrofolate reductase; results in impaired protein synthesis

Dosage

ADULT: 1 double-strength tablet po bid or 15–20 mg/kg/24 hr (based on trimethoprim component) IV in 3 to 4 divided doses

PEDS: 8–10 mg/kg trimethoprim and 40–50 mg/kg sulfamethoxazole/24 hr po in divided doses

Supplied: Tablets, regular and double-strength (double-strength contain 160 mg trimethoprim and 800 mg sulfamethoxazole); oral suspension, 40 mg trimethoprim and 200 mg sulfamethoxazole in 5 ml; injectable forms

Notes: Synergistic combination; reduce dosage in renal failure; if creatinine clearance 15–30 ml/min, use ½ dose.

Triprolidine-Pseudoephedrine (Actifed)

Indications: Symptomatic relief of allergic and vasomotor rhinitis

Actions: Triprolidine, an antihistamine; pseudoephedrine, a decongestant

Dosage

ADULT: 1 tablet po tid–qid or 2 tsp (10 ml) tid–qid

PEDS

4 Months to 2 Years: ¼ tsp tid–qid

2 to 4 Years: ½ tsp tid–qid

4 to 6 Years: ¾ tsp tid–qid

6 to 12 Years: 1 tsp tid–qid

Supplied: Tablets, syrup

Valproic Acid (Depakene)

Indications: Absence seizures (petit mal)

Actions: Anticonvulsant, mechanism unknown

Dosage: Initially, 15 mg/kg/24 hr; can be increased by 5–10 mg/kg/24 hr at weekly intervals for desired effect (maximum 30 mg/kg/24 hr)

Supplied: Capsules, syrup

Vancomycin (Vancocin)

Indications: Serious infections due to penicillin-resistant staphylococcal and enterococcal endocarditis, staphylococcal enterocolitis

Actions: Bactericidal, inhibits cell wall synthesis

Dosage

   ADULTS: 2 gm/day po or IV bid–qid

   PEDS: 10–40 mg/kg/24 hr po or IV in 2 to 4 divided doses

Supplied: Powder, injectable forms

Notes: Not a first-line drug; ototoxic and nephrotoxic; to prevent GI side effects, divide dose when daily dosage exceeds 250 mg.

Vasopressin (Pitressin)

Indications: Treatment of diabetes insipidus, relief of gaseous GI tract distention, limited usefulness for GI bleeding

Actions: A posterior pituitary hormone (ADH); potent vasoconstrictor of smooth muscle (especially GI tract)

Dosage
   • Diabetes insipidus: 5–10 units SQ or IM tid–qid or 1.5–5.0 units IM q1–3days of the tannate

Supplied: Injectable, SQ or IM use; tannate (oil base) should be given IM only

Notes: Should be used with caution with any vascular disease.

Verapamil (Isoptin)

Indications: Supraventricular tachyarrhythmias (PAT, Wolff-Parkinson-White syndrome, atrial flutter or fibrillation), vasospastic (Prinzmetal's) and unstable (crescendo, preinfarction) angina, chronic stable angina (classic effort-associated)

Actions: Slow-channel calcium blocking agent

Dosage

ADULT
- Tachyarrhythmias: 5 to 10 mg IV over two minutes (may repeat in 30 minutes)
- Angina: 240–480 mg/24 hr divided in 3 to 4 doses

PEDS

<1 Year: 0.1–0.2 mg/kg IV over two minutes (may repeat in 30 minutes)

1 to 15 Years: 0.1–0.3 mg/kg IV over two minutes (may repeat in 30 minutes)

Supplied: Injectable form, tablets

Notes: Contraindications include severe hypotension, cardiogenic shock, second-degree and third-degree AV block, sick sinus syndrome, CHF, beta-blocking drugs; caution with elderly patients.

Vitamin K: See phytonadione

Warfarin Sodium (Coumadin)

Indications: Prophylaxis and treatment of pulmonary embolism and venous thrombosis, atrial fibrillation with embolization, other post op indications

Actions: Anticoagulant, inhibits hepatic production of vitamin K-dependent clotting factors in this order: VII-IX-X-II

Dosage: Need to individualize dosage to keep PT (prothrombin time) at 1.5 to 2.5 times control; initially, 10–40 mg po, IM, or IV qd for one to three days; then maintenance, 2–10 mg po, IV, or IM qd; follow daily PT during initial phase to guide dosage

Supplied: Tablets, 2, 2.5, 5, 10, 25 mg; injectable forms

Notes: PTs need to be checked periodically while on maintenance dose; beware of bleeding caused by overanticoagulation (PT >3 times control); caution patient on effects of taking Coumadin with other medications, especially aspirin; to rapidly correct overcoumadinization, use vitamin K or fresh frozen plasma or both.

Zomepirac (Zomax)

Zomepirac (Zomax), a non-steroidal antiinflammatory agent, was withdrawn by the manufacturer in March, 1983 due to serious allergic reactions associated with it's use. This drug should no longer be prescribed and all supplies should be destroyed or returned to the manufacturer.

CHEMOTHERAPEUTIC AGENTS

The following table is a guide to chemotherapeutic agents most commonly used against cancer. Dosages vary greatly depending on the protocol used at a particular center.

Chemotherapeutic Agents in Treatment of Cancer

Trade Name (Generic)	Category (Action)	Type of Cancer	Toxicity*		Route
			Acute	Delayed	
Adriamycin (doxorubicin)	Antibiotic (depolymerizes DNA)	Breast Bladder Lymphomas Lung, Sarcoma Hodgkin's Testicular	N,V Red urine TN, A	BM Cardiotoxicity (Lifetime dose 550 mg/m² or 450 mg/m² with cytoxan)	IV
Adrucil (fluorouracil/ 5-FU)	Antimetabolite (blocks DNA synthesis)	Stomach Colon, Breast Prostate Bladder	N, V, D	Oral and GI ulcers, A, BM (7–14 days), Dermatitis, Ataxia Photosensitivity	IV
Alkeran (melphalan)	Alkylating agent (blocks DNA synthesis)	Breast Myeloma Ovarian	N	BM (10–12 days) Pulmonary fibrosis, L	PO
BiCNU (carmustine/ BCNU)	Synthetic Alkylating agent (see Alkeran)	Brain, Lung Lymphomas Multiple myeloma	N, V, A	BM (progressive) Pulmonary fibrosis Delayed renal damage	IV

*CODE: N = nausea; V = vomiting; D = diarrhea; A = alopecia; S = stomatitis; BM = bone marrow suppression; L = leukemogenic; TN = tissue necrosis, if given SQ OR IM.

Chemotherapeutic Agents in Treatment of Cancer (Continued)

Trade Name (Generic)	Category (Action)	Type of Cancer	Toxicity* Acute	Toxicity* Delayed	Route
Blenoxane (bleomycin)	Antibiotic (damages DNA, prevents repair)	Cervix Head and Neck (squamous) Lymphoma Hodgkin's Testicular	N, V Fever Anaphylaxis	Pneumonitis Pulmonary fibrosis (rales detected on exam), Hyperpigmentation Lifetime dose 300–400 units, S, A	IV IM SQ
CeeNU (lomustine/CCNU)	Synthetic	Brain Lymphoma Lung Renal Hodgkin's	N, V, A	Delayed leukopenia and thrombocytopenia (4–6 wk) S, A Renal damage	PO
Cosmegen (dactinomycin/ actinomycin D)	Antibiotic (intercalate DNA)	Melanomas Sarcomas Testicular	N, V, D TN	Potent BM (15 days) A in 47%, S	IV

*CODE: N = nausea; V = vomiting, D = diarrhea; A = alopecia; S = stomatitis; BM = bone marrow suppression; L = leukemogenic; TN = tissue necrosis, if given SQ or IM.

Chemotherapeutic Agents in Treatment of Cancer (Continued)

Trade Name (Generic)	Category (Action)	Type of Cancer	Toxicity*		Route
			Acute	Delayed	
CytosarU (cytosine arabinoside/ ARA-C)	Antimetabolite (blocks DNA synthesis)	Acute leukemia Lymphomas	N, V Anaphylaxis A	Rare hepatic dysfunction BM (7–14 days)	IV
Cytoxan (cyclophospha- mide)	Alkylating agent (see Alkeran)	Breast Leukemia Lymphoma Lung Multiple myeloma Hodgkin's Prostate	N, V Anaphylaxis	BM (7–14 days) Hemorrhagic cystitis (prevented by increasing fluid intake and voiding frequently) Bladder cancer Sterility, A, L	IV PO IM
Daunomycin (daunorubicin)	Antibiotic (depolymerizes DNA)	Acute lymphocytic leukemia (ALL) Acute myelog- enous leukemia (AML)	N, V Red urine TN	BM (10–14 days) Cardiotoxicity A (complete body alopecia) S	IV

*CODE: N = nausea; V = vomiting; D = diarrhea; A = alopecia; S = stomatitis; BM = bone marrow suppression; L = leukemogenic; TN = tissue necrosis, if given SQ or IM.

Chemotherapeutic Agents in Treatment of Cancer (Continued)

Trade Name (Generic)	Category (Action)	Type of Cancer	Toxicity*		Route
			Acute	Delayed	
DTIC (dacarbazine)	Synthetic	Hodgkin's Melanoma Sarcoma Lymphoma	N, V Anaphylaxis Fever, TN	BM, Flu-like syndrome A	IV
Elspar (L-asparaginase)	Enzyme (deaminates L-asparagine)	ALL	N, V Fever Anaphylaxis	CNS depression, Acute hemorrhagic pancreatitis, Coagulopathy Anaphylaxis	IV IM
Hydrea (hydroxurea)	Synthetic (blocks DNA synthesis)	CML Head and Neck Melanoma	N, V	BM, A, S Fever Hyperpigmentation	PO IV
Leukeran (chlorambucil)	Alkylating agent (see Alkeran)	Breast, Chronic lymphocytic leukemia (CLL) Testicular Lymphoma Hodgkin's Ovarian		BM (particularly platelets) Pulmonary fibrosis, L	PO

*CODE: N = nausea; V = vomiting; D = diarrhea; A = alopecia; S = stomatitis; BM = bone marrow suppression; L = leukemogenic; TN = tissue necrosis, if given SQ or IM.

Chemotherapeutic Agents in Treatment of Cancer (Continued)

Trade Name (Generic)	Category (Action)	Type of Cancer	Acute	Delayed	Route
Matulane (procarbazine)	Synthetic (degrades DNA)	Lymphoma Lung Brain Hodgkin's	N, V, Rash CNS depression	BM (2–3 wk) S, Dermatitis Peripheral neuropathy	PO
Methotrexate (MTX/ methotrexate)	Antimetabolite (folic acid antagonist)	ALL Breast Lymphoma Head and Neck Lung Sarcoma	N, V, D Fever Anaphylaxis (give leukovorin rescue)	S BM (7–14 days) Hepatotoxicity Rare renal toxicity (check BUN, Cr)	PO IM IV
Mithracin (mithramycin)	Antibiotic (see Mutamycin)	Embryonal Testicular (Also refractory hypercalcemia)	N, V, D Fever, TN	BM, Bleeding abnormalities Hepatic damage Hypokalemia Hypocalcemia	IV
Mustargen (mechlorethamine)	Alkylating agent (see Alkeran)	Hodgkin's Lymphomas Lung	N, V, TN Skin necrosis	BM (7–14 days) A, D, L	IV

*CODE: N = nausea; V = vomiting; D = diarrhea; A = alopecia; S = stomatitis; BM = bone marrow suppression; L = leukemogenic; TN = tissue necrosis, if given SQ or IM.

Chemotherapeutic Agents in Treatment of Cancer (Continued)

Trade Name (Generic)	Category (Action)	Type of Cancer	Toxicity* Acute	Toxicity* Delayed	Route
Mutamycin (mitomycin C)	Antibiotic (depolymerizes DNA)	Breast Lung GI	N, V, Fever	BM (cumulative, 5–6 wk), S, A, Renal toxicity, Pulmonary fibrosis, L	IV
Myleran (busulfan)	Alkylating agent (see Alkeran)	CML (Also polycythemia vera)	N, V	Pulmonary fibrosis, L, A BM (11–30 days)	PO
Oncovin (vincristine)	Mitotic inhibitor	ALL Breast Lymphoma Lung Hodgkin's	Metallic taste, TN (avoid extravasation)	A (in 12% to 45% of patients) Neurotoxicity (foot drop) Constipation Maximum dose 2 mg	IV
Platinol (cisplatin/DDP)	Synthetic (cross-links DNA)	Testicular Ovarian Cervix, Lungs Head and Neck Bladder	N, V Fever Anaphylaxis	Renal damage Ototoxicity BM Hypomagnesemia Neurotoxicity	IV

*CODE: N = nauseac; V = vomiting; D = diarrhea; A = alopecia; S = stomatitis; BM = bone marrow suppression; L = leukemogenic; TN = tissue necrosis, if given SQ or IM.

Chemotherapeutic Agents in Treatment of Cancer (Continued)

Trade Name (Generic)	Category (Action)	Type of Cancer	Toxicity* Acute	Toxicity* Delayed	Route
Purinethol (mercaptopurine/ 6-MP)	Antimetabolite (purine antagonist)	ALL	N, V, D	BM (7 days), S Cholestasis Hepatic necrosis (rare)	PO
Thioguanine (6-TG/thioguanine)	Antimetabolite (purine antagonist)	AML ALL	Occasional N, V	BM, S	PO
Velban (vinblastine)	Mitotic inhibitor	Breast, Renal Lymphoma Hodgkin's Testicular	N, V, TN	BM (5–9 days) A, S	IV
VP-16 (etoposide)	Miscellaneous	Oat cell Testicular Hodgkin's	N, V, D Fever Hypotension	BM, A Peripheral neuropathy	IV

*CODE: N = nausea; V = vomiting; D = diarrhea; A = alopecia; S = stomatitis; BM = bone marrow suppression; L = leukemogenic; TN = tissue necrosis, if given SQ or IM.

DRUG LEVELS

The following tables are a general guide to drug levels commonly monitored. Each lab may have its own set of values that may vary slightly from those given.

Drug Levels

Drug	Therapeutic Level	Toxic Level
Carbamazepine (Tegretol)	8.0–12.0 μg/ml	>15.0 μg/ml
Digitoxin	13.0–25.0 ng/ml	>40.0 ng/ml
Digoxin	0.8–2.0 ng/ml	> 2.4 ng/ml
Ethosuximide (Zarontin)	40.0–100.0 μg/ml	>150.0 μg/ml
Lidocaine	1.5–6.5 μg/ml	>6.0–8.0 μg/ml
Phenobarbital	15.0–40.0 μg/ml	>45.0 μg/ml
Phenytoin (Dilantin)	10.0–20.0 μg/ml	>25.0 μg/ml
Procainamide (Pronestyl)	4.0–10.0 μg/ml	>16.0 μg/ml
Quinidine	—	>6.0 μg/ml
Salicylate	15.0–25.0 mg/dl	>30.0 mg/dl, >60.0 lethal
Theophylline	10.0–20.0 μg/ml	>20.0 μg/ml

Drug Levels: Antibiotics

Antibiotic	Trough (μg/ml)	Peak (μg/ml)
Amikacin	5.0–7.5	<35
Gentamicin	1.5–2.0	<6–8
Kanamycin	5.0–7.5	<35
Tobramycin	1.5–2.0	<6–8

Drug Levels: Miscellaneous

Drug	Level*	Condition
Ethanol	100–200	Legally drunk, labile behavior
	150–300	Confusion
	250–400	Stupor
	350–500	Coma
	>450	Death
Lithium	0.5–1.0	Therapeutic maintenance
	0.9–1.4	Acute treatment
	>1.5	Toxic

*Levels for ethanol (blood level) given in mg/100 ml; for lithium, in mmol/liter.

AMINOGLYCOSIDE DOSING

The aminoglycosides are primarily excreted unchanged in the urine. Toxicities associated with aminoglycoside therapy necessitate careful monitoring of serum levels, especially during renal impairment. See the previous table, "Drug Levels: Antibiotics" for the trough and peak levels of the aminoglycosides gentamicin, tobramycin, and amikacin.

Therapy can be initiated with the recommended guidelines that follow.

Procedure

1. Calculate the estimated creatinine clearance (CrCl) based on serum creatinine (SCr), age, and weight (in kg). A formal creatinine clearance can also be ordered, if time permits (see Chapter 8).

$$\text{CrCl: male} = \frac{(140 - \text{age}) \times (\text{weight})}{(\text{SCr}) \times (72)}$$

$$\text{CrCl: female} = 0.85 \times (\text{CrCl male})$$

2. Select the loading dose:

   - Gentamicin — 1.5–2.0 mg/kg
   - Tobramycin — 1.5–2.0 mg/kg
   - Amikacin — 5.0–7.5 mg/kg

3. By using the following table you can now select the maintenance dose (as a percentage of the chosen loading dose) most appropriate for the renal function of the patient based on CrCl and dosing interval. Shaded areas are the suggested percentages and intervals for any given creatinine clearance.

Percentage of Loading Dose Required for Dosage Interval Selected*†

CrCl (ml/min)	Dosing Interval		
	8 hr	12 hr	24 hr
90	90	—	—
80	88	—	—
70	84	—	—
60	79	91	—
50	74	87	—
40	66	80	—
30	57	72	92
25	51	66	88
20	45	59	83
15	37	50	75
10	29	40	64
7	24	33	55
5	20	28	48
2	14	20	35
0	9	13	25

*From Hull JH, Sarubbi FA: Gentamicin serum concentrations: pharmacokinetic predictions. *Ann Int Med* **85**:183–189, 1976. Used with permission.
†Shaded areas indicate suggested dosage intervals.

Example

- Age = 65 years
- Sex = male
- Weight = 60 kg
- SCr = 3.1 mg/dl

1.
$$\text{CrCl: male} = \frac{(140 - 65) \times (60)}{(3.1) \times (72)} = 20 \text{ ml/min}$$

2. Loading dose = 120 mg gentamicin IV

3. From the table calculate the percentage of the loading dose that will be the maintenance dose:

- CrCl = 20 ml/min
- Suggested interval = 12 hr
- Maintenance dose = (0.59) × (120 mg) = 70 mg q12h

Note: This is only an empirical dose to begin therapy. Serum levels should be monitored routinely for optimal therapy. Use the previous table, "Drug Levels: Antibiotics."

Appendix

ABBREVIATIONS

Instructions

ac: before meals
ad lib: as often as desired
amb: ambulate
ASAP: as soon as possible
bid: twice a day
BRP: bathroom privileges
c: with
dl: deciliter
gr: grain
gtts: drops
HOB: head of bed
hs: at bedtime
IM: intramuscular, given intramuscularly

IV: intravenous, given intravenously
KOR: keep open rate
KVO: keep vein open
ml: milliliter
mmol: millimole
ng: nanogram
NPO: nothing by mouth
OOB: out of bed
pc: after meals
pg: picogram
po: by mouth, given orally
pr: by rectum, given rectally
prn: as needed
q: every
qd: every day
qh: every hour
qid: four times a day
qod: every other day
q6h: every six hours
s: without
sig: label
SL: sublingual
SQ: subcutaneous, given subcutaneously
STAT: immediately
tid: three times a day
TKO: to keep open
wnl: within normal limits

Description and Diagnosis

AAA: abdominal aortic aneurysm
A&B: apnea and bradycardia
A-aDO$_2$:   A-a gradient
A-a gradient: alveolar to arterial gradient
AAS: acute abdominal series
AB: antibody, abortion, or antibiotic
A/B Index: ankle brachial index
ABD: abdomen
ABG: arterial blood gas
ACLS: advanced cardiac life support
ACTH: adrenocorticotropic hormone

A.D.C. VAN DISSEL: mnemonic for Admit, Diagnosis, Condition, Vitals, Activity, Nursing procedures, Diet, Ins and outs, Specific drugs, Symptomatic drugs, Extras, Labs
ADH: antidiuretic hormone
AEIOU TIPS: mnemonic for Alcohol, Encephalopathy, Insulin, Opiates, Uremia, Trauma, Infection, Psychiatric, Syncope
AF: afebrile, aortofemoral, or atrial fibrillation
AFB: acid-fast bacilli
AFP: alpha-fetoprotein
AI: aortic insufficiency
AKA: above-the-knee amputation
ALL: acute lymphocytic leukemia
AML: acute myelogenous leukemia
AOB: alcohol on breath
AODM: adult onset diabetes mellitus
AP: anteroposterior, abdominal-perineal
ARDS: adult respiratory distress syndrome
AS: aortic stenosis
ASCVD: atherosclerotic cardiovascular disease
ASD: atrial septal defect
ASO: antistreptolysin O
AV: atrioventricular
A-V: arteriovenous
$A\text{-}VO_2$:   arteriovenous oxygen
B I&II: Billroth I and II
BBB: bundle branch block
BCAA: branched chain amino acids
BE: barium enema
BEE: basal energy expenditure
BKA: below-the-knee amputation
BMR: basal metabolic rate
BOM: bilateral otitis media
BP: blood pressure
BPH: benign prostatic hypertrophy
BPM: beats per minute
BS: bowel or breath sounds
BS&O: bilateral salpingo-oophorectomy
BUN: blood urea nitrogen
BW: body weight
CA: cancer

CAA: crystalline amino acids
CABG: coronary artery bypass graft
CAD: coronary artery disease
CAT: computerized axial tomography
C&S: culture and sensitivity
CBC: complete blood count
CBG: capillary blood gas
CC: chief complaint
CCU: clean-catch urine or cardiac care unit
CCV: critical closing volume
CEA: carcinoembryonic antigen
CHF: congestive heart failure
CHO: complex carbohydrate
CI: cardiac index
CML: chronic myelogenous leukemia
CMV: cytomegalovirus
CN: cranial nerves
CNS: central nervous system
CO: cardiac output
C/O: complaining of
COAD: chronic obstructive airways disease
COLD: chronic obstructive lung disease
COPD: chronic obstructive pulmonary disease
CPAP: continuous positive airway pressure
CPK: creatinine phosphokinase
CPR: cardiopulmonary resuscitation
CrCl: creatinine clearance
CRP: C-reactive protein
CSF: cerebrospinal fluid
CT: computerized axial tomography
CVA: cerebrovascular accident or costovertebral angle
CVP: central venous pressure
CXR: chest x-ray
DC: discontinue, discharge, or direct current
D&C: dilation and curretage
D5LR: 5% dextrose in lactated Ringer's solution
D5W: 5% dextrose in water
DIC: disseminated intravascular coagulation
DOA: dead on arrival
DOE: dyspnea on exertion
DPL: diagnostic peritoneal lavage
DPT: diphtheria, pertussis, tetanus

DTR: deep tendon reflexes
DVT: deep venous thrombosis
DX: diagnosis
EAA: essential amino acids
EBL: estimated blood loss
ECG: electrocardiogram
EDC: estimated date of confinement
EFAD: essential fatty acid deficiency
EMV: eyes, motor, verbal response (Glasgow Coma Scale)
EOM: extraocular muscles
ESR: erythrocyte sedimentation rate
ET: endotracheal
ETOH: ethanol
EUA: examination under anesthesia
FBS: fasting blood sugar
FEV_1:   forced expiratory volume-1 second
FFP: fresh frozen plasma
FLK: funny looking kid
FRC: functional residual capacity
FTA-ABS: fluorescent treponemal antibody-absorbed
FU: follow up
FUO: fever of unknown origin
FVC: forced vital capacity
Fx: fracture
G: gravida
GC: gonorrhea (gonococcus)
GFR: glomerular filtration rate
GI: gastrointestinal
GNID: gram-negative intracellular diplococci
GSW: gunshot wound
GTT: glucose tolerance test
GU: genitourinary
GXT: graded exercise tolerance (cardiac stress test)
HAA: hepatitis-associated antigen
HB_sAg: hepatitis B surface antigen
HCG: human chorionic gonadotropin
HCT: hematocrit
HEENT: head, eyes, ears, nose, throat
Hgb: hemoglobin
H/H: Henderson-Hasselbach equation, hemoglobin/
    hematocrit
HIAA: 5-hydroxyindoleacetic acid

HJR: hepatojugular reflex
HPF: high power field
HPI: history of the present illness
HR: heart rate
HSM: hepatosplenomegaly
I&D: incision and drainage
I&O: intake and output
ICU: intensive care unit
ID: identification
IDDM: insulin-dependent diabetes mellitus
IHSS: idiopathic hypertrophic subaortic stenosis
IMV: intermittent mandatory ventilation
INF: intravenous nutritional fluid
IPPB: intermittent positive pressure breathing
IRBBB: incomplete right bundle branch block
IRDM: insulin-resistant diabetes mellitus
ITP: idiopathic thrombocytopenic purpura
IVC: intravenous cholangiogram
IVP: intravenous pyelogram
JODM: juvenile onset diabetes mellitus
JVD: jugular venous distension
KUB: kidney, ureter, bladder
L: left
LAD: left axis deviation or left anterior descending
LAE: left atrial enlargement
LAHB: left anterior hemiblock
LAP: left atrial pressure or leukocyte alkaline phosphatase
LBBB: left bundle branch block
LDH: lactate dehydrogenase
LE: lupus erythematosis
LLL: left lower lobe
LMP: last menstrual period
LP: lumbar puncture
LPN: licensed practical nurse
LUL: left upper lobe
LUQ: left upper quadrant
LVEDP: left ventricular end diastolic pressure
LVH: left ventricular hypertrophy
MAO: monoamine oxidase
MAP: mean arterial blood pressure
MAST: military (medical) anti-shock trousers

MBT: maternal blood type
MCH: mean cell hemoglobin
MCHC: mean cell hemoglobin concentration
MCV: mean cell volume
MI: myocardial infarction or mitral insufficiency
MLE: midline episiotomy
MMEF: maximal mid expiratory flow
MMR: measles, mumps, rubella
MS: mitral stenosis or morphine sulfate
MVA: motor vehicle accident
MVI: multivitamin injection
MVV: maximum voluntary ventilation
NAACP: mnemonic for Neoplasm, Allergy, Addison's
     disease, Collagen-vascular diseases, Parasites
NAD: no active disease
NAVEL: mnemonic for Nerve, Artery, Vein, Empty space,
     Lymphatic
NED: no evidence of disease
NERD: no evidence of return disease
NG: nasogastric
NIDDM: non-insulin-dependent diabetes mellitus
NKA: no known allergies
NKDA: no known drug allergy
NRM: no regular medicines
NS: normal saline or neurosurgery
NSR: normal sinus rhythm
NT: nasotracheal
OB: obstetrics
OCG: oral cholecystogram
OD: overdose or right eye
OM: otitis media
OPV: oral polio vaccine
OR: operating room
OS: opening snap or left eye
OU: both eyes
P: para
PA: posteroanterior
PAC: premature atrial contraction
pAO_2:   alveolar oxygen
paO_2:   peripheral arterial oxygen content
PAP: pulmonary artery pressure

PAT: paroxysmal atrial tachycardia
P&PD: percussion and postural drainage
PCWP: pulmonary capillary wedge pressure
PDA: patent ductus arteriosis
PDR: *Physicians Desk Reference*
PE: pulmonary embolus
PEEP: positive end expiratory pressure
PERRLADC: pupils equal, round, reactive to light accomodation directly and consentually
PFT: pulmonary function tests
PI: pulmonic insufficiency
PID: pelvic inflammatory disease
PKU: phenylketonuria
PMH: past medical history
PMI: point of maximal impulse
PMN: polymorphonuclear leukocyte (neutrophil)
PND: paroxysmal nocturnal dyspnea
POD: post op day
PP: pulsus paradoxus or postprandial
PPD: purified protein derivative
PRBC: packed red blood cells
PS: pulmonic stenosis
PT: prothrombin time, physical therapy
Pt: patient
PTH: parathyroid hormone
PTHC: percutaneous transhepatic cholangiogram
PTT: partial thromoplastin time
PUD: peptic ulcer disease
PVC: premature ventricular contraction
PVD: peripheral vascular disease
PZI: protamine zinc insulin
Q: mathematical symbol for flow
Qs: volume of blood (portion of cardiac output) shunted past nonventilated alveoli
Qs/Qt: shunt fraction
Qt: total cardiac output
R: right
RAD: right axis deviation
RAE: right atrial enlargement
RAP: right atrial pressure
RBBB: right bundle branch block

RBC: red blood cell (erythrocyte)
RDA: recommended dietary allowance
RDW: red cell distribution width
RIA: radioimmunoassay
RLL: right lower lobe
RLQ: right lower quadrant
RML: right middle lobe
RNA: ribonucleic acid
R/O: rule out
ROM: range of motion
ROS: review of systems
RRR: regular rate and rhythm
RT: rubella titer, respiratory therapy
RTA: renal tubular acidosis
RU: resin uptake
RUG: retrograde urethrogram
RUL: right upper lobe
RUQ: right upper quadrant
RV: residual volume
RVH: right ventricular hypertrophy
Rx: treatment
SA: sinoatrial
SAA: synthetic amino acids
S&A: sugar and acetone
SBE: subacute bacterial endocarditis
SBFT: small bowel followthrough
SBS: short bowel syndrome
SCr: serum creatinine
SG: Swan-Ganz
SGGT: serum gamma-glutamyl transpeptidase
SGOT: serum glutamic-oxaloacetic transaminase
SGPT: serum glutamic-pyruvic transaminase
SIADH: syndrome of inappropriate ADH
SIMV: synchronous intermittent mandatory ventilation
SKSD: streptokinase-streptodornase
SLE: systemic lupus erythematosis
SMO: slips made out
SOAP: mnemonic for Subjective, Objective, Assessment,
  Plan
SOB: shortness of breath
SVD: spontaneous vaginal delivery

Sx: symptoms
T&C: type and cross
TAH: total abdominal hysterectomy
T&H: type and hold
TB: tuberculosis
TBG: thyroid binding globulin
TBLC: term birth, living child
TC&DB: turn, cough, and deep breathe
TIA: transient ischemia attack
TIBC: total iron binding capacity
TIG: tetanus immune globulin
TLC: total lung capacity
TNTC: too numerous to count
TORCH: toxoplasma, rubella, cytomegalovirus, herpes virus
TPN: total parenteral nutrition
TPR: total peripheral resistance
TSH: thyroid stimulating hormone
TTP: thrombotic thrombocytopenic purpura
TU: tuberculin units
TUR: transurethral resection
TURBT: TUR bladder tumors
TURP: TUR prostate
TV: tidal volume
TVH: total vaginal hysterectomy
Tx: treatment
U/A: urinalysis
UGI: upper gastrointestinal
URI: upper respiratory tract infection
US: ultrasound
UTI: urinary tract infection
UUN: urinary urea nitrogen
VC: vital capacity
VCUG: voiding cystourethrogram
VMA: vanillymandelic acid
V/Q: ventilation-perfusion
VSS: vital signs stable
WB: whole blood
WBC: white blood cell or white blood cell count
WD: well-developed
WF: white female
WM: white male

WN: well-nourished
YO: years old

APGAR SCORES

Apgar scores (see the following table) are a numerical expression of the condition of a newborn infant. Usually determined one minute after birth and again at five minutes, the score is the sum of points gained on assessment of color, heart rate, reflex irritability, muscle tone, and respirations.

Apgar Scores

	Score		
Sign	0	1	2
Appearance (color)	Blue or pale	Pink body with blue extremities	Completely pink
Pulse (heart rate)	Absent	Slow (<100/min)	>100/min
Grimace (reflex irritability)	No response	Grimace	Cough or sneeze
Activity (muscle tone)	Limp	Some flexion	Active movement
Respirations	Absent	Slow, irregular	Good, crying

GLASGOW COMA SCALE

The Glasgow Coma Scale (EMV Scale) gives a fairly reliable, objective way to monitor changes in levels of consciousness. It is based upon eye opening, motor responses, and verbal responses (EMV). A person's EMV score is based upon the total of the three different responses. The score ranges from three (lowest) to 15 (highest).

Glasgow Coma Scale

Parameter	Response		Score
EYES	Open	Spontaneously	4
		To verbal command	3
		To pain	2
	No response		1
BEST MOTOR RESPONSE	To verbal command	Obeys	6
	To painful stimulus	Localizes pain	5
		Flexion-Withdrawal	4
		Decorticate (flex)	3
		Decerebrate (extend)	2
		No response	1
BEST VERBAL RESPONSE		Oriented, converses	5
		Disoriented, converses	4
		Inappropriate responses	3
		Incomprehensible sounds	2
		No response	1

SCHEDULE FOR CHILDHOOD IMMUNIZATIONS AND TINE TESTS

The following list gives the ages for childhood immunizations and tine tests.

- 2, 4, 6 months: DPT (diphtheria, pertussis, tetanus)
- 6 months: OPV (oral polio vaccine), optional
- 12 months: TB tine test (repeat every one to two years)
- 15 months: MMR (measles, mumps, rubella)
- 18 months: DPT, OPV
- 4–6 years: DPT, OPV
- 14–16 years: Tetanus, diphtheria (then every 10 years)

ISOLATION

Respiratory Isolation

Required

- Masks for visitors
- Wash hands after contact
- Patient wears mask while being transported

Indications

- Meningococcal meningitis
- Meningococcemia
- Mumps
- Pertussis
- Q fever
- Rubella
- Rubeola
- Respiratory TB

Wound and Skin Isolation

Required

- Masks when changing dressings
- Gown with direct contact
- Wash hands after contact

Indications

WITH DRAINING LESIONS
- Actinomycosis
- Brucellosis
- Clostridia
- Cryptococcosis
- Norcardiosis
- *S. aureus*
- Group A streptococci
- Extrapulmonary TB
- Tularemia
- Anthrax

OTHERS
- Bacterial conjunctivitis
- Granuloma inguinale
- Localized *Herpes zoster*
- Lymphogranuloma venereum

Strict Isolation

Required

- Masks, gowns, gloves
- Strict handwashing

- All specimens sent to the lab in specially marked isolation bags

Indications

- Anthrax
- Diphtheria
- Chickenpox
- Disseminated herpes
- Lassa fever
- Marburg virus disease
- Plague
- Rabies
- *S. aureus*: Pneumonia, enterocolitis, or major ward infection
- Group A streptococci: Pharyngitis, pneumonia, or major ward infection

Enteric Isolation

Required

- Gowns and gloves with direct contact
- Wash hands after contact
- Specimens sent to the lab in specially marked bags

Indications

- Cholera
- Severe diarrhea (undiagnosed)
- Enteropathogenic or enterotoxic *E. coli*
- *Salmonella*
- *Shigella*
- Typhoid
- *Yersinia enterocolitica*
- Hepatitis A

Protective Isolation

Required

- Masks and gowns
- Gloves with contact
- Patient wears mask while being transported

Indications

- Agranulocytosis
- Burns
- Leukemia
- Leukopenia
- Immunosuppressed patients

Blood Precautions

Required

- Gowns and gloves with direct contact
- Blood specimens in specially labeled, impermeable bags

Indications

- Active hepatitis B
- HAA-positive patient

TEMPERATURE CONVERSION

The following table gives information for converting temperatures from the Fahrenheit (F) scale to the centigrade or Celsius (C) scale and vice-versa.

Temperature Conversion Table*

F	C	C	F
0	−17.7	0	32.0
95.0	35.0	35.0	95.0
96.0	35.5	35.5	95.9
97.0	36.1	36.0	96.8
98.0	36.6	36.5	97.7
98.6	37.0	37.0	98.6
99.0	37.2	37.5	99.5
100.0	37.7	38.0	100.4
101.0	38.3	38.5	101.3
102.0	38.8	39.0	102.2
103.0	39.4	39.5	103.1
104.0	40.0	40.0	104.0
105.0	40.5	40.5	104.9
106.0	41.1	41.0	105.8
$C = (F - 32) \times 5/9$		$F = (C \times 9/5) + 32$	

*F = degrees Fahrenheit; C = degrees Celsius.

WEIGHT CONVERSION

The following table gives information for converting weights in pounds (lb) to weights in kilograms (kg) and vice-versa.

Weight Conversion Table

lb	kg	kg	lb
1	0.5	1	2.2
2	0.9	2	4.4
4	1.8	3	6.6
6	2.7	4	8.8
8	3.6	5	11.0
10	4.5	6	13.2
20	9.1	8	17.6
30	13.6	10	22.0
40	18.2	20	44.0
50	22.7	30	66.0
60	27.3	40	88.0
70	31.8	50	110.0
80	36.4	60	132.0
90	40.9	70	154.0
100	45.4	80	176.0
150	68.2	90	198.0
200	90.8	100	220.0
kg = lb × 0.454		lb = kg × 2.2	

DESIRABLE BODY WEIGHTS

The table on p. 461 gives desirable body weights for men aged 25 years and over and for women aged 18 years and over.

STANDARD ANTHROPOMETRIC MEASUREMENTS

The table on p. 462 gives the standard measurements for triceps skinfold and midarm muscle circumference.

Desirable Weights*†

Height		Small Frame	Medium Frame	Large Frame
		MEN OF AGES 25 AND OVER		

(with shoes on)
1-inch heels

Feet	Inches	Small Frame	Medium Frame	Large Frame
5	2	112–120	118–129	126–141
5	3	115–123	121–133	129–144
5	4	118–126	124–136	132–148
5	5	121–129	127–139	135–152
5	6	124–133	130–143	138–156
5	7	128–137	134–147	142–161
5	8	132–141	138–152	147–166
5	9	136–145	142–156	151–170
5	10	140–150	146–160	155–174
5	11	144–154	150–165	159–179
6	0	148–158	154–170	164–184
6	1	152–162	158–175	168–189
6	2	156–167	162–180	173–194
6	3	160–171	167–185	178–199
6	4	164–175	172–190	182–204

WOMEN OF AGES 25 AND OVER

For girls between 18 and 25, subtract 1 pound for each year under 25.

(with shoes on)
2-inch heels

Feet	Inches	Small Frame	Medium Frame	Large Frame
4	10	92–98	96–107	104–119
4	11	94–101	98–110	106–122
5	0	96–104	101–113	109–125
5	1	99–107	104–116	112–128
5	2	102–110	107–119	115–131
5	3	105–113	110–122	118–134
5	4	108–116	113–126	121–138
5	5	111–119	116–130	125–142
5	6	114–123	120–135	129–146
5	7	118–127	124–139	133–150
5	8	122–131	128–143	137–154
5	9	126–135	132–147	141–158
5	10	130–140	136–151	145–163
5	11	134–144	140–155	149–168
6	0	138–148	144–159	153–173

*Courtesy of The Metropolitan Life Insurance Co, New York.
†Weight in pounds according to frame (in indoor clothing). New weight tables now in the process of being formulated will show that desirable weights for men and women today probably are higher than those in the tables above which were based on statistical studies made 25 years ago.

Standards for Anthropometric Measurements*†

Age‡	Triceps Skinfold (mm)		Midarm Muscle Circumference (cm)	
	MALE	FEMALE	MALE	FEMALE
0–5 mo.	8	8	10.6	10.4
6–17 mo.	9	9	12.3	11.7
1.5–2.5	10	10	12.7	12.5
2.5–3.5	9	10	13.2	12.8
3.5–4.5	9	10	13.5	13.2
4.5–5.5	8	10	14.1	13.8
5.5–6.5	8	10	14.6	14.0
6.5–7.5	8	10	15.1	14.6
7.5–8.5	8	10	15.8	15.1
8.5–9.5	9	11	16.1	15.7
9.5–10.5	10	12	16.8	16.3
10.5–11.5	10	12	17.4	17.1
11.5–12.5	11	13	18.1	17.9
12.5–13.5	10	14	19.5	18.5
13.5–14.5	10	15	21.1	19.3
14.5–15.5	9	16	22.0	19.5
15.5–16.5	9	15	22.9	20.0
16.5–17.5	8	16	24.5	19.6
17.5–24.5	10	17	25.8	20.5
24.5–34.5	11	19	27.0	21.3
34.5–44.5	12	22	27.0	21.6

*From Center for Disease Control, Publication 72-8131, US Dept Health, Education, and Welfare, 1972.
†These standards indicate the 50th percentiles derived from data obtained in the United States Ten-State Survey of 1968–1970.
‡Age given in years unless otherwise specified.

BODY SURFACE AREA: ADULT

Fig. A-1 is a nomogram for determining the body surface area of an adult.

BODY SURFACE AREA: CHILDREN

Fig. A-2 is a nomogram for determining the body surface area of children.

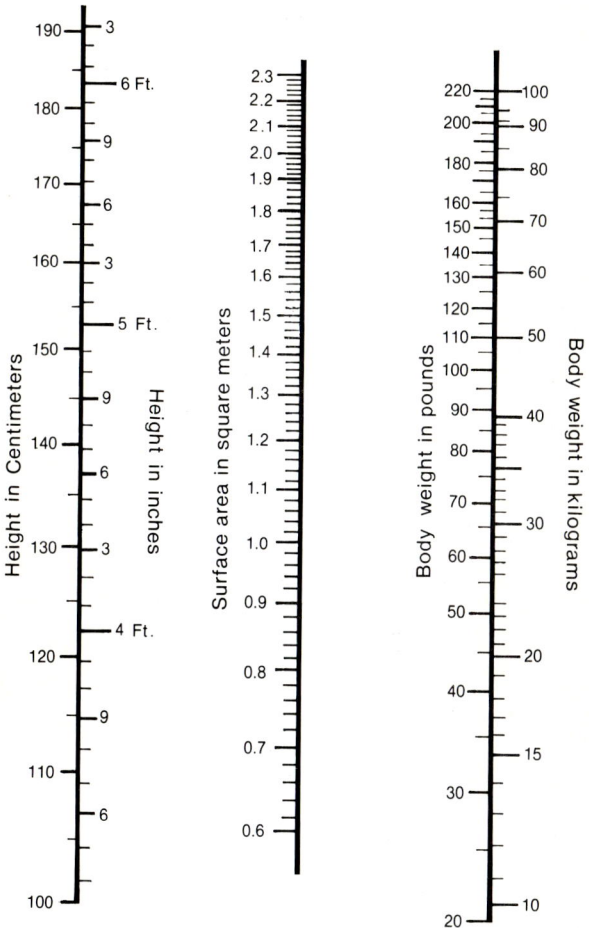

Fig. A-1 Nomogram for determining body surface area in adults. Find height on the left-hand scale and weight on the right-hand scale. Connect these two points with a straightedge and read the surface area from the middle scale. *(From Wilmore DW: Metabolic Management of the Critically Ill. New York, Plenum Medical Book Co, 1977. Used with permission)*

NOMOGRAM

| HEIGHT cm in | For children of normal height for weight | SA M² | WEIGHT lb kg |

For children of normal height for weight

Weight in pounds

Surface area in square meters

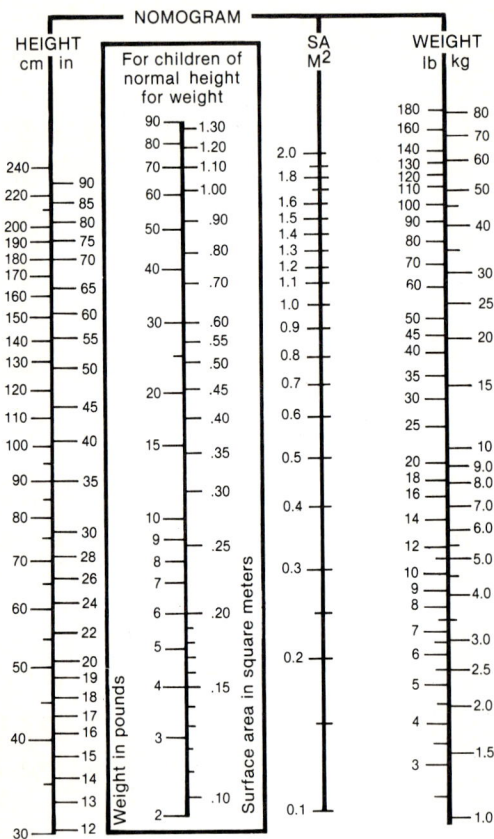

Fig. A-2 West nomogram for determining body surface area in children. Find height on the far left-hand scale and weight on the far right-hand scale. Connect these two points with a straightedge and read the surface area from the SA column. If the patient is roughly of average size, the surface area may be determined from weight alone by using the scale in the enclosed area. *(From Vaughan VC, III, et al: Nelson Textbook of Pediatrics, ed 11. Philadelphia, WB Saunders Co, 1979. Used with permission.)*

Index

Y

Z

Telephone Numbers

Telephone Numbers

Telephone Numbers

Telephone Numbers

Telephone Numbers

Pearls

Pearls

Pearls

Pearls

Pearls

Pearls

Pearls

Pearls

Pearls